Advance Praise for *Fragments*

"Fragments of Real Presence represents feminist Catholic theology at its best. Teresa Berger attends closely to the wisdom of wo/men making meaning of liturgy and theology because they hunger and thirst for glimpses of a life-giving G*d. I highly recommend these essays to all those seeking for a spirituality that is life-giving. The book will be especially useful to all those engaged in feminist ministry and liturgy."

> —Elisabeth Schüssler Fiorenza, Krister Stendahl Professor of Divinity, Harvard Divinity School

"With luminous writing, this book weaves together the cycles of women's lives and the liturgical year with great skill. By turns poignant and humorous, and studded with simple yet profound examples, it wrestles with the long liturgical tradition to bring forth a rich feast of insight and prayer. Liturgy can be alienating to women. This is a story of its beauty when filtered through the experience of contemporary, busy women."

> —Elizabeth A. Johnson, Distinguished Professor of Theology at Fordham University, New York

"This compelling volume integrates liturgical feasts and seasons with the liturgies of our lives, revealing what liturgy and life look like when seen through a feminist lens. May it help to hasten the day when the spiritual leadership of women is not the exception but the norm."

> —Miriam Therese Winter, Medical Mission Sister, and professor of liturgy, worship, and spirituality at Hartford Seminary in Connecticut

"Teresa Berger guides us through the cycle of the liturgical year with startling and gentle insights into the contradictions of our lives lived simultaneously in a grotesquely secular 21st century America and an ancient round of symbols of renewal of life in God. In her vision of divine real presence in women's lives the waters of birth and the waters of baptism flow together to transform one another."

> —Rosemary Radford Ruether, Carpenter Professor of Feminist Theology, Graduate Theological Union, Berkeley, California

FRAGMENTS of REAL PRESENCE

Liturgical Traditions in the Hands of Women

TERESA BERGER

A Herder & Herder Book
The Crossroad Publishing Company
New York

The Crossroad Publishing Company
481 Eighth Avenue, Suite 1550, New York, NY 10001

This book is set in 11/13 Garamond Antiqua.
The display type is Nueva Roman.

Printed in the United States of America

Library of Congress Cataloging-in-Publication Data

Berger, Teresa.
    Fragments of real presence / Teresa Berger.
        p. cm.
    Includes bibliographical references (p.   ).
    ISBN 0-8245-2295-8 (alk. paper)
    1. Feminist theology. 2. Women in the Catholic Church. 3. Church year meditations. 4. Worship programs. I. Title.
    BT83.55.B48 2005
    264'.02'0082—dc22

                                                    2005004033

1   2   3   4   5   6   7   8   9   10   09   08   07   06   05

*To the foremothers
whose names I know:*

Heta

Hedwig and Maria Theresia

Clara and Elisa, Viktoria and Mariana

Therese, Sophia, Katharina,
Anna, and Anna, Genofeva,
Karolina, and Theresia

*and to those
whose names are lost
yet whose lives are known to God*

Contents

Preface

T HE ORIGINS OF THIS BOOK, I like to think, reach back almost a half-century, to the day of my baptism at the ripe age of ten days. A photo taken that day shows me in an extravagant floor-length white baptismal gown. My mother holds me in her arms; to her left is my grandmother, to her right the Vincentian sister who midwifed my birth (her pre-Vatican II religious habit as elaborate as my baptismal gown). This is the faith into which I was baptized: a faith of both extravagant and austere materiality, a faith of mothers and sisters and midwives, the faith and face of the Catholic Church in one of its most ancient mysteries. It is this faith that will shape my days and my nights, my longings and my rebellions, my work and my vision of a God-sustained universe. It is the faith that has shaped *Fragments of Real Presence*.

Between the day of my baptism and the writing of this book, I have learned to attend closely to the wisdom of women making meaning of liturgy in the crucible of their own lived lives. With these women—those before me and those around me—I make meaning by conspiring through, with, in, and against the liturgy in the crucible of my own life. I hunger and thirst for glimpses of a life-giving God. Together with the whole cosmos, I groan for redemption as a woman in labor pains longs for the birth of her child. This, indeed, is a vast vision; a book can embody no more than a fragmentary glimpse of such a vision.

Nevertheless, given the fact that a half-century has passed since the seeds of this vision were first planted, I have incurred numerous and profound debts of gratitude. I delight in naming some of these here.

To begin with, there are my women friends (and I have been blessed with a startling abundance of them). Among these are three Faithful Companions of Jesus, Sisters Carmel, Ellen, and Joanna, who pondered and prayed some of the texts as I wrote them, and who by their presence next door to my own home made sure that a fragment of Real Presence was always close.

To Mary McClintock Fulkerson, whose friendship I have cherished for twenty years. It was Mary who pointed out to me that the anagram

I had seen in a *New York Times* layout on the day of the Beatification of Mother Teresa ("saint"—"satin") could be decoded in yet another way (namely, as "stain"). As a Roman Catholic, I am blessed to have a friend and colleague with Calvinist sensibilities who keeps me mindful of the intrinsic flaws in the fabric of the real.

To Lorna Collingridge, with whom I share a love for Hildegard of Bingen, a passion for moonflowers, a deep devotion to both the Holy Spirit and *La Virgen de Guadalupe,* and a desire for creating women-identified liturgies. A couple of the liturgies we have celebrated together are included in this book, as are some of Lorna's own compositions. My life has been profoundly blessed by Lorna's gift of real presence.

To Kazuyo Hirose, for embracing me across the Pacific Ocean, and to Sr. Chris Gellings, IHM, for lightening a walk through hell.

To Rev. Jennifer Copeland, for loving a good glass of white wine as much as I do, and for helping me live well at Duke.

To the women of my parish, for sustaining me along the way (and for the gift of champagne one Saturday when life was hard).

To Rev. Teresa Holloway, for helping me confront the fight against breast cancer.

Since gender is nothing if not a relational category, a book about women's lives cannot but be shaped by the "other" (gender) in some ways. I thus—joyfully and unapologetically—give thanks for a number of men who have accompanied the writing of this book.

For my Jesuit uncle, Fr. Francis X. Weiser, SJ (1901–1986), whose own books on the liturgical year I continue to cherish even if they are very different from my own.

For Fr. David McBriar, OFM, whose life has spelled grace for mine.

For Fr. Emmanuel Katongole, for postcolonial cartographies of friendship.

For Mark Burrows, who added *Lachfalten* to the last months of writing.

For Hansjakob Becker, whose scholarly passion and profound faith first lured me into a life shaped by the liturgical tradition. *Ich werde Dir ewig dankbar sein, Hansjakob.*

Finally, for my son Peter Ludwig Berger, who taught me much about liturgy by his deep impatience with it and his sporadic curiosity about it.

My scholarly work at Duke Divinity School is generously supported by a host of co-workers. I mention here in particular the staff of Duke libraries, and especially Roberta Schaafsma: friend, fountain of wisdom, and magic librarian par excellence. Dr. Mary Deasey Collins ably translated the essay "The Waters of Birth and the Waters of Baptism" from my original German text; I am profoundly grateful to her.

I also am grateful to the Department of Theology of Uppsala University, Sweden, and to Ninna Edgardh Beckman, for an invitation to spend six wonderful summer weeks there in 2001. A number of the fragments of this book originated in Uppsala, most notably the one for Pentecost Sunday.

The Franciscan Friars of the Atonement, especially Fr. Jim and Fr. Brian, welcomed me, in May of 2002, to Sant'Onofrio and the Centro Pro Unione in Rome. An afternoon visit to Santa Maria in Trastevere inspired and burdened me with the piece that is now "A Gypsy Mother and the Mother of God."

The editorial support I have received from Dana Polanichka, Carol Shoun, and Anne Weston, who have skillfully edited my texts, has been invaluable. Dana Dillon, In-Yong Lee, Rachel Maxson, and Sarah Sours have been my graduate research assistants, with diligence and good spirit. I am also fortunate to work in close proximity to other theological scholars and gratefully here acknowledge the insights and help of James Crenshaw, Richard Hays, Susan Keefe, Joel Marcus, and Geoffrey Wainwright.

It remains for me to thank John Jones, Maria Devitt, Rachel Greer, and Gwendolyn Herder of Crossroad Publishing for seeing these texts from manuscript form into a book.

Fragments of Real Presence is dedicated to those women who in ways invisible to the reader accompanied the writing of this book: my foremothers, who have handed down the faith through the centuries. I both live and believe because of them.

TERESA BERGER
DURHAM, NC

Acknowledgments

Grateful acknowledgment is made to the following for permission to quote copyrighted material:

Anselm of Canterbury, "Prayer to St Paul," in *The Prayers and Meditations of St Anselm with the Proslogion*, trans. Sister Benedicta Ward, Penguin Classics (Harmondsworth: Penguin, 1973), 153ff. Copyright © Benedicta Ward, 1973. Reproduced by permission of Penguin Books Ltd., London.

Angela Berlis, Psalm 71. English translation by Teresa Berger. Copyright © 2004. Used by permission of Angela Berlis and Teresa Berger.

Lorna Collingridge. Unpublished original compositions ("Circle of Wisdom," Antiphon for Psalm 18, and "Divine Love"). Copyright © 2004 by Lorna Collingridge. Used with permission.

Virgil Elizondo, *Guadalupe, Mother of the New Creation*, 5th ed. (Maryknoll, N.Y.: Orbis Books, 2001), 5-22. Copyright © 1997 by Virgil Elizondo. Used with permission.

Hildegard of Bingen, *The Book of the Rewards of Life*, trans. Bruce W. Hozeski, The Garland Library of Medieval Literature 89 Series B (New York: Garland Publishing, 1994), 136. Copyright © 1994 by Bruce W. Hozeski. Used with permission.

Hildegard of Bingen, Letter to the Monk Guibert [no. 103r], in *The Letters of Hildegard of Bingen*, Vol. II, ed. and trans. Joseph L. Baird and Radd K. Ehrman (New York: Oxford University Press, 1998). Copyright © 1998 by Oxford University Press, Inc. Used with permission.

Hildegard of Bingen, *Scivias*, trans. Mother Columba Hart and Jane Bishop, The Classics of Western Spirituality (New York: Paulist Press, 1990), 59f., 244, 246, 254, 336. Copyright © 1990 by Abbey of Regina Laudis, Bethlehem, Connecticut. Used with permission.

J. Michael Joncas, "God ever-faithful." Copyright © (1994) by GIA Publications, Inc. All Rights Reserved. Printed in U.S.A. 7404 S. Mason Ave., Chicago, Ill. 60638, www.giamusic.com, 800.442.1358. Used with permission.

Journal of Feminist Studies in Religion, for permission to reprint, in slightly rewritten form, my essay "Of Claire and Clairol," which first appeared in the *Journal of Feminist Studies in Religion* 18 (2002): 53–69. Copyright © *The Journal of Feminist Studies in Religion*, 2002. Used with permission.

I myself hold the copyrights for the following texts:

A Note on Scripture Quotations

In essays that directly engage a liturgical reading, the Scripture texts usually are taken from the New American Bible with Revised New Testament and Revised Psalms © 1991, 1986, 1970 Confraternity of Christian Doctrine, Washington, D.C. This is the translation used in the Lectionary for Mass for Use in the Dioceses of the United States of America, second typical edition © 1998, 1997, 1970 Confraternity of Christian Doctrine, Inc., Washington, D.C. In some cases, I have preferred the Revised New American Bible as used in the yearly Workbooks for Lectors and Gospel Readers. In essays that deal with biblical materials beyond a narrow focus on their liturgical reading, I quote from the New Revised Standard Version. Occasionally, I privilege my own translations of biblical texts. This is clearly marked in each instance, as are cases where, in one essay, different biblical translations are used.

Illustrations

No. 1
Hildegard of Bingen, by Robert Lentz. © Robert Lentz. Color reproductions available from Bridge Building Images • www.BridgeBuilding.com. Reproduced by permission.

No. 2
Juan Diego, by Robert Lentz. © Robert Lentz. Color reproductions available from Bridge Building Images • www.BridgeBuilding.com. Reproduced by permission.

No. 3
The Annunciation [with Mary in priestly vestments!]. Gengenbach Evangeliary (ca. AD 1150). Württembergische Landesbibliothek, Cod. bibl. 2° 28. Reproduced by permission of Württembergische Landesbibliothek, Stuttgart, Germany.

No. 4
The Visitation. Attributed to Master Heinrich Constance (ca. 1310 AD), from the Dominican Nunnery of Katharinental. The Metropolitan Museum of Art, Gift of J. Pierpont Morgan, 1917 (17.190.724). Reproduced by permission of The Metropolitan Museum of Art, New York.

Introduction

Gathering the Fragments

A group of older women has gathered in a dimly lit church. The women kneel in front of a statue of Mary and begin to recite the rosary. Their low voices fill the church. The women know by heart the ancient greeting between two mothers pregnant with God's future: "Blessed are you among women, and blessed is the fruit of your womb."

A woman in a wheelchair serves as eucharistic minister. She smiles broadly at people who have to bow low to receive the real presence of Christ.

A woman leaves the Sunday liturgy during the sermon, giving up on her effort to make meaning of the words.

Another woman remains behind, struggling throughout the liturgy with her active child. At the end of the service, the woman is exhausted. She remembers little of the readings and prayers; she always dreads the sermon, since she has to work especially hard to keep her young child still.

A woman sings the songs and prays the texts of the liturgy, but consciously changes words so as to avoid straightjacketing God into being no more than a "He."

A woman hurries to church with her infant son. Her babysitting arrangement fell through, and it is too late to find another person to take her place as lector in this liturgy. The woman processes in with her baby in her arms. After the liturgy, one of the women in the congregation says: "I saw my life brought into the sanctuary today."

A woman comes to a Good Friday service with bruises on her body from yet another domestic assault. She moves forward slowly at the Veneration of the Cross. As she kisses the body on the crucifix, tears well up in her eyes.

A woman enters the church halfway through the liturgy. She carries a large image of the Virgin of Guadalupe. While the priest continues with the prayers, the Latina grandmother self-confidently places her image on the altar steps. The priest, when sharing communion, will have to find a way around this mestiza Virgin Mother.

A woman accompanies her daughter to the child's First Reconciliation in church, painfully aware that the girl has suffered her father's sexual advances and now is asked to receive the sacrament of reconciliation from a "Father."

A woman attends Sunday worship after having given birth. Her body bears the evidence of her nursing a child. The woman delights in going to communion, making her own the ancient image of the Eucharist as God's breast milk.

A lesbian couple rises together on Mother's Day. The presiding minister has invited all mothers to stand and be recognized.

A group of women gathers on the Feast of Saint Mary Magdalene to celebrate the memory of this "apostle to the apostles." The liturgy has been written by one of the women in the group. Anticipation fills the church.

These are just twelve of the innumerable ways in which women's lives shape, enrich, disturb, own, and contest the life of the liturgy. Women's real presence is woven into all moments of worship, whether a Sunday morning Mass at a Roman Catholic parish in the southeastern United States or a feminist ritual celebrated in a private home nearby that same evening. Wherever women's lives and liturgy touch each other, a distinct way of living the faith materializes. This way of living faith, birthed of liturgy inflected by women's lives, is fundamental to the life of the church. It is also, for the most part, hidden. Women's real presence continues to be veiled. Glimpses of this presence are all around, to be sure; the twelve moments described above witness to this. But these glimpses—as fragments of a larger whole—must be gathered in order to become visible, so that "nothing may be lost" (John 6:12). *Fragments of Real Presence* embodies such a gathering, dedicated to moments of encounter between the life of the liturgy and the lives of women.

Fragments of Struggle

Why hold the complexities of women's lives and the liturgy together in the first place? Much has been written on the alienating and conflictual relationship between contemporary women and the church, especially its liturgical life. Sometimes this conflictual relationship between women and worship has led women to distance themselves from traditional liturgies, even if not from ritualizing their lives. Alternative rituals for women abound, from life cycle celebrations and seasonal rituals to those for women-identified realities such as stillbirth or breast cancer. Within the church itself, there is a host of new songs, meditations, creeds, prayer books, and liturgies specifically for women.

Why, at this point, return to the liturgical tradition itself as a site of women's wisdom and faith, when so many alternative ritual sites have opened? Three reasons in particular lead me to reclaim the liturgy as a site of women's lives of faith.

"Behold, the Women"

To begin with, there is the simple fact that women today continue to be a (or is it *the*?) real presence in liturgical life. Of the twenty million Roman Catholics who attend Mass on an average Sunday in the United States, the majority are women. Women also constitute the majority in most other worship services in North America and Europe, and, indeed, around the globe. Of the roughly one billion women worldwide who self-identify as Christian, many bear eloquent witness to this. *Fragments of Real Presence,* on one level, simply takes seriously the fact of women's continuing presence in the churches' liturgical life.

There are, however, more compelling reasons than numbers and statistics for attending to liturgy as inflected by women's lives. Liturgy and women's lives have always been intertwined in lived experience. Our mothers, grandmothers, and great-grandmothers lived their faith to the rhythm of the feasts and fasts of the church. Where they lived their faith in *conflictual* engagement with this rhythm, the liturgy remained the fundamental backdrop even of their subversions. Why do without this site today, a part of such a rich heritage of women's lives of faith? Interestingly, many contemporary women, even if they struggle with a sense of alienation from the church, remember traditional liturgies and devotions as extraordinarily beautiful and life-giving.[1]

The relationship between women's lives and the rituals of faith has obviously been complex and ambiguous. Liturgical life was deeply marked by its own gendered asymmetries. The privilege of masculinity in liturgical leadership, logistical arrangements that distanced women from the Holy, liturgical taboos related to women's bodily and reproductive labor, constraints on women's voices, as well as the clearly gendered domestic sphere and forms of popular religiosity peculiarly linked to women are just a few examples. As a scholar of liturgy, I know of many more.[2]

I also know that the relationship between women and rituals of faith has at points been destructive even of women's very lives. The biblical story of the unnamed secondary wife of a Levite (Judg. 19–20) is a terrifying witness to that truth. The woman's gang-raped body literally was fragmented, cut into twelve pieces, and sent throughout Israel as a ritual call to arms.[3] "Behold, the woman," the author of the book of Judges exhorts the readers (Judg. 19:27 KJV). I dare not forget. Our sacred Scriptures hold a painful memory of the broken and fragmented body of a woman, long before the broken body of a man becomes the sign of redemption.

Breaking Open the Liturgical Tradition

While liturgy can be a deeply painful space for women, liturgy also has been a rich site of encounter with God's life-giving presence, my second reason for reclaiming liturgy as a site of women's lives of faith. The liturgical tradition, including the wealth of popular devotions, has offered meaning, strength, and solace to generations of women—not least of all as a site of subversion of established gender identities. From the image of the Eucharist as God's breast milk or of Jesus as a woman in labor pains on the cross to the profound connection between women and eucharistic devotions, the liturgical tradition in all its breadth has always empowered women's lives of faith. *Fragments of Real Presence* seeks to break open and rediscover, in the richness and complexity of the liturgical tradition, those fragments able to sustain and empower women's lives today. Breaking open the liturgical tradition, wrestling with it until it yields fragments of blessing, is of fundamental importance for the present and the future of the church. If we continue to see this tradition through the dominantly androcentric reception history of the past, we may be tempted simply to discard it as sexist and patriarchal—the impulse of our feminist older sisters. But the past, when sifted, realigned, and reappropriated,[4] is much richer than its androcentric and traditionalist interpreters ever imagined. What counts as liturgical tradition, after all, is never fixed. Its individual elements—its fragments—are always susceptible to new alignment. Liturgical tradition, in other words, is open to being reclaimed. As such, it can become a site of life and flourishing as well as a space for lament for women today. Even if the claim to liturgy as a site, then, is a seemingly traditional move, the reconfiguration of liturgical tradition in light of women's lived lives expands the very meaning of tradition within the life of the church.[5]

One story from our history might illustrate both the tradition's stark problems in relation to women's lives and the wonderful subversions it always engendered. Embedded in the story that follows is such a subversion, even if the story itself follows the traditional script of a named, male hero as its central figure.

> Somewhere around A.D. 1114, Robert d'Arbrissel, the founder of several monasteries in which ascetic women and men lived together under the authority of an abbess (!), wanted to preach at the little church of Menat in Auvergne. He was told by the locals that women had been forbidden from entering this church ever since a saint, five hundred years earlier, had decreed it so. Any woman defying the ban would die. Robert d'Arbrissel, in a simple and forthright response, proceeded to enter the church with a group of women. He then eloquently defended his defiance of the local saint by insisting that if women ate and drank the body and blood of Christ—the real presence of God—what folly it was to believe that these women could not bring their own real presence into this church.[6]

Robert's twelfth-century challenge to a tradition of distancing women's lives from God's real presence is worth claiming as our own. Against a tradition that has distanced the presence of women from the presence of God, I argue with Robert d'Arbrissel (and other fragments of the liturgical tradition) that the real presence of women and the real presence of God are, in fact, co-constitutive of each other.

An Everyday God?

Confronted with a God intricately woven into women's lives, one might wonder, once again, why the turn to liturgy as a site? Why not the everyday lives of women, or the struggles for justice, for the future of our children and, indeed, of this whole fragile and threatened planet? It should be obvious by now that turning to the liturgical tradition is not a turning away from other sites of encounter with the Holy One. It is, rather, a turning to all other sites with utmost passion and clarity—but a clarity sharpened, deepened, and nourished by liturgy.

There is an additional reason for (re-)turning to the liturgical tradition at this time, beyond women's continuing presence in contemporary worship and the rich insights offered by the liturgical tradition itself. The third and last reason for turning to the liturgy has to do with contemporary spiritual sensibilities and the worlds they invite us into. I want to suggest that the "Everyday God"[7] celebrated in much of contemporary spirituality needs more than the everyday for us to comprehend that "there is nothing ordinary about an incarnate God."[8]

Spiritual sensibilities today are attuned to the everyday sites of God's presence in the world. These sites, to be sure, are of fundamental importance, especially for women's lives of faith. The vibrant contemporary (re-)discovery of a spirituality of the everyday was a necessary reaction to a particular construal of the spiritual and the sacred as otherworldly, church-focused, and priest-centered. Today, we have learned to claim the "quotidian mysteries"[9] of our lives as deeply sacramental, pregnant with holiness and divine presence. Whether it is the love shared around a breakfast table, or insights based on the playfulness of our cats, or the deep wisdom of a compost heap that turns dead stuff into something life-giving, it is the ordinary that inspires. I cannot but affirm this shift of spiritual gravity; it has been richly important for women's lives, which in our culture are still coded as ordinary, domestic, and oftentimes trivial. *Fragments of Real Presence,* with its commitment to the lived lives of women, claims the sacrament of the ordinary as a site of encounter with God. God redeems concrete women's lives, with all their particular cultural codes, distinct bodily characteristics, gendered identities, and concrete struggles, pains, and passions. There is no redemption outside of material reality in all its holy splendor and its abysmal pain.

And yet, "there is nothing ordinary about an incarnate God." Our deepest spiritual intuitions will need more than breakfast tables, cats, and compost heaps in order to grasp that truth. It is here that the liturgical tradition yields its power. Having discovered, exuberantly, the sacramentality of the everyday, we do well to reclaim the sacramentality of the liturgy itself—the church's feasts and fasts, its symbols and images—for the lives of women. The liturgical tradition, after all, is not beyond or opposed to material reality. Indeed, it has its own deep materiality inscribed in its very fabric: water and wine, oil and bread, light and incense, stones and flowers. With its ancient materiality, the liturgical tradition opens up a world beyond either the religious flavor of the day or my own contingent life-world with its kitchen table, cats, and compost heap. There is more to encountering the divine presence than the spiritual experiences mediated by my middle-class existence and its trappings.

Sometimes, in fact, the liturgical tradition is clearly ahead of the contemporary everyday imagination and its attendant spiritual sensibilities. The Milk and Honey Ritual celebrated at the Re-Imagining Conference, which was held in Minneapolis in 1993 to mark the midpoint of the Decade of Churches in Solidarity with Women, might serve as an example. The woman who crafted the ritual had sought to celebrate women's bodies and sensuality, not least of all by invoking the feminine symbols of milk and honey for the Creator God's abundant goodness and care. After the Re-Imagining Conference, this ritual became a focal point of conservative indignation, since the ritual was seen as beyond the boundaries of the Christian tradition. The critics seemed unaware that in the early centuries, Christian communities blessed a chalice filled with milk and honey at the Easter Vigil and offered the consecrated cup to the newly baptized together with bread and wine. Texts of ancient prayers over this milk and honey chalice are extant; they invoke God to make the elements of milk and honey signs of God's abundant care. Is it not worth (re-)discovering these and other fragments of the tradition, broken open for the sake of women's lives today?

"That Nothing May Be Lost"

Obviously, the impulse to gather fragments is shaped by the times we live in, especially the multiple fragmentations so evident in contemporary, disparate postmodernities.[10] But the desire at the heart of *Fragments of Real Presence*—however consonant with postmodern sensibilities—has its roots in more ancient times. In some small way, the impulse to gather fragments simply responds to a command of Jesus himself. In times past, such "dominical commands," that is, explicit mandates of Jesus, were crucial for what came to be considered a sacrament. "Do this in memory of me," or "Go into all the world and baptize" are dominical commands at the heart of the sacramental life of the church. The dominical command to "gather up the fragments" (John 6:12), however, has hardly ever inspired the sacramental imagination. Or has it?

The biblical story that leads up to Jesus' command to gather fragments is the story of the multiplication of five loaves and two fish. With these loaves and fish, Jesus feeds a large crowd—"about five thousand men, besides women and children"[11]—by the Sea of Galilee. The way this story is told in the Gospel of John richly echoes Israel's Scriptures. There is the memory of the gift of manna, the bread from heaven, in the wilderness (Exod. 16). There are the five loaves of the "bread of the Presence" that sustained David (1 Sam. 21:3–6). And there is the invitation of Lady Wisdom to the feast of life, for which she has prepared bread and wine (Prov. 9:5, cf. Sir. 24:19–21). Bread spells life in such a context. But the story in the Gospels does not end with the feeding of the five thousand.

> When they were satisfied, [Jesus] told his disciples, "Gather up the fragments left over, so that nothing may be lost." So they gathered them up, and from the fragments of the five barley loaves, left by those who had eaten, they filled twelve baskets. (John 6:12ff.)

The Greek words in John 6:12, "that nothing may be lost" (*hina mē ti apolētai*), are the same words used in the worn, yet at heart dramatic text of John 3:16: "For God so loved the world that he gave his only Son, so that everyone who believes in him *may not perish* but may have eternal life." The same Greek verb for "to perish/lose" reappears in John 6 when Jesus defines the meaning of his own life: "that I should lose nothing of all that [the Father] has given me, but raise it up on the last day" (John 6:39).[12] Unmistakably, Jesus' command to gather fragments "so that nothing may be lost" has a redemptive vision embedded in it. A part of this redemptive vision is linked to bread, that material reality which is the fragments. In the Gospel of John, the feeding of the multitude and the gathering of the fragments lead to Jesus' wonderful words about himself being the true Bread of Life, a bread that "gives life to the world" (John 6:33).[13] To taste Jesus, in other words, "is to taste life."[14] No wonder early Christians wove the language of Jesus' gift of bread, of gathering, and of fragments into their own eucharistic reflections.[15] Here, after all, are both the reality of brokenness and a hope of wholeness, all in one. Here are the hunger of the world and God's wild desire to become for us ever new Bread of Life. Fragments may just be "our best possession."[16] And gathering them may just hold its own promise of wholeness.

Fragments of Time and Rhythms of Grace

But how to break open and how to gather the liturgical tradition for the sake of women's lives today? How to map liturgy inflected by women's lives? *Fragments of Real Presence* privileges the rhythm of time in intertwining women's lives and the life of the liturgy; that is to say, it follows the rhythm of the year with its times and seasons. In part, this is an acknowledgment of how women's cycles and the liturgical cycle have shaped each other. For centuries, women's days of feasting and fasting, of labor and of rest were largely those of the church's calendar. Gendered asymmetry did, of course, mark these realities as it marked all others. A Sunday under the conditions of nineteenth-century, white, middle-class domesticity, for example, with food on the table for a large family and guests, would not have been the same "day of rest" for the wife that it was for the husband. Many of the ways in which women's lives and the life of the liturgy interrelated have become unusable today. This is the case not least of all because the gender constructions of the past and their interpretive powers have begun to crumble. An example from the mid-twentieth century illustrates this point.

Beyond the Liturgical Year in the Kitchen

In the renewal movement known as the Liturgical Movement, women actively sought and found ways their daily lives could be shaped by the power of the church's liturgy.[17] A telling example is the little book by Florence S. Berger, *Cooking for Christ: The Liturgical*

Year in the Kitchen, published in 1949. Far more than a simple cook-book, *Cooking for Christ* provides something like liturgical catechesis for women living under the conditions of traditional domesticity (*aka* housewives). The book highlights domestic devotional practices linked with the worship of the church, narrates family anecdotes in relation to liturgical celebrations, and, of course, provides recipes, mostly for traditional dishes connected in one way or another with liturgical feasts and seasons. In her preface, Berger (1909–1983), a well-known activist Catholic laywoman, writes:

> To some it may seem sacrilegious to connect cookery and Christ, but that is exactly what this book means to do. If I am to carry Christ home with me from the altar, I am afraid he will have to come to the kitchen because much of my time is spent there. . . . Liturgists have called us back to a vision of early Christian worship and have begged for more active lay participation in the Lord's service. . . . Now perhaps mothers and daughters can lead their families back to Christ-centered living and cooking. Foods can be symbols which lead the mind to spiritual think-ing.[18]

Berger's little volume, connecting Catholic women's lives and the liturgical tradition, was by no means alone in the mid-twentieth century. The *Feast Day Cookbook* by Katherine Burton and Helmut Ripperger and the *Cookbook for Fridays and Lent* by Irma Rhode appeared just a couple of years later. Berger herself added a companion volume to *Cooking for Christ,* subtitled *Your Kitchen Prayer Book.* These books witness to a grandiose attempt to relate traditional domestic life to the liturgical life of the church (at a point in the twentieth century when the two were beginning to part ways). Such attempts were not focused on the kitchen alone; they *were,* however, focused almost exclusively on the domestic sphere. The Catholic Women's Union, to name but one other example, adopted a series of resolutions at its annual convention in 1933 that illustrates this point. The resolutions outline a detailed liturgical turn in women's lives: from removing "unworthy pictures" from the walls and the blessing of a home by a priest to placing holy water fonts in individual rooms; from making baptismal garments to abolishing birthday parties in favor of celebrating the children's saints' days and baptismal anniversaries; from cultivating a "Catholic Saturday evening spirit" to "[s]uper-naturalizing" the Christmas Eve celebration.[19]

Cycles of Women's Lives

These examples from the mid-twentieth century illustrate why the maps of the past for the relationship between women's lives and liturgical life need to be critically sifted. These maps are problematic because the geographies of women's lives have undergone profound changes. A new cartography is needed that accounts for the immense cultural shifts that have taken place in recent decades. These shifts have effectively broken off the traditional narrative of what it means to be "woman." The diversity of contemporary women's lives was unimaginable when our grandmothers were young. Women now routinely work outside the home; our lives have been shaped not only by professional opportunities but also by diversifying family patterns, new reproductive technologies, and an increasing awareness of the manifold cultural constraints on women. Essentializing presuppositions about "womanhood" have lost their explanatory power, and women's lives have come to be acknowledged as always locally situated and context-specific. Women in the church have been shaped by these cultural shifts as much as anyone else. The church, indeed, now has its own chorus of voices struggling to articulate a "perspective of diverse women's flourishing."[20]

While women's lives have changed dramatically, so has liturgical life. The Tridentine Mass of our grandmothers is little more than a memory. In addition, the liturgy can no longer simply be assumed to yield the dominant categories that women's lives will be made to fit. There is no un-knowing the ambiguity of the liturgical tradition for our lives. This ambiguity, after all, is one of the reasons why other sites of meaning, such as the everyday, have come to the spiritual foreground in recent years. If liturgy and women's lives are to relate, the potential of *both* to render real the presence of God will have to be acknowledged from the outset.

In light of all this, *Fragments of Real Presence* chooses to privilege the rhythm of times and seasons for its own explorations. Time has become one of the scarcest of all resources that shape contemporary lives, especially women's lives. But beyond the sheer scarcity of time, its very rhythm is a good illustration of the multiple subject positions women inhabit today. Not least of all as women of faith, we live synchronously within different calendars and their distinct mappings of time. There is the calendar of the liturgy, to be sure, with its feasts and fasts, its moments of celebration and reconciliation. This liturgical calendar itself is already shaped by a number of cycles that fuse in ever-changing ways each unfolding year. There is, within the liturgical calendar, the lunar cycle, which determines the central date of Easter and thereby also the dates of Lent and Pentecost. There is the daily cycle of prayer from dawn to nightfall, the cycle of movable feasts and fasts, and the sanctoral cycle that patterns each year. Within the complexity of the liturgical calendar, there are different cultural memories and accents that will, for example, make a Hispanic liturgy for El Día de Los Muertos look very different from a Mass on the same All Souls' Day in a "white" parish. But beyond the differences already present in the liturgical calendar, even the most pious lives today are also marked by other rhythms of time. There is the civil calendar, which tells us, for example, when to pay taxes and when to vote—never mind when to celebrate Women's History Month or Thanksgiving. There are our work-related calendars and the school calendars of the children (some-how these two calendars seem designed to conflict on a regular basis). There is our very own personal calendar and rhythm of life, with its birthdays, anniversaries, and monthly days when our bodies obey the pull of the moon, at least between menarche and menopause. There are the "global" days, a phenomenon spawned by the rapid process of globalization through the twentieth century. These days, from the International Day of Remembrance of the Rwandan Genocide, World AIDS Day, and International Women's Day to World Turtle Day, are celebrated with varying degrees of intensity around the globe. Finally, there are extraordinary moments that inscribe themselves across most calendars, forever marking a particular date. 9/11 was such a moment.

Fragments of Real Presence mirrors lived life in that it holds different calendars together in its journey through the year. Even if the liturgical calendar provides the framework for the book, the texts do not begin (as does the church year officially) with the First Sunday in Advent. Rather, the book picks up—as do most of our lives—somewhere in the middle of a given year. And as do our lived lives, the texts move from fragment to fragment, following a pattern of their own making.[21] No grand narrative supports the movement, only a basic impulse that might be put thus: In case of a fragment, gather.

Fragments Are Our Best Possession

As the twelve glimpses of encounters between the lives of women and the life of the liturgy at the beginning of this introduction show, "women" is not a one-size-fits-all category. There is no universal "woman" who celebrates a universal liturgy.[22] If nothing else, women's lives today have to be respected in their radical diversity; women are not a unified or homogeneous subject. One way to honor this diversity is through a variety of genres that speak the diverse truths of women's lives. In the texts that follow, the different genres—meditations, stories, prayers, theological reflections, historical reconstructions, biblical and cultural analyses, liturgies, letters—witness to the variety of registers in which women make meaning with the liturgical tradition.

This variety of registers points to a deeper truth that might be described as the multiplicity inherent in all liturgical meaning. We are, in fact, all familiar with this in lived life. Think of this simple example. The biblical image of God's abundant grace as an "overflowing torrent" (Isa. 66:12 NAB) will "mean differently" for a woman running through a torrential downpour to get her infant son to the church for baptism, than for a woman in a drought-stricken part of the world who walks twelve miles every day to fill buckets of water at a well. It will mean differently again for a woman in rural eastern North Carolina who, years after Hurricane Floyd swept through, still has not been able to return to her flood-ravaged home. With its different genres, *Fragments of Real Presence,* then, is an invitation neither to sameness nor to wholeness, but to a gathering of always diverse and ever-new fragments in women's lives as they are inflected by the rhythm of the liturgical tradition.

Liturgy and Women's Lives: A Concelebration

One way of imagining the intertwining between liturgy and women's lives is to think of a concelebration: a concelebration between the liturgical tradition, with its texts and celebrations, and the realities of the lives women bring to every liturgical celebration. In the past, scholars have identified the meaning of a liturgy with the texts of the liturgy in question and with what these texts govern. But just as there is no generic woman, there also exists no generic liturgy. There is consequently no simple way to identify liturgical meaning, since there never is a single meaning in any liturgical event that can be said to be definitive.[23] The particularities of liturgical subjects, that is, the worshipers, are co-constitutive in the making of liturgical meaning. Moreover, not only are there "as many interpretations, or 'meanings,' for any liturgical act as there are people attending,"[24] but there are actually *more* meanings than there are people attending, since, rather than being a unified self, most people are better understood as sites of multiple and contesting meanings. And liturgical meaning-making does not stop when people file out of the sanctuary. Much liturgical meaning-making happens outside of the specific time frame of the liturgy itself, as women ponder, find solace in, resist, and subvert liturgical celebrations and their power in lived life.

Liturgical meaning, in short, is created by people (in the case of this book, women) conspiring with the biblical texts, the rubrics, the priests, and each other—but regularly also "against" them—to discern the presence of the living God and their own lives as graced within that presence. In that sense, every liturgy is a concelebration: Women, as indeed all present, always concelebrate with the presider. Concelebration is not a particular priestly "special." It is the basic form of all liturgy. And liturgy is a concelebration not only in terms of a multitude of celebrants, but also in terms of the material givens of the celebrants' lived lives and the wider cultures they inhabit. Rain or drought, race and gender, our baptismal or our funeral liturgies—all of these mean differently for each of us. Our lives do inflect liturgical meaning-making in particular ways.[25]

Twelve Baskets of Leftovers: Or, Toward a New Wholeness

Having gathered *Fragments of Real Presence,* I cannot but wonder what happened to the twelve baskets of leftovers, once those fragments had been gathered in response to Jesus' charge. The writer of the Gospel of John did not find this a question worth pondering. I am therefore left without an answer. Close to two thousand years later, however, someone else pondered the meaning of fragments and of their gathering, this time not at a lakeshore but in a prison cell. The insights born in this prison cell shed light both on the story told in John 6 and on the texts that follow in this book.

On February 20, 1944, Dietrich Bonhoeffer saw his life as "split . . . into fragments, like bombs falling on houses."[26] The violence of an inhuman war that he witnessed and lived through had shattered any sense of wholeness in his own life. Yet, out of this painful experience grew a profound insight about the very meaning of wholeness: "[T]his very fragmentariness [in the German original simply *das Fragment*] may, in fact, point towards a fulfillment beyond the limits of human achievement," Bonhoeffer wrote in his prison cell.[27] A day later, the same theme is still with him, this time in even greater clarity and depth:

> The important thing today is that we should be able to discern from the fragment of our life how the whole was arranged and planned, and what material it consists of. For really, there are some fragments that are only worth throwing into the dustbin . . . and others whose importance lasts for centuries, because their completion can only be a matter for God, and so they are fragments that must be fragments.[28]

Bonhoeffer knew from the violent fragmentation of his own life that if brokenness is to become a new wholeness, this wholeness will have to be born of something stronger than human making. Such wholeness beyond our own making can only be received as gift, made by a power beyond our own. As the medievalist Caroline Walker Bynum puts it in her own moving reflection on fragments: "Only supernatural power can reassemble fragments so completely that no particle of them is lost, or miraculously empower the part to *be* the whole."[29]

But if the gathering of fragments is all we can ever do, since wholeness is beyond our power to make, there is nevertheless a gesture toward a new wholeness inscribed in the very act of gathering. In this act of gathering itself, we catch glimpses of a wholeness yet to be, even if this wholeness itself remains elusive. These glimpses of wholeness are not devoid of power. As gestures of defiance and hope, they do inspire, shape, and nurture ways of living beyond fragmentariness in this world. The gospel story of the gathering of fragments itself points to this. The leftovers, after all, are said to have filled twelve baskets, not eleven or thirteen. The symbolic number twelve will have evoked wholeness and completion not only for the descendants of the twelve tribes of Israel but also for those who remember twelve being called as apostles. The twelve baskets, then, spell wholeness—all the while holding only fragments, gathered. Jesus himself strengthens that spell. His charge to the disciples to "gather up the fragments left over" includes a glimpse of redemptive possibilities: "so that nothing may be lost." Surely those words, in the mouth of the One who came precisely for the lost, evoke a redemptive vision beyond brokenness. The gathering of fragments itself can be said to embody hope, namely, for a wholeness beyond that which a gathering of fragments itself can give. Such gathering, at the same time, is an act of defiance against the ever-present forces of fragmentariness in our lives. The gathering of fragments denies to these forces the last and defining word on fragments.

What might emerge from the gesture toward wholeness and the act of defiance and hope embodied in this book? On one level, the fragments simply offer glimpses of the liturgical tradition as a site of life, natality, and flourishing,[30] as well as a space of lament, endurance, and solace for women's lives. The new wholeness that beckons in the gathering of these fragments will, however, have to be larger than our own lives or even the whole of "women's lives," if it is to be true to God's own redemptive desire for wholeness. It is for this reason that *Fragments of Real Presence* ultimately must not only speak of women's lives and liturgy but must open up a passionate commitment to the whole cosmos "groaning" for redemption (Rom. 8:22ff.). The world we inhabit is nothing if not in violent labor pains. It is a world that desperately needs midwives, women who know how to be "with" (from the word's origins in Middle English). Without women who are "with," how will this world glimpse a God who is "with," God-with-us, Emmanuel?

I will never know what happened with the twelve baskets of leftovers that day by the lake, after Jesus had wondrously multiplied five loaves of bread and two fish. But I suspect it was left to the women to figure out what to do with the fragments. Women, after all, were responsible for making bread in Jesus' time. Bread making was a distinctly female, often communal, and overall time-intensive labor.[31] Jesus, in multiplying five loaves, took this distinctly female labor upon himself. And the twelve baskets of leftover fragments of bread that were the result of this generous bread making? I imagine that women simply continued the labor that was theirs with these fragments of bread. The women will have taken the baskets of leftovers and done with them what they knew to do: to feed a world so very hungry, and to let the fragments become glimpses of a God who always and everywhere desires to become the Bread of our Lives.

We, who two thousand years later still claim that tradition, know well that God's wild desire to be the Bread of Life ultimately had to mean the fragmentation of God's own body, broken for us. Fragments of real presence, indeed.

Saint Mary of Magdala (July 22)

Framing the Apostle to the Apostles

F OR A GROWING NUMBER OF WOMEN around the world, July 22 has become one of the highlights of the calendars we keep in our hearts. It is the feast day of a biblical woman who, until quite recently, was seen more through the eyes of a tradition that had framed her as a prostitute than through the biblical story itself. Since the publication of Dan Brown's furiously successful novel *The Da Vinci Code,* on the other hand, she has become best known as the (conjectured) wife of Jesus of Nazareth and the mother of their child. Contrary both to Dan Brown's domesticating and romanticizing image of Mary Magdalene as wife and mother, and to the traditional image of her as a repentant prostitute, the biblical story frames her along very different lines. Mary is a key disciple; she is also the first witness to the resurrection, and as such, an apostle to the apostles. Given that Mary of Magdala's picture has been framed in distinct ways over the course of two millennia, how can we frame her today? And how does she help us frame our own images of ourselves and what it means to be women who witness to life out of death? To answer these questions, I begin with a look at the biblical frame.

The Biblical Frame

The picture of Mary of Magdala framed by the biblical witness is quite small, and the frame is fairly simple. It looks something like this: What we know historically about Mary of Magdala comes from the four gospels, and it is much less than the later framing of her life would lead us to believe.[1] But the little that is there is telling. First, Mary, in contradistinction to other biblical women, is not identified by relationality, that is, as daughter, wife, or mother of a male figure. Rather, she is identified by her native city, Magdala. Magdala was a Jewish commercial fishing village on the edge of the Sea of Galilee, just north of Tiberias (the Aramaic *magdala* means tower or fortress, which is why Mary of Magdala is sometimes represented in Christian iconography with a tower in her hands). This identification of Mary's name with a city, rather than with a man, probably means that she was both independent and wealthy, a privileged position for a woman of her time. The Gospel of Luke (8:2) tells us that Mary suffered a profound illness ("seven demons" is the description that the gospel writer uses), but that in her encounter with Jesus, she is healed. Mary becomes one of Jesus' disciples and one of several women on whom the Jesus movement depends for financial support. Again, this is a position of relative privilege and power for a woman of Mary's time.

Mary of Magdala is present at the central events that the gospels witness to: Jesus' crucifixion, burial, and resurrection. The Gospel of John describes Mary as the first to encounter the risen Lord. She is charged with proclaiming the Good News of the resurrection to the "brothers." Mary's subsequent proclamation has become the foundational witness of our faith: "I have seen the Lord" (John 20:18).[2] It is no wonder that, in the gospels, the name of Mary of Magdala routinely leads the list of women disciples in much the same way that the name of Simon Peter heads the list of male disciples. It is also no wonder that Hippolytus, in the early third century, describes her in his *Commentary on the Song of Songs* as someone who is like an apostle to the apostles (25.6ff.). Others in the history of the church—from Rhabanus Maurus in the ninth century to Abelard and Bernard of Clairvaux in the twelfth century to Thomas Aquinas in the thirteenth century to Pope John Paul II in our own time—have followed Hippolytus in this.[3] It is not surprising that in early noncanonical accounts of Jesus' life, death, and resurrection, Mary of Magdala can be described as the most beloved disciple of Jesus (*Gospel of Philip* 55) or as the one who has a deeper understanding of Jesus than any of the other disciples. The latter is the case in a noncanonical gospel named after Mary of Magdala, the *Gospel of Mary*.[4] Given that the earliest framing of Mary of Magdala shows a woman leader in the Christian community, the first one to whom the risen Christ appears and the first one commissioned to proclaim the resurrection, why have most of us grown up with images of Mary as a beautiful whore, albeit repentant? The answer lies with the second frame —this one very lavish and elaborate—which came to envelop the figure of this Mary.

Further Framing

Already in the New Testament, the witness to Mary of Magdala is not uniform. The Gospel of Luke, for example, passes over any apostolic charge given by the risen Christ to Mary of Magdala and the other women witnesses to the resurrection. The apostle Paul does the same in his well-known list of witnesses to the resurrection: "Christ . . . appeared to Cephas, then to the twelve. Then he appeared to more than five hundred brothers and sisters . . ." (1 Cor. 15:5ff.). Indeed, Mary of Magdala is conspicuously absent from the Acts of the Apostles and the New Testament epistles.[5] As centuries passed by, these accounts seemed to gain in importance; Mary of Magdala as first witness to the resurrection consequently receded into the background. But how did she ever come to be framed as a prostitute? The answer lies in the fact that a number of New Testament stories, which, in the gospels themselves, are quite separate, came to be read together. Out of this conflation of stories emerged a composite picture of a "Magdalene." Here is how this frame was put together: The biblical Mary of Magdala came to be identified with other women and other Marys (the "muddle of Marys," as Marina Warner has called it), especially with the unnamed woman in the Gospel of Mark (Mark 14:3–9, par. Matt 26:6–13) and Mary of Bethany in the Gospel of John, who anointed Jesus with costly perfume (John 12:1–8). Luke similarly describes a woman anointing Jesus' feet but knows her as a public sinner, that is, a prostitute (Luke 7:36–50). This conflation, in turn, invited a further conflation. The woman caught in adultery and brought to Jesus (John 8) was also added to the composite picture of a "Magdalene." In this conflation of several biblical stories into one, Mary of Magdala's frame was significantly enlarged beyond the original biblical testimony to this particular woman. Mary of Magdala had now become a prostitute, an adulteress, and the sister of Martha and Lazarus of Bethany, all in one. This (con-)fusion is clearly established by the time of Pope Gregory the Great at the end of the sixth century. Gregory was convinced that Mary of Magdala, Mary of Bethany, the unnamed woman who anointed Jesus' feet, and the public sinner were all one and the same woman. Interestingly enough, the Eastern churches never combined all these stories in the same way the Western church did, although, as early as Hippolytus's *Commentary on the Song of Songs,* Mary of Magdala was identified with Mary of Bethany. Against the clear witness of Scripture, Hippolytus imagined the two sisters, Mary and Martha, both of Bethany, to be the first to encounter the risen Christ. Some Eastern traditions even conflated the Virgin Mary and Mary Magdalene, so that the former could be the one to encounter the resurrected Jesus in the garden.

The lavish framing of Mary of Magdala in the Western church did not stop with Gregory the Great or the conflation of several biblical stories into one. By the time of the *Legenda Aurea,* a widely read thirteenth-century collection of saints' lives, the image of the Magdalene had acquired a most elaborate frame indeed. Mary now is of royal lineage, as are her siblings, Martha and Lazarus. Their parents are even named: Syrus and Eucharia. Furthermore, Mary's story in the *Legenda Aurea* by no means ends with a repentant prostitute encountering the risen Christ. Mary Magdalene now sails across the Mediterranean to southern France and preaches the gospel there, converting the ruling family and the peoples. The legend thus describes a double apostolate of Mary: one oriented toward the male apostles immediately after the resurrection and one exercised much later in southern France.[6] Mary then withdraws to the wilderness and lives in stark ascetic penitence for thirty more years until she dies. This Mary Magdalene is buried in what is surely one of the most beautiful cathedrals in Europe, Vézelay.

What a rich story! It is no wonder that by the time of the Renaissance, Western art had made this Mary Magdalene a beloved subject. Under the guise of depicting an edifying biblical story, many painters welcomed the opportunity to display a female body, highly eroticized and sexualized, and have the church gaze approvingly at it. Harriet Beecher Stowe later noted disapprovingly in her *Woman in Sacred History:* "Many artists seem to have seen in the subject only a chance to paint a voluptuously beautiful woman in tears."[7]

Nevertheless, even in times of heightened interest in Mary Magdalene as a repentant prostitute, knowledge about Mary of Magdala's apostolic function was never lost.[8] In fact, the veneration of an apostolic Mary Magdalene gained strength with the twelfth century.[9] In the above-mentioned *Legenda Aurea,* after all, Mary of Magdala is shown as preaching and converting. And the twelfth-century St. Albans Psalter (probably commissioned by the anchoress Christina of Markyate) depicts Mary authoritatively proclaiming the resurrection to the eleven remaining apostles.[10] The illustration invites the interpretation that Mary is the twelfth apostle. The Dominicans in the later Middle Ages also foregrounded Mary of Magdala as a preacher, no doubt in order to strengthen their own preaching mission. In the early sixteenth century, the humanist scholar Faber Stapulensis contended that three different biblical women had come to be conflated and confused in the traditional image of Mary Magdalene. Faber's contention was condemned. It would take another almost five hundred years for this insight into the problem with the traditional framing of Mary Magdalene to become commonplace.

Given the overlap of the different frames that Scripture and tradition have handed us for the images of Mary of Magdala and Mary Magdalene, how do we look at her today? In the last few decades, there has been a renewed interest in taking a fresh look at this biblical woman. A multitude of books and articles, films and videos, images, icons, cards, songs, and stained-glass windows witness to this interest. And the nearly seven million copies sold of Dan Brown's *Da Vinci Code* have brought to the forefront yet another framing of Mary Magdalene: the secret lover and wife of Jesus who is also the mother of his child. But years before Dan Brown framed Mary thus, women around the world had begun to mark the feast day of St. Mary of Magdala with celebrations, gatherings, liturgies, and prayers. A great reclaiming of this woman is taking place in our time, and, as with every reclaiming, this one also involves a reframing.

What frames are available to us today? Dan Brown's framing of Mary Magdalene as Jesus' lover, the mother of his child, and an embodiment of the "divine feminine"—even if part of a wonderful read—is precisely what its title says—a novel, a fictional narrative.[11] What other frames are available? One possibility is simply to go back to the biblical frame and to reclaim Mary of Magdala as a leader in the early Jesus movement, as the first to witness the resurrection and as the apostle to the apostles. This is, indeed, how much of the contemporary scholarly rediscovery of Mary of Magdala has proceeded. The second frame— that of the repentant prostitute Mary Magdalene—then simply has to be discarded as fraudulent. Mary of Magdala was indeed "framed" by a tradition that made her into someone she, according to the biblical witness, clearly was not. The traditional, deceptive framing of Mary of Magdala can then be read as an expression of a wider problematic, namely, how a woman leader in the early Jesus movement had to be remade into a more traditional image of "woman": the sexual temptress who, for God, leaves her body and her sexuality behind and transforms herself through a life of ascetic renunciation.

But leaving behind this framing of Mary Magdalene as a repentant prostitute also means leaving behind the manifold ways in which our mothers and grandmothers, and so many women through the centuries, have found meaning and solace in this image of Mary Magdalene. Women throughout the Christian tradition have loved Mary precisely as that sinful woman whom Jesus so loved. Teresa of Ávila is only one among many who were deeply devoted to this "glorious Magdalene" (*Book of Her Life* 9.2). As an older woman friend of mine cautioned me, "I would not deprive the world of this beloved character!"

Can this traditional framing of Mary Magdalene as a repentant prostitute bear any wisdom for us today? I will take for granted that we would not want to frame Mary of Magdala as a repentant prostitute to detract from her ministry as the apostle to the apostles or to mark women's bodies and women's sexuality as a problem for a life of faith. I will also take for granted that we do not need that image of Mary Magdalene to be able to defend her position as the patron saint of hairdressers, and comb and perfume makers. But saving the traditional framing of Mary of Magdala as a repentant prostitute, rather than discarding it, does offer intriguing possibilities for today. Let me suggest just one.

Today, we no longer have to read prostitution primarily as a sign of women's lust. That interpretive lens is outdated and does not do justice to the stark reality of what prostitution means for women today. I read prostitution primarily not as an evil of women's lust, but as an evil of sexual exploitation of women's bodies, often forced on women out of economic necessity. In fact, sex trafficking of young women today is one of the fastest growing criminal enterprises in the global economy. As Amnesty International reports:

> Women are recruited on false pretenses, coerced, transported, and bought and sold for a range of exploitative purposes. . . . Women who are trafficked for sexual exploitation are often sexually abused and raped to break them mentally and emotionally, in order to force them into sex work. Many are beaten and raped to punish them for trying to escape or for refusing to have sex for money. Despite the risks of HIV/AIDS, women are often punished for refusing unprotected sex.[12]

What does this have to do with Mary of Magdala and Mary Magdalene? I think that opening our eyes to the present reality of women's lives might help us create a new frame for this Mary that can hold the older frames together in ways that speak to us today. I imagine framing Mary of Magdala as a symbol of a misused, exploited, and trafficked woman who was freed and healed in the encounter with Jesus. The powerful attraction that drew this woman to Jesus undid all other ways of living for her. The encounter with Jesus thus freed Mary from "seven demons"—why should the sexual exploitation of women's bodies not be one of these? It is certainly a demon that has plagued women's lives for millennia. But there is more to this Mary than her demons. It is this woman's body, with its history of abuse and exploitation, that becomes the first site of encounter with Christ's resurrected body. It is precisely this woman—not the Virgin Mother or any other immaculate figure—whom the risen Jesus chooses to appear to first. And it is precisely this woman—with a history of abuse and exploitation—who is charged to be the apostle to the apostles. Granted, the biblical witness itself does not make this connection, but the Scriptures also do not render it impossible. There may be something precisely in this framing of Mary Magdalene as a prostitute-turned-apostle that can evoke for us the power of redemption, of the wholeness of very concretely broken women's lives and bodies, and of the beauty of a God who does not shun the messiness of our lived lives.

Finally, then, I come back to us, women at the beginning of the twenty-first century. In attempting to frame Mary of Magdala for our times and for the lives of women today, we are, to some degree, framing ourselves. Mary's story, the image of her that we decide to frame, becomes a frame for seeing the histories and struggles of all women, especially in the church. In understanding her, she can help us understand ourselves. In rendering her visible, we also become visible. In reclaiming her, she reclaims us as women witnessing to a God who calls forth life out of death. There are questions that she asks of us with which to frame our own lives and ministries as women: How do we continue her solidarity in suffering and her apostolic witness to life? Where are the crosses of our day and age that others run from and that we are called to stand by? Who are the gardeners in our lives, the ones we mistake? How does our name have to be called for us to recognize the voice of God? Which ways of living as "woman" are we called to resist and leave behind in order to live the gospel?

Our own framings of Mary of Magdala will be incomplete until we allow her to frame these questions for our lives, for her apostolic witness in our midst continues. Every time we profess that we believe in the one, holy, catholic, and apostolic church, Mary of Magdala herself stands at the very foundation of this apostolicity.[13] She proclaims to us, as she proclaimed to the male disciples so long ago: "I have seen the Lord." May this apostle to the apostles encourage us to go and do likewise.

Sunday in Ordinary Time
Proclaiming Life

A WOMAN HURRIES TO CHURCH with her infant son. Her babysitting arrangement fell through at the last minute. It is too late to find another person to take her place as lector in this liturgy. Arriving at church, the woman hesitates for a moment, then asks the young priest to carry the gospel book in procession, a task that belongs to the lector. The woman herself takes her place behind the altar servers and processes into the sanctuary, carrying her sleeping baby. Slowly making her way down the aisle, the woman catches surprised looks as people take note of the infant in her arms. With a measure of defiance, she lifts the baby higher, almost as high as the gospel book she is supposed to carry into the sanctuary. She is struck by the promise of life in both.

As is the custom in the parish, the woman sits next to the priest throughout the liturgy. Today, she cradles her infant, wondering what she will do should the little one awake and want to nurse. Rising to proclaim the Scriptures, she knows no better than to entrust her sleeping baby to the young priest. She reads more rapidly than usual, but her voice carries as the ancient exuberant words of the prophet Isaiah begin to fill the sanctuary:

> Rejoice with Jerusalem and be glad because of her,
>   all you who love her;
> exult, exult with her,
>   all you who were mourning over her!
> Oh, that you may suck fully
>   of the milk of her comfort,
> that you may nurse with delight
>   at her abundant breasts!
>
> For thus says the Lord:
> Lo, I will spread prosperity over Jerusalem like a river,
>   and the wealth of the nations like an overflowing torrent.
> As nurslings, you shall be carried in her arms,
>   and fondled in her lap;
> as a mother comforts her child,

so will I comfort you;
   in Jerusalem you shall find your comfort.
When you see this, your heart shall rejoice,
   and your bodies flourish like the grass;
the Lord's power shall be known to his servants.
(Isa. 66:10–14c)[1]

Reading Isaiah's words, the woman all but forgets the puzzling advice from her *Workbook for Lectors:* "If you are initially uncomfortable with the image of a woman nursing her child, practice the passage until you are confident that you can proclaim it as God's message of tender love."[2] The woman's voice, which only an hour ago sang to her child as she breast-fed, carries all imaginable fullness of confidence in Isaiah's words.

Hearing his mother's voice now at a distance, however, the infant begins a wailing protest in the priest's arms, evoking soft laughter from among the congregation. The mother quickly returns to her seat and gathers her child in her arms. The priest is free to proceed to read the Gospel for the day, struggling to proclaim words of life for the women and men in front of him.

At the end of the liturgy, the woman processes out of the sanctuary with her child in her arms. She sees some of the women in the pews smiling at her, knowingly. As she leaves the church, one of the women catches her. She whispers: "I saw my life brought into the sanctuary today."

Sunday in Extra-Ordinary Time
Voiceless Women

T HE PREVIOUS STORY about a Sunday in ordinary time also is a story
about extra-ordinary time. Rarely in Sunday liturgies are women's
concrete life experiences and struggles rendered as visible as they are in
that story. Not only did a woman choose to bring the concreteness of
her life, with all its inevitable complications, into the liturgy, but the
Old Testament reading also was rich in metaphors taken from a
woman's life, in this case from the practices of mothering and nursing.
Unfortunately, biblical readings that resonate clearly with women's
lives are rare. There are three main reasons for this. To begin with, the
Scriptures as a whole have a decidedly androcentric bias. The textual
representation of women in the Bible simply is limited. Second, the
androcentric bias of the biblical witness is heightened by the politics of
translation that for most Christians mediate the biblical witness.
Unless one reads Hebrew and Greek, translation is the only way to
encounter Scripture. Translation, however, is no innocent enterprise.
Two examples with regard to biblical women "lost in translation"
make this clear. There is, first, the apostle Junia, whom Paul greets in
his Letter to the Romans (Rom. 16:7). This apostle—someone who had
seen the risen Christ and been called to preach the Good News—was
imprisoned at the same time as Paul, was "prominent among the apostles," and "in Christ" before Paul himself embraced the faith. So much
for Paul's description of this person. Although early Christian commentators praised this Junia as a female apostle, later commentators
interpreted the Greek name to refer to a male Junias (a name nowhere
attested in Greek). Only recently have interpreters come to acknowledge that the name is that of a woman apostle, Junia.[1] For almost a mil-
lennium, however, readers of the New Testament not familiar with the
intricacies of both the Greek language and its attendant cultural context had to assume this apostle to be male. This is no minor accident.
Much in relation to women's vocations and ministries hinges on the
biblical witness, after all. Another example of the politics of biblical
interpretation for the reality of women's lives is the parable of the

Widow and the Unjust Judge (Luke 18:1–8). Jesus here makes a woman and her unrelenting struggle for justice the symbol of what it means to pray persistently and without losing heart. Many translations, however, soften Jesus' image of this woman's relentless struggle for justice. In Jesus' parable, the unjust judge actually becomes worried that the woman might "hit him under the eye" (so the quite literal translation of *hypōpiazō*). Many translations soften this feared blow and render the woman's powerful presence as merely one of "wearing out" the unjust judge (Luke 18:5).[2] Such translations are a far cry from the fearless image of this woman portrayed by Jesus. The translations do come quite close, however, to cultural stereotypes of women as whining their way through life.

The androcentric bias of the biblical witness and of its translators comes to be further heightened by the choice of passages for reading in the liturgy. The lectionary that governs this choice simply has not attended carefully enough to biblical stories about women and their faith.[3] These absences speak loudly in the liturgical assembly, particularly to women who have learned to ask why their foremothers seem voiceless.

Readings That Render Women Voiceless

Take for example the following omissions of biblical women's stories from the lectionary readings.[4] The moving narrative of the two Hebrew midwives Shiphrah and Puah, who set the scene for the story of the Exodus by defying Pharaoh, is simply cut out of the liturgical reading of Exodus 1:8–22. The liturgical reading of this passage inexplicably jumps from v. 14 to v. 22, thus "disappearing" Shiphrah and Puah from sight. As a result, we will never, in a liturgical assembly, hear the stories and names of these two foremothers of ours—although, in a wonderful irony of history, the biblical witness *does* remember their names, while it has forgotten the name of "the pharaoh." It is painful to realize that today this wonderful irony of the biblical witness has almost been undone. Most people will know something about the pharaoh and nothing about the two Hebrew women who defied him. There are other lectionary omissions of women's stories in the midst of longer narratives. Such omissions have rendered invisible, among others, the Hebrew prophet Hulda (2 Kgs. 22:14–20). Hulda's story is that of a temple prophet who is asked to validate a scroll found in the temple during repairs. Hulda validates this "book of the law" with a prophetic word of judgement.[5] Feminist scholars have argued that through this validation, Hulda in fact authorizes what will become the core of our Scriptures: "Her validation of a text . . . stands as the first recognizable act in the long process of canon formation."[6] It is painful that our lectionary thinks nothing of Hulda's authoritative act.

Unfortunately, Shiphrah, Puah, and Hulda are not alone. There are other women whom the lectionary renders invisible through its choice of texts, such as Phoebe, the co-worker of the apostle Paul and "deacon" or "minister" of the church at Cenchreae (Rom. 16:1). The same is true for Lois and Eunice, the grandmother and mother of Timothy, both of whose faith the apostle Paul applauds (2 Tim. 1:5). Additionally, the prophet Deborah, a judge and military leader of Israel, is not allowed to speak to a liturgical assembly, although she is a decisive figure in Israel's settling in Canaan. In the Book of Judges, Deborah's deeds fill two whole chapters (Judg. 4–5). The lectionary, however, knows nothing of this woman. Similarly, short excerpts from the Book of Ruth appear only twice in the lectionary and then only in weekday liturgies. This is especially unfortunate, since Ruth is named explicitly in the New Testament as a foremother of Jesus (Matt. 1:5), making her one of only four women named in the genealogy of the Messiah.

Weekdays are also the only times that we might hear from Esther, the Jewish exile who becomes queen of the Persian empire and who, with her resourcefulness and courage, saves her people. The Book of Esther is particularly striking in its weaving together of two unusual narrative features. The protagonist of the book is a woman, and God as an actor is conspicuously absent (there is simply no mention of God in this biblical book). The people are saved by a woman—and that is all there is to the story. Esther, sadly, is not the only female savior of her people whom the lectionary hides; Judith, too, is an "undocumented" character in the lectionary. We find no trace of this pious widow who saved her people in the choice of readings (except within the common of saints). Interestingly, unlike the heroine of the Book of Esther, Judith is very clear about her divine collaborator: "the Lord will deliver Israel by my hand" (Jdt. 8:33). Judith is also the only biblical woman who pleads with God to make her a good liar. In this, she is one of a larger company of biblical women who practice deceit in order to survive and flourish.[7] Would that we had the complicated richness of the biblical witness of both Esther and Judith to ponder in our liturgical assemblies and for our lives!

There are other biblical women-identified texts that, according to the lectionary, are read only on weekdays, such as Mary's song of praise at her encounter with Elizabeth (Luke 1:46–55). This text is never read on a Sunday. The same applies to the story of Jesus' healing of a crippled woman (Luke 13:10–17). This story—the only text in which Jesus calls a woman "daughter of Abraham"—is not proclaimed on any Sunday. Neither is the story of Jesus appearing to Mary Magdalene and charging her with proclaiming the Good News of the resurrection to the "brothers" (John 20:17).

Optional Presences, Eloquent Absences

The lectionary also assigns women's stories the status of "optional" in a number of readings; that is, these women's stories form part of a longer biblical passage that may be shortened by the presider if he(!) considers the passage too long. The presence of the prophet Anna at the presentation of Jesus in the temple (Luke 2:36–38) thus is rendered optional. Anna's optional presence is especially painful because the biblical witness itself has already left this woman voiceless. While the gospel writer puts a beautiful prayer into the mouth of Simeon ("Master, now you are dismissing your servant in peace, according to your word"), we are left guessing about Anna's eloquence. We hear only that "she came, and began to praise God and speak about the child [Jesus] to all who were looking for the redemption of Jerusalem" (Luke 2:38). Here is a woman who witnesses to Jesus long before any of the apostles embrace that task, and yet her witness in our liturgical assemblies is considered optional!

It is hardly a consolation that Anna at least is not alone in her liturgical status. She is joined in her optional presence by the woman with a hemorrhage who is healed by Jesus (Mark 5:25–34). Since this nameless woman makes her appearance in Mark within the larger narrative of the healing of the daughter of Jairus, this woman also has become liturgically optional. Her presence within the story of the healing of Jairus's daughter does, no doubt, lengthen and complicate the narrative. But cannot this very complication serve as a pointer to the willingness of Jesus to be a healing presence in the often complicated ways in which women's lives intersect? The writer of the Gospel of Mark did not consider this woman's healing optional and neither did Jesus, so why should we? The same applies to the beautiful parable in which Jesus likens the coming of God's reign to a woman baking (Matt. 13:33). This passage, too, is optional on the only Sunday when it might be read, although this is one of the precious few biblical texts that show Jesus drawing on women's everyday lives to image God's reign.

There are yet other ways in which women's presence in the Scriptures and the lectionary readings come to be veiled. Take the reading of Proverbs 31 as just one example. The lectionary omits precisely those verses that show the woman of Proverbs 31 as a powerful and productive household manager and makes us focus instead on her service to her husband. This is a particularly unfortunate decision, since the choice of the gospel text for that Sunday, Matthew 25:14–30, is Jesus' parable of the skilled management of resources. The corresponding verses from Proverbs would be those that show the woman praised in this text as an able household manager, rather than as her husband's "unfailing prize," as the lectionary reading emphasizes (Prov. 31:11).

The Easter Vigil and Women's Menstrual Cycles

Not every omission of women-identified texts in the lectionary is cause for lament. A case in point is one of the biblical readings for the central liturgical celebration of the church year, the Easter Vigil. Right in the heart of the appointed reading from the prophet Ezekiel is a verse in which the prophet proclaims a word from God that indicts the house of Israel: "their conduct in my sight was like the uncleanness of a woman in her menstrual period" (Ezek. 36:17b). While voices from the past can only speak a word from God within the possibilities and constraints of their own cultural contexts, I for one am glad not to have to wrestle with the ancient, powerful imagery of women's menstrual cycles as defilement, especially not in a liturgy that celebrates the very journey from death into life. There are more important issues at hand that night. I therefore appreciate a lectionary selection that spares me the confrontation with Ezekiel 36:17b at that moment and makes me skip from v. 17a to v. 18. On the other hand, being allowed to skip v. 17b suggests that this half-verse is the whole of the problem and that not reading its words takes care of the problem at hand. In reality, this half-verse is only part of a much larger picture. The Book of Ezekiel as a whole uses the metaphor of "woman" to describe idolatry, impurity, profanation, and sinfulness.[8] And so, while I appreciate the possibility of ignoring this reality during the Easter Vigil, we surely need to make room somewhere to confront the fact that our Scriptures contain divine words that use "woman" to spell "evil."

But returning to the lectionary and its women-friendly omissions, I do appreciate a couple of other possible omissions introduced with the second typical edition of the Roman Missal. For the Feast of the Holy Family and its appointed reading of Colossians 3:12–21, there is now the option to stop short of the instruction to wives to submit to their husbands (the longer form had already stopped short of the instruction to slaves to submit to their masters). There is a similar optional shorter form for the reading of Ephesians 5 in ordinary time. Here again, the instruction to wives to submit to their husbands has become optional.

But these possibilities of women-friendly omissions do not undo the larger problem. What do we—as women who entrust our lives of faith, at least to some degree, to the liturgy—do with the fact that there is a limited number of stories about biblical women's faith and that the lectionary omits and veils some of the beautiful stories that we do have? Women who want to make meaning of liturgy will have to resist the ways in which the lectionary renders women voiceless and asks us to be complicit in this. Maybe we need to begin to celebrate, in our hearts and with our lives, extra-ordinary Sundays in which some of the liturgically voiceless women of the Bible begin to be heard again. What might it look like if we gave voice, for example, to the women at prayer in the Bible?

Giving Voice to Biblical Women

Looking for women at prayer in the Scriptures offers a glimpse both of the problems and of the possibilities of hearing the voices of our foremothers. As far back as the early parts of the Hebrew Scriptures, songs and prayers were put in the mouths of women. Nonetheless, only about ten of the nearly three hundred instances of recorded prayers or allusions to prayer in the Hebrew Scriptures purport to be those of women.[9] And not one of the 150 psalms in the Book of Psalms can be attributed to a woman beyond the shadow of a doubt. If we look for biblical voices of women at prayer, then, the stark asymmetry in the amount of evidence is striking. Although nothing would lead us to assume that women invoked the Holy One with any less frequency or fervor than did their male counterparts, the Scriptures record only a fraction of women's prayers in comparison to those of men.

The content of the recorded prayers also speaks to the power of gender in shaping faith. The majority of prayers put in women's mouths in the Hebrew Scriptures are related to women's reproductive and maternal roles. There is, for example, Hagar's desperate plea in the face of her dying child (Gen. 21:16ff.), Leah's praise of God at the birth of her son (Gen. 29:35), the blessing of Naomi by her women friends on the occasion of Ruth's marriage to Boaz (Ruth 4:14), and Hannah's agonizing prayer for a son (1 Sam. 1:10), followed by her exuberant praise when the prayer is answered (1 Sam. 2:1–10). Women's prayers, as represented in Scripture, are disproportionally shaped by women's reproductive and maternal roles (which, to be sure, are coded differently in ancient times, much more broadly than those today).

That these roles exhaust neither women's lives nor women's prayers becomes apparent in two powerfully prophetic voices of prayer and praise in the Hebrew Scriptures. First, there is Miriam's triumphant song after the crossing of the Red Sea, which is part of a larger women-centered ritual under Miriam's leadership: "Then the prophet Miriam, Aaron's sister, took a tambourine in her hand; and all the women went out after her with tambourines and with dancing. And Miriam sang to them: 'Sing to the Lord, for he has triumphed gloriously; horse and rider he has thrown into the sea'" (Exod. 15:20–21). The passage, tellingly, is not included in any lectionary reading. Similarly, there is the mighty song of Deborah, sung after Jael, the "most blessed of women," had killed Sisera (Judg. 5:1–31). This passage, too, is never read in a liturgical assembly.

In the apocryphal books, prayer "often undergirds female actions that are courageous, unconventional, and subversive."[10] The best-known female figures of these books are probably Susanna and Judith. Susanna stands against two lecherous judges. She remains voiceless throughout most of the story, except when she chooses death over and against the sexual advances of the two men. At this point, it is her prayer that leads God to intervene: "O eternal God, you know what is secret and are aware of all things before they come to be; you know that these men have given false evidence against me. And now I am to die, though I have done none of the wicked things that they have charged against me" (Sus. 42). The biblical writer then introduces the turning point in Susanna's story with the simple acknowledgment that "The Lord heard her cry" (Sus. 44). In the story of Judith, the protagonist is presented as a woman of prayer who single-handedly delivers Israel from Assyrian aggression. The book is faithful to this depiction of its heroine by including several prayers of Judith. In fact, it is Judith's practice of nightly prayer in the mountains that allows her to escape the Assyrian camp unharmed after she has killed Holofernes. Like Miriam enacting her triumphal song, Judith leads the women in a victory dance (with the men following) and sings a song of praise: "Begin a song to my God with tambourines, sing to my Lord with cymbals. Raise to him a new psalm" (Jdt. 16:1). Sadly, the lectionary knows nothing about Judith's courage or her prayer.

Looking to the New Testament, we find traces both of the tradition of Judith—that is, images of courageous and subversive women at prayer—and of the maternal concerns that again and again dominate women's prayers as recorded in the Scriptures. We also find a continuing story of voicelessness of women at prayer. Interestingly, two New Testament prayers put in the mouths of women have, indeed, become part of the liturgical tradition of the church. Mary's song of praise at her encounter with Elizabeth (Luke 1:46–55) has its place in the daily evening prayer of the church. As mentioned above, however, the lectionary does not include this text in a Sunday liturgy. Elizabeth's prophetic blessing of Mary, "Blessed are you among women, and blessed is the fruit of your womb" (Luke 1:42), is a part of the Hail Mary and is recited again and again in the rosary (surely making Elizabeth the most frequently quoted woman in the Christian tradition, at least in its catholic embodiment). These two songs of praise, like their counterparts from the Hebrew Scriptures, are situated within women's reproductive and maternal roles. But Mary's song also has subversive overtones, especially in its critique of established power relations: "he [God] has scattered the proud in the thoughts of their hearts. He has brought down the powerful from their thrones, and lifted up the lowly; he has filled the hungry with good things, and sent the rich away empty" (Luke 1:51–53).

Beyond the powerful voices of these two pregnant women, however, the other women described in the New Testament as praying and praising God remain speechless in the recorded testimony—from the prophet Anna (Luke 2:38) to "certain women" devoting themselves to prayer with the other disciples of Jesus after the Ascension (Acts 1:14) to the four nameless daughters of Philip who prophesy (Acts 21:9).

Of Voices and Visibility:
"The Names of the Mothers Have Been Lost"

The uneven witness of the Scriptures to the voices of women is part of our tradition and heritage. As one biblical scholar has said quite matter-of-factly, "the words attributed to women are fragments in a Bible that is thoroughly androcentric in its perspective, authorship and cultural background."[11] We simply have to acknowledge that (even) the most foundational texts of our faith leave invisible much of women's practices of faith. In our liturgies, however, this uneven witness of Scripture is exacerbated by what the lectionary chooses to render visible—and what it chooses to occlude—of biblical women's faith. When women's practices of faith do become visible, they are often related to women's bodily and reproductive functions.

The implications of these observations for a (re-)construction of the lives of our foremothers are sobering. Whereas earlier feminists might have celebrated, in the prayers of biblical women, the voices of these foremothers, scholars today increasingly confront questions of representation. Can we, through these texts, really encounter Miriam and Judith, Mary and Elizabeth? Past women's lives, after all, are accessible only through multiple mediations, especially the mediation of (always gender-specific) texts, and through the politics of documentation that made these texts, rather than others, accessible. Whether and how "real" women and their faith can be uncovered in the midst of these mediations is a real question. To put it more sharply and use a concrete example, can we assume that the author of the Gospel of Luke, writing after the resurrection, had knowledge of the words exchanged between Mary and Elizabeth? Does Luke preserve the words spoken between these women? If the answer is not a wholehearted yes, then how much room for error do we need to leave for a male author's construction of what women could, should, and did do and say? These and other questions about the way in which women are represented in past texts haunt our reading not only of the Scriptures but also of the whole of the Christian tradition.

Moreover, much of the past neglect of women's voices simply can no longer be undone. This truth is movingly expressed in a feminist Advent reading of a "different genealogy of Jesus, the son of Miriam, the daughter of Anna." This genealogy begins with what we can recover of the foremothers of Jesus: "Sarah was the mother of Isaac. Rebekah was the mother of Jacob. Leah was the mother of Judah. Tamar was the mother of Perez." The reading then continues, "The names of the mothers of Hezron, Ram, Amminadab, Nashon, and Salmon have been lost," and the communal response affirms, "The names of the mothers have been lost."[12] The fact that the names of the mothers have, indeed, been lost does not mean that we should not strive to reconfigure the way in which the past has been narrated so that women can become much more present in history than ever before. It does mean, however, that there are limits to this reconfiguration.

Voicing Our Selves

The complications that confront us when pondering the biblical witness to women's voices have not emerged in a vacuum. The recognition of the loss of our foremothers' voices (and the tools of feminist analysis that birthed this recognition) also stands at the cradle of an amazing new life. I am thinking of the wonderful outpouring, in our own day, of prayers, songs, blessings, meditations, hymns, litanies, and yes, even whole feminist lectionaries and readings for the liturgical year, written by and for women. As we become ever more aware of how few of the prayers and songs of our foremothers in the faith have survived, and we render visible their absence and mourn their loss, we have also begun to cherish the act of voicing ourselves and fill the void left by the voiceless women of the past with the voices of women today, with our own songs of faith and defiance, prayer and hope, sadness and vision. And while the scriptural witness simply does not offer us the possibility of extravagance when it comes to women's presence, such extravagance is precisely what we do have in the contemporary surge of women-identified prayers and songs.

Nevertheless, against the backdrop of this extravagance of contemporary prayers, the scarcity of biblical voices and their heightened invisibility in the lectionary are doubly painful. One part of voicing ourselves today, then, will be a continuing restlessness about the biblical women who remain voiceless in our liturgies. But the surge of women-identified prayers and songs has also given us ways of re-imagining the voices of our foremothers. And so, while I work for the day when I will hear the story of the prophet Anna proclaimed in the liturgical assembly, I also cherish the imaginative reconstruction of Anna's voice that I find in contemporary women's texts. For I do not find it far-fetched to ponder what Anna might have prayed when seeing Jesus:

> How long, O God, have I waited
> for a sure sign of liberation,
> waited with hope,
> waited in faith
> for the dawning of this day.
> And now my heart has feasted upon the One
> Who is my salvation.
> I have looked into a human face
> And have seen the face of God.[13]

Extra-ordinary Sundays are those times when we honor biblical women whose faith sustains our own faith, but who are voiceless in our liturgical assemblies. "Anna's Psalm" might be a good reading for one of those times, even if this psalm cannot be found in either our Scriptures or our official lectionary.

Summer Days

Every Woman of This Earth Is Sacred to My God

E VERY WOMAN OF THIS EARTH is sacred to my God. I remember how something deep within me stirred when I first heard these words, and how I kept repeating them for days afterwards.[1] And then the sudden longing: Why is this sentence not in our Holy Scriptures? How would it sound if it were proclaimed as sacred text? This summer especially, these words would sound good news, in the midst of terrifying news all around as far as women's lives are concerned. Not that terrifying news is anything really new. Most women have known for a long time that being born a woman is a risk in this world. As Amnesty International put it when launching its global campaign to stop violence against women: "From the battlefield to the bedroom, women are at risk."[2] Statistics only confirm that knowledge.[3]

> Although the world's population continues to grow, the number of women actually is declining. Already there are sixty to one hundred million fewer girls than boys as a result of selective abortions, selective infanticide, neglect, and the widespread uneven allocation of basic resources such as food, health care, and education.

> Despite these millions of women who are "missing" (Amartya Sen),[4] women are overrepresented among the world's poor, the world's illiterate adults, and the world's children not in primary school. Seventy percent of the world's poor are women, over 60 percent of the world's illiterate adults are women, and 60 percent of children not in primary school are girls, according to the UN's Human Development Report from 2002.

> UNICEF reports that violence against girls and women is the most widespread violation of human rights. And this is not a third-world problem by any means. Many of the violent crimes committed—and almost 90 percent are committed by men—have women as their victims. More than 50 percent of all women will experience violence from intimate partners; battering of women

37

results in more injuries requiring medical attention than auto acci-
dents, mugging and rape combined, according to the Center for
the Prevention of Sexual and Domestic Violence.

Every year, four million women and girls are sold into marriage,
prostitution, and slavery, the UN World Population Report 2000
states.

Every minute, according to UNICEF, a woman dies somewhere
on this globe due to complications surrounding pregnancy and
birth.

These statistics only scratch the surface of what Elisabeth Schüssler
Fiorenza has described as "structural normative practices"[5] of physical
and sexual violence against women. Schüssler Fiorenza reckons in
these structural normative practices not only overt physical violence,
including that of neglect, but also the cultural constructions of docile
feminine bodies. Such cultural constructions of docile feminine bodies
take place, for example, through the disciplining obsessions with food
and dieting, and the shaping of youthful and glamorous (but also
constrained) bodies through clothing, rigorous exercise, cosmetic products, and cosmetic surgery. The latter, now sometimes called "Aes-
thetic Services," covers a growing range of interventions, among them
facelift, eyelid surgery, laser skin resurfacing, brow and forehead lift,
skin rejuvenation, cheek and chin augmentation, liposuction/body con-
touring, breast augmentation/reduction or lift, and abdominoplasty. I
have this list of possible interventions readily available. My university
saw fit to send this list to every employee, with a special offer of a free
consultation and a 10-percent discount off professional fees for surgery
(the woman in the ad, by the way, is young, blonde, beautiful, inno-
cent-looking, and clad in nothing but lily-white underwear). "Obsessions" these might well be called. The beauty business alone is a $160
billion-a-year global industry. North Americans spend more on this
business than on education.[6]

Those are some of the large contours. Women's lives seem to be
everything but sacred on this earth. Then there is the individual news
of women's lives this summer, which gives names and faces to the
global statistics:

Mukhtaran Bibi is forced to world attention when the young
woman is sentenced by a Punjab tribal council to being gang-
raped by four men because her younger brother had allegedly

been seen with a woman of a higher social class. After the rape, Mukhtaran Bibi is forced to walk home naked.

A nameless Thai woman is mentioned on the radio, BBC World Service News. Her husband has been sentenced to two years in prison for beating her to death.

Spogmai, a six-year-old Afghan girl, can find her photo in the *New York Times.* She has lost both parents and her oldest sister in a U.S. bombing raid.

Sarah Baartman is laid to her final rest in a solemn burial ceremony in the Eastern Cape Province of South Africa, from where she was taken almost two hundred years earlier to be paraded naked in Europe as a "Hottentot Venus."

And, close to (my) home: an abusive husband takes his rage out on his daughter, her lesbian partner, and a child when he cannot find his wife at home. The two women and the child are killed. Four other women in the area are similarly murdered by fiancés and husbands in these summer months.

What, in the face of this news, do we hear as good news this summer? Grieving over women's news, I long to hear "Every woman of the earth is sacred to my God." But those are not sacred words, at least they are not found in our Scriptures. Is there anything in our Scriptures that spells Good News in the face of the terrifying news of women's lives? It is not until the late summer that something like these words, "Every woman of this earth is sacred to my God," emerges from the Scriptures, even if hidden amidst other truths. It is the Twentieth Sunday in Ordinary Time, according to the liturgical year. The Gospel is Matthew 15:21–28:

> At that time, Jesus withdrew to the region of Tyre and Sidon.
> And behold, a Canaanite woman of that district came
> and called out,
> "Have pity on me, Lord, Son of David!
> My daughter is tormented by a demon."
> But Jesus did not say a word in answer to her.
>
> Jesus' disciples came and asked him,
> "Send her away, for she keeps calling out after us."
> He said in reply,
> "I was sent only to the lost sheep of the house of Israel."

But the woman came and did Jesus homage, saying,
"Lord, help me."
He said in reply,
"It is not right to take the food of the children
and throw it to the dogs."
She said, "Please, Lord, for even the dogs eat the scraps
that fall from the table of their masters."

Then Jesus said to her in reply,
"O woman, great is your faith!
Let it be done for you as you desire."[7]
And the woman's daughter was healed from that hour.

"My daughter is tormented." The Canaanite woman[8] will have known what women have known throughout history, namely, that being born a woman is a risk. How much *more* of a risk is it to be born a woman with some form of disability, mental illness, demon posses-sion, or other marker of difference and infirmity?[9] The Canaanite woman's daughter was such a girl, doubly at risk for being female and disabled. Moreover, as inhabitants of the border region of Tyre and Sidon, both women were ethnically and religiously "other." They therefore bore a triple—and for the girl a quadruple—challenge in the encounter with the Jewish male prophet.[10] No wonder that the narra-tive is ambiguous as to where precisely their encounter took place. This can only be an encounter in the borderlands, transgressive of established boundaries.[11] What seems clear is that the woman does not hesitate to meet Jesus, the Jewish male prophet, in a public place, and yet alone, without a male protector. Yes, the woman's "faith," her desire for the healing of her tormented daughter is great indeed—even greater than Jesus might have realized. As Elisabeth Schüssler Fiorenza has described her: "the woman has broken all the rules of conduct. . . . Concern for the well-being of her daughter, who signifies the future, impels the woman to enter the public domain of men."[12]

Between the torment of her daughter and the depth of her own desire for the girl's healing, the Canaanite finds the strength to chal-lenge Jesus to believe: *Every woman of this earth is sacred to my God. Heal my daughter. It should not have to be a double risk to be born a woman. . . .* No wonder that by the third or fourth century, the Canaanite and her desire have been given a name. She is Justa, the one who desires justice, the justice-seeking and justice-making one.[13] Named or nameless, however, her struggle is not an easy one. Jesus takes his time in acknowledging the depth of the woman's claim, and makes her argue her case.[14] He initially ignores her, then insists that his mission is only to Israel, and lastly denigrates her. But the Canaanite woman, as any mother who wants her daughter to live, is both relentless and resourceful, neither willing nor able to give up on the child's well-being. Jesus finally surrenders to her desire: "O woman, great is your faith! Let it be done for you as you desire." The story in Matthew leaves off where for the mother the crucial moment has only just come: Her tormented daughter is healed—at least from one of the burdens that made her life as a woman so very risky, namely, her infirmity, her demon possession.

But where is there healing for the tormenting, truly demonic reality that millions of women are at risk on this globe simply because they were born female? Where is the missing link between the biblical Good News and the news of contemporary women's lived lives? If the story of the Canaanite woman from the Gospel of Matthew is any indication, then this woman herself, with her unquenchable desire for her daughter's flourishing and wholeness, is this missing link. Given the cultures in which women's lives have to be lived, both then and now, that desire and longing for wholeness often go unfulfilled, and in many women, the desire and the longing themselves die in the face of overwhelming odds against them. In this Canaanite, however, we encounter a woman in whom this desire and longing have not died, and who remains unwilling to take no for an answer, even from God.

In her, Jesus himself is forced to confront the depth of a woman's desire for flourishing and wholeness, for a glimpse of redemption. Ultimately, Jesus affirms the power of that longing: "Let it be done for you as you desire." Surely it was the depth of this longing that sustained the Canaanite woman's unrelenting challenge to Jesus. In that sense, this mother, with her commitment to her daughter's flourishing, is the missing link between the biblical Good News and the news of women's lives today. She herself embodies the Good News for women's lives, because she, for one, knows how to bring women's lives and the Good News of God's redemptive presence together. In this, she calls us to follow her, to struggle and argue and not give up, to claim our desire for wholeness as right and just, to be women who seek and make justice for all the daughters of this earth, against whatever forms their torment takes.

Whether the sentence itself is in our Sacred Scriptures or not, its truth is right there, in the story of the Canaanite mother: Every woman of this earth is sacred to my God.

Saint Clare of Assisi (August 11)

Of Clare and Clairol:
Imaging Radiance and Resistance

Saint Clare Appears at the Magazine Rack

THIS YEAR, THE FEAST OF SAINT CLARE OF ASSISI fell on the day of the week that I had, reluctantly, marked for a pilgrimage to the grocery store. The thirteenth-century noblewoman Chiara di Offreduccio, who had forsaken the world for a life of radical poverty that would make her into Saint Clare, seemed an unlikely companion, never mind inspiration, for a woman in the twenty-first century making her way through the rows of a supermarket. As I gathered all the items on my shopping list, I was struck by the depth of irrelevance of Saint Clare's life for my own.

The only reason Clare came with me to the supermarket that day was that I had wasted much of the prior week wondering whether and how to attend to this woman saint, given that her feast was approaching. The lives of the saints had long struck me as a rich yet little known resource for women's lives today—little known at least among those of us who were professional women with children and for whom daily Mass, with its attention to the sanctoral cycle, mostly was not an option. Clare, however, as soon as she appeared on the horizon with her feast day, began to pose problems. Saints such as Hildegard of Bingen, Catherine of Siena, and Teresa of Ávila seemed so much more amenable to a women-identified reading today, and these women had, in fact, received sustained attention from scholars of women's histories and beyond. And then there was Clare. Hardly any feminist scholar had made Clare central to her thinking. Granted, the Franciscan interest in Clare was lasting and had deepened significantly in the past decade as Clare began to be read as a woman in her own right, not simply as the dependent or complementary "other" to Saint Francis.[1] But as one scholar had rightly noted, both the growing interest in Clare and in her portrayal as "uniquely feminine" or as "feminine franciscanism" mostly bypassed how social constructions of femininity functioned within writings by and about Clare.[2] Clare continued to be imaged as the "specifically feminine" and complementary "other" Franciscan without attention to how such femininity comes to be constructed in the first place, either in the thirteenth or in the twenty-first century.

And what about the majority of women today—most of them neither Franciscans, nor scholars of women's histories, nor, for that matter, feminist theorists? How could Clare and her feast in the liturgical calendar be rendered intelligible in the crucible of *their* lives?

In my childhood book of saints—a gift from my grandmother—Clare had been portrayed as a heroic ascetic, and as the female (that is, dependent) counterpart to Francis. Not that such a portrayal in and of itself spelled problems for me at that point in time. I was only six months old when my devoutly Catholic grandmother thought it important for me to have a book with the lives of the saints. (I hope to God she knows that almost fifty years later her handwritten dedication, "to dear little Teresa, on the feast day of Saint Teresa of Ávila," evoked pure delight.) I simply grew up with other saints than Clare around me. There were the women saints of my region: the eighth-century Anglo-Saxon Lioba, whom Boniface asked for help with his mission; the twelfth-century Hildegard of Bingen, who was visionary, prophet, composer, and scientist all in one; and, for a heroic ascetic, we had thirteenth-century Elizabeth of Thuringia, whose (empty) golden shrine we admired as children and whose name graced our local Catholic parish church. Added to the women saints whose lives had left their imprint on the geography of my childhood were the saints whose names graced the lives of women in my family, especially Teresa of Ávila and Hedwig of Silesia, strong and determined women both. Granted, my mother's middle name was Klara (the Teutonic version of Chiara) and my great-grandmother had been named after the woman of Assisi—but my great-grandmother was dead, Assisi was far away, and a life of stark renunciation was not something that captured my postwar childhood imagination.

Neither did heroic renunciation capture my imagination as I made my way to the long line of shoppers in front of the cash register on this Feast of Saint Clare. How does one keep the feast of a woman such as Clare in a world such as mine? As I joined the line of other shoppers, my eyes began to wander over the magazine racks that bordered the path to the cash register. "Good-health Secrets for a Steamier Love Life," one women's magazine promised; "Five Minute Cures for Bad Hair," another. "She Lost 140 Pounds on the Internet," triumphed a third. Life advice for women abounded, from "bouquet basics," "salon smooth legs," "smile makeovers," and "no-cook dinners, plus 86 kitchen timesavers," to "how to reel in bunches of boys," "increase breast size & firmness naturally," and "achieve a to-die-for derriere."

As the cashier began to sort through the groceries of another woman ahead of me, I picked up one of the glossy magazines from the rack. Idly turning the cover, I saw rich golden tresses filling the page; with them came the enticement: "Give your hair the strength to shine." I am uncertain whether I needed the additional prompt of the brand name Clairol to conjure up the image of Saint Clare, beckoning me to a scene eight hundred years earlier.

It was the night after Palm Sunday of the year 1212. Clare had left her stately home under the cover of darkness and made her way to the little chapel of Saint Mary of the Portiuncula, where Brother Francis and a handful of his companions were waiting. What happened next is illustrated in *The Franciscan Book of Saints* on a full page: the hand of Francis, holding a pair of scissors, hovers over Clare's head. Francis has begun to cut her luxurious and luminous tresses. Clare's companion Pacifica kneels in the background, crying. In her hands Pacifica holds the thick tresses Francis has already clipped from Clare's hair. The image of Clare's rich and flowing hair in this picture is a match for any Ms. Clairol; and Francis with scissors in hand makes one ponder *Elle*'s claim that "women everywhere still seem to melt around a sexy man wielding a pair of scissors." But the story of Clare does not end here. Francis cuts Clare's hair, she exchanges her noble clothes for a coarse habit and takes the monastic vow of obedience. Several days later, when Clare's enraged family attempts to bring her back to the family fold by force, Clare symbolically renounces her previous life by baring her shorn head for all to see. A similar story is repeated when Clare's sister Agnes attempted to join Clare and her mendicant vision of life. Their enraged kinsmen literally tried to pull Agnes back into the family fold by her hair. Not surprisingly, Agnes's hair was cut off as soon as the kinsmen desisted from their efforts.

What is noticeable in both Clare and Agnes, as well as in the other women who joined them, is that their embrace of radical poverty took symbolic form in the women's hair being cut. Granted, this had been part of the monastic repertoire for men and women ever since monas-

tic life began; but in the thirteenth-century mendicant renewal movements more radical symbols of renunciation surfaced, at least for the
men. None of the women, after all, could or did take off all her clothes
and walk away naked, as did Francis. Instead, women's hair was a
defining site of bodily renunciation. Later hagiography, such as it is
reflected in *The Franciscan Book of Saints,* imaged that hair as long and
luxurious, and there are written accounts (as well as a film) that, without any hesitation, image Clare as a blonde.[3] Incidentally, *The Franciscan Book of Saints* with its wonderful illustration of Clare's luxurious
hair being cut was published in the same years in which "Lady Clairol"
pleaded: "If I've only one life . . . let me live it as a blonde."

Of Radiant and of Real Women

Following this mental journey to the thirteenth century, I was
brought back to the supermarket by the elderly woman in front of me
who now began to put her groceries on the line. As I looked closer at
the women around me, it struck me that none of us resembled a Saint
Clare; neither did any of us come close to a Ms. Clairol. The cashier
was a competent and energetic young woman with a ready smile, but
she did not seem to spend much time in front of the mirror. The Hispanic woman packing the groceries seemed tired, timid, and preoccu-
pied. Last week, when I had seen her for the first time and had thanked
her after she packed all my groceries, she had looked up surprised and
made no response. The elderly woman in front of me who was now
emptying her cart wore an eye-catching pink dress, and, despite the
sweltering heat outside, pantyhose; her white summer shoes had heels.
This woman seemed to come closer to the women's magazines than the
rest of us, yet her particular age group was not represented on any of
the magazine covers.

Clare and Clairol, so far apart from each other—and yet both equally
distant from the women whose lives intersected in the grocery line that
morning on the Feast of Saint Clare! Was this what Clare and Clairol
had in common, after all? Images of radiance, of a "strength to shine,"
that hardly any woman ever embodied in her daily life? Are Clare and
Clairol both symbols of a woman script that is unattainable for most
of us—Clare's script being written with the church's grammar of sanctity, Clairol's script with the grammar of late capitalist advertising? I
had to think of a postcard I cherished with the image of a fat, beautiful
red-haired woman. The caption read: "There are three billion women

who don't look like supermodels and only eight who do." Translating this truth into the grammar of sanctity, the caption could read: There are billions of Christian women who have lived the gospel faithfully throughout history, but only a few whose mothers heard a voice informing them, "You will give birth to a light that will shine brilliantly in the world."[4] Clare's mother did hear such a voice, and even if the women using Clairol today far outnumber the followers of Saint Clare, I for one had begun to find both Clare's and Clairol's promise of brilliance testing.

Claire, Clairol, and Complicity

As I continued to stand in line in the supermarket, both Clare and Clairol more and more spoke of radiant unattainability. They also in a startling way began to seem complicit in their women scripts. "Radiant femininity" then and now was imaged by way of a compelling fixation on women's bodies, desires, hair, and food. The energetic, if not exactly radiant, cashier interrupted my meditations on this Feast of Saint Clare. My time had come to empty my shopping cart of its possessions. On the spur of the moment, I turned to the magazine rack and gathered all the women's magazines available. A question had begun to haunt me: How on earth can we make meaning of our lives as women in the twenty-first century with the images of femininity that surround us—in the media, on the one hand, but also in the church that puts before us on this day in August the figure of Saint Clare?

There is an easy—alas, all too easy—answer to this question. This answer images Clare as the one who resists all that Clairol stands for. Clare, with her love of radical poverty, becomes the shining icon of countercultural resistance to Clairol and all forms of late capitalism (Clairol's worldwide sales were estimated, conservatively, at $1.6 billion in the year 2000.[5]) Clare spells "exile from the fake highs of a soap-opera life," an alternative to "what fails us in a consumer-saturated society," and the promise of "a journey toward inner peace" for our "burning-out friends in high-powered jobs."[6] I am all for icons of countercultural resistance to late capitalism, but I desperately need these icons to spell more than utter irrelevance when it comes time for the weekly pilgrimage to the grocery store. The grocery store might, after all, be one of the crucial sites in women's lives for practicing resistance to capitalism. On the other hand, the church wants me to believe that what the weekly pilgrimages to the grocery store sustain—namely, family life—is rooted in a sacrament itself.

But there is another reason why pitting the image of Clare over and against the cultural icons of Clairol and the like is all too easy: imaging both as opposites masks the complexities and complicities between the two. Clare's radiance, for example, was overshadowed for many centuries. With all her strength to shine, Clare for more than eight hundred years has stood in the shadow of the overpowering male saint of Assisi. Even if the *poverello* seems an unlikely candidate for the role of "overpowering male," in relation to Clare's reception history, Saint Francis has undoubtedly played that role. The lack of scholarly interest in Clare is indicative: "While the numerous documents by and about Francis of Assisi have been repeatedly—one is tempted to say 'endlessly'—published, edited, interpreted and debated, Clare's brief corpus did not even appear together in the original Latin until 1970."[7] Until well into the twentieth century, Clare has been imaged primarily as dependent on Francis, or as an *alter Franciscus,* another Francis.[8] Clare's own rhetoric of dependence on Francis (the "little plant"), coupled with traditional gender constructions that naturalized such images, rendered the position of Clare in the shadow of Francis credible for many centuries. Today, Clare's story can be read as the story of a woman struggling to become visible in her own right. And it is precisely the women of today who are finding ways to image Clare at the center of her story and to render visible Clare's *own* strength to shine.[9]

But connections are detectable also in the opposite direction. The world that Clairol and friends image for women today has usurped the language of Clare's world. The ever-present powerful imagery of "light," "radiance," and "brilliance" in advertising is only one intriguing example. Whether it is the assurance of "glowing energy," a "mega-dose of shine," or a "light-reflecting shimmer," lipsticks, makeup, and rouge seem to sell better when promising to "infuse your entire face with radiance." And for hopeless causes—good-bye, Saint Jude—there is the "artificial light luminizing lotion," and the "color vitality solar power highlighter." The women's magazines I picked up on the Feast of Saint Clare revealed other connections between the worlds of Clare and Clairol. There were the ads for a "divine moisturizer," a "healing essence," and a "heavenly hydrotherapy." There were remedies for "seven deadly beauty skin sins," and the same number of "tips for saving face." There was the invitation to "believe in beauty." Finally there was the world of perfumes, a more deeply religious world than that of any other beauty product. With names such as Truth, Eternity, Angel, Beyond Paradise, and Miracle, these perfumes either claimed to be "touched by grace," or to be "an expression of purity," or to be able to create "the look of simplicity"—for close to fifty dollars, that is. Even if I struggled with understanding why a mixture of "basil, blackcurrant, white peppar [sic], mandarin, sweet pea, jasmine, and white rose, with a base of sandalwood and chestnut tree" would be "an expression of purity," one thing was clear: women's perfumes today evoke an imagery that in previous centuries was that of the sacred.

But this connection functions both ways. Clare's own story draws not only on the powerful imagery of light and radiance but also on the imagery of fragrance. The *Bull of Canonization* joins both when it describes Clare in the following way:

> It should not be surprising that a *light* so *enkindled,*
> so *illuminating* could not be kept from *shining brilliantly*
> and giving *clear light* in the house of the Lord;
> nor could a vessel filled with *perfume* be so hidden
> that it would not emit its *fragrance*
> And suffuse the Lord's house with a *sweet aroma.*[10]

There are less pure and more complex connections between the worlds of Clare and Clairol. One connection is the importance of food and of food control as a shaper of women's lives in the thirteenth and twenty-first centuries. From eyewitnesses whose testimonies are captured in the *Acts of the Process of Canonization* we know that Clare for much of her life practiced severe food asceticism. Again and again, sisters from the community at San Damiano, some of whom had lived with Claire for close to forty years, stressed the severity of Clare's asceticism: "[S]he was so very strict in her food that the sisters marveled at how her body survived."[11] Even if we read such severe food asceticism as a way of women claiming power over a crucial women-identified resource (food production and consumption) and not as a disturbing sign of female self-mutilation,[12] the fact remains that for Clare, food intake was a central site for embodying her way of life. This is true in relation not only to food asceticism but also to food consumption. Clare's piety, including miracles related to the Eucharist or even noneucharistic foods, witnesses to the importance of food in her life.[13]

Turning to the twenty-first century, food and food deprivation clearly are dominant themes for women's lives. The more traditional women's magazines I had brought home from the grocery store and spread out on my kitchen table all attended to food production and its accessories, including an irresistible offer of a "free poster: two months of menus." But there are other indications that food and its production and intake are of consuming importance for women in the twenty-first century. There are the images of models and supermodels whose bodies speak of a caloric intake that borders on that of Clare. There are the growing numbers of young women whose lives and bodies are shaped by eating disorders, including life-threatening forms of anorexia. There is the fact that each year, Americans spend almost forty billion dollars trying "to get skinny."[14] Thinking back to the checkout line in the grocery store, I realized that there had been only one man in sight. From what he carried in his arms—no cart for him, thank you—it was obvious that he was not on a weekly shopping tour that supported a family. Quite the contrary . . .

But back to Clare and Clairol. Another connection between their worlds is that Clare, like those in religious life in general, has not stood apart from the world of commerce, capitalism, and "the market"; and both have profited. One only has to listen to the never-ending chagrin of pilgrims over how much Clare would have hated Assisi's tourist industry to realize that this industry has shaped the story of Clare quite profoundly. The chagrin itself has become a part of this story. This chagrin, of course, assumes that the two stories of cult and capitalism could or should be strictly separate, when in fact the making of an ecclesial object of devotion, such as a Saint Clare, has always involved the production of cultural and material "icons."[15] Beyond Assisi, there are the Saint Clare medals for the television set or, more cutting-edge, the Saint Clare greeting cards on the Web. The church itself laid claim to this connection when it elevated Saint Clare to the (dubious) honor of patron saint of television. One could sharpen these observations: at the heart of both Clare's world and that of Ms. Clairol and friends is a powerful struggle with materiality, for Clare in the grammar of "have not," for the Ms. Clairols of this world, as well as for some of the reception history of Clare, in the grammar of "have." But both share the same defining power behind their struggles: materiality.

Did She . . . or Didn't She?[16]

Finally, there is another shared feature between the worlds of Clare and Clairol: the language of love and of passion. I will assume that the omnipresence of this language in women's magazines does not need to be substantiated. In fact, the language of desire can now be invoked in relation to hair ("hair lust") as well as to any other subject. From the magazines I brought home from the supermarket on the Feast of Saint Clare, it was obvious that the magazines' producers thought women desperately wanted to read about (the media's construction of) women's desires. It may be less obvious to women today that love and passion also were at the heart of Clare's life—and I am not thinking of Clare and Francis here at all. Whether Clare felt passionate about Francis, and in which way, strikes me as uninteresting. This question has died the death of having been asked too many times and of having been answered with a script that presupposes that women's lives need relationality with a male to qualify as meaningful. As far as Clare and Francis are concerned, I find sufficient the recognition that Clare's relationship with this man does not need to have been dispassionate. But there were other passions that guided Clare's life as a whole (she outlived Francis by three decades, after all), and these are the passions that interest me. First and foremost is Clare's language of love and passion in relation to "Lady Poverty." It bears remembering that since poverty was gendered female, loving poverty for Clare would have been a woman-identified love, in distinction to the male mendicant's love of the same Lady Poverty. And love her she did. As the *Bull of Canonization* succinctly described Clare: "She was, above all, a lover . . . of poverty."[17] This love of poverty, so pronounced in the religious renewal movements sweeping Europe in the thirteenth century, had a christological orientation. It was ultimately oriented toward Christ, who was imaged as poor. Thus, Clare passionately described Christ as the one

> Whose affection excites, . . .
> Whose delight replenishes,
> Whose remembrance delightfully shines,
> By Whose fragrance the dead are revived.[18]

Clare wrote these words, not as a young woman, but close to her own death at about age sixty. Love of poverty and love of God, however, were not the only loves that evoked Clare's language of passion. In the *Blessing* traditionally assumed to have been given by Clare shortly before her death, she commanded the sisters always to be "lovers of your souls and those of all your sisters."[19] Such love Clare herself expressed most clearly in her last letter to Agnes of Prague, whom she described as "half of her soul and the special shrine of her heart's deepest love."[20] And even while pouring her love for Agnes out in exquisite Latin, Clare—like any lover—knew that "the love I have for you . . . can never be fully expressed by the tongue of the flesh."[21]

Clare did not have available twenty-first-century women's magazines' "relationtips" on how to live "the ins and outs of intimacy," but her religious sensibilities and passions also did not exist in a cultural no-woman's land. Clare's language of passion was nourished by the love lyrics of the courtly culture of the urbanized aristocracy of her time, particularly the troubadour songs, but also by the much older love poetry of the Song of Songs. Drawing on those traditions, Clare could write to Agnes of Prague:

> From this moment, then, O Queen of our heavenly King, let yourself be inflamed more strongly with the fervor of charity. As you further contemplate His ineffable delights, eternal riches and honors, and sigh for them in the great desire and love of your heart, may you cry out: . . .

> O heavenly Spouse!
> I will run and not tire,
> Until you bring me into the wine-cellar,
> Until Your left hand is under my head
> And Your right hand will embrace me happily,
> [and] You will kiss me with the happiest kiss of Your mouth.[22]

The culture of Clare's day fused religious passion, Hebrew love poetry, and the language of the troubadour songs to create the possibility of a distinctly sensual world of sexual renunciation. Thus, while Clare would not have known what to do with "good-health secrets for a steamier love life," this was not because she lacked a "love life."

But what can one make of all these connections between the worlds of Claire and Clairol? If a simple opposition between Clare and Clairol masks the complexities of their relationship, could one not argue that even where these two women's worlds share common ground—say, in practices of food deprivation—Clare's practices are born of a God-sustained vision, and the practices of today are not. Such an interpretation, however, is only a slightly more sophisticated rendition of the previous image of Clare as an icon of countercultural resistance. In this more sophisticated version, Clare is acknowledged to engage in practices that have equivalents in the twenty-first century, but her motives now are said to differ from those of the Ms. Clairols of this world. In other words, where the differences between Clare and Clairol can no longer be located simply and starkly on the level of practices, they come to be located in the realm of what remains invisible: the interior motives. I am not denying that such an image holds explanatory power. Clare herself comes close to such an interpretive strategy when describing religious life for Agnes of Prague using images of women's glamorous appearance. Clare described Jesus Christ as the one

> In Whose embrace You are already caught up;
> Who has adorned Your breast with precious stones
> And has placed priceless pearls on Your ears
> And has surrounded You with sparkling gems
> As though blossoms of springtime
> And placed on Your head a golden crown
> As a sign of Your holiness.[23]

Here is a woman who knows the glamorous world of women's appearance but who uses that imagery as a powerful signifier of a spiritual, otherworldly passion. The clothes Clare herself wore and the ones she prescribed for her community were, of course, quite the opposite of such glamour. As Clare wrote in her Rule: "I admonish, beg, and exhort my sisters to always wear cheap garments out of love of the most holy and beloved Child Who was wrapped in such poor little swaddling clothes."[24] The interpretive strategy I have in mind and its explanatory power thrive precisely on this contrast: what is real—ultimately real—is beyond that which is visible. The lives of many women who have lived the gospel faithfully are written according to this script. But what is occluded when the "real," on the one hand, and "materiality," on the other hand, come to be severed?

Resisting Clare?

As I pondered the inescapable materiality of the groceries I had brought home on this Feast of Saint Clare, it struck me that both Clare and Clairol ask for an act of faith. The story of Saint Clare asks me to see beauty in the emaciated body of a strictly cloistered nun who secretly wore a shirt of horsehair on her body. Clairol asks me to believe a few drops of shampoo from a bright green bottle will make my hair—and me?—"up to five times stronger."

I realized that I wanted to resist some powerful markers of Clare's existence just as much as I resisted "renewing" my life with the help of a bright green bottle. Even if I set aside the fact that I do know women with eating disorders, and even if I ignored the painful feeling of violence I experience when confronted with these emaciated women's bodies, I resist other markers of Clare's life. There is the male-dominated religious universe of which Clare was a part, and which she accepted as a given. There is the imagery of light and darkness that marked Clare's life wonderfully—but that also meant that she could see evil personified as a black child. There is the fact that the community in San Damiano did not break through status barriers between women as profoundly as one might have thought. Divisions between an educated elite who could read (and therefore use breviaries) and women who could not and therefore were unable to engage in the same prayer practices are as evident in San Damiano as the divisions of labor between "sisters" and "serving sisters." And there are larger issues at stake here, such as an understanding of sanctity that centers on poverty, chastity, and obedience and that has produced a communion of saints that includes few women who look anything like the women I see in church, never mind in the grocery store.[25] Finally, there is a certain sadness that Clare's vision of a life of radical poverty was clearly circumscribed by her gender, so that she did not (because she could not?) find a concrete embodiment for this vision in a mendicant and itinerant way of life for women, but only in a strictly cloistered community. I will leave to scholars of Saint Clare the struggle over what exactly enclosure might have meant for her, given that she wanted to live radical poverty.

A simple antithesis, then, between Clare and Clairol is not an option. In the last analysis, such an option also assumes that only the seductiveness of slick advertising renders Clairol's promise of radiance more credible for women today than the church's own promises. Matters are not so simple. The history of the church with its women is not uninterruptedly luminous and life-giving. And Clairol and friends could also be taken as a form of resistance to ecclesial women scripts. The suntan ad that admonishes women: "Don't get burned for your sins" is no more (in-)credible than the church's traditional inscription of what counts as "sinful" in women's lives. And when in our own time have we seen the public face of the church bear the features of a radiant woman? Should it really be legitimate to credit slick advertising—and, one is forced to assume, women's inability to see through this advertising—with the church's ineffectiveness in convincing women of the church's own radiance for them?

What does Clairol stand for? What meaning do women make with it? Could Clairol's promise of radiance ultimately be about the condition of the possibility of women's lives being more than opaque? Is there a hint, in the image of golden tresses, of the knowledge that everything in life is capable of transcendent meaning, even the ordinary of women's lives? Is there a glimpse here of "quotidian mysteries"[26] in the profound trivialness of women's beauty practices? And why is it only a little bit harder to believe Clairol's promise of radiance for women's lives than the church's promise?

A Clare for the Daughters of Clairol?

Maybe one should leave Clare to the religious women (and men) who most depend on making meaning of her life for their own lives and who also have fewer stones than I to roll away when doing so. But Saint Clare is one of the women who for centuries have been recognized in the liturgical calendar; she supposedly holds meaning not only for her own time, region, monastic family, or even gender, but for all those struggling with living a God-sustained vision of life. As one of the contemporary women scholars of Saint Clare put it succinctly: "In that reality which we know as the communion of saints these persons exist in relationship to us."[27] Besides, since there are not that many women in the liturgical calendar of saints to begin with, we dare not assign any of them to oblivion, at least not until we are surrounded by so great a cloud of women witnesses that we can afford to do so.

Here, then, is one way of making meaning of Saint Clare for all who dare to acknowledge multiple belongings and who do not want to close their eyes to the fact that they inhabit worlds of Clare and Clairol at the same time and that, indeed, these worlds interrelate. Here, then, is a Saint Clare for the daughters of Clairol. Recent scholarly work on Clare has suggested new ways of imaging her that resonate with women's lives today. They resonate much more readily than the older narratives of Clare with their script of dependence and heroic asceticism, or even than the newer narratives with their stress on femininity, complementarity, and collaboration between male and female lovers of radical poverty.

The image of Clare that emerges out of the shadows of traditional hagiography is one in which Clare resists her own traditional image and claims Clairol's promise of a new "strength to shine." This image, to begin with, is one of a strong-willed, daring, and determined woman who charted a new course for women of her time, namely, a life of radical communal poverty within the church. Clare did not fit into a prefabricated Franciscan way of life—there was none for women when Clare decided to embrace holy poverty. She created such a life.

Such a reading of Clare also necessitates an image of this woman as one who knew how to live with conflict, and who had her share of defiance and skills of resistance. These become visible in Clare's "no" to traditional woman scripts, including religious ones—after all, she could simply have entered one of the established women's religious communities and given up on her vision of a communal life of radical poverty for women. She did not, and instead forged her path by practices of resistance that began with her family and that culminated in Clare's rejection of the papal offer to absolve her from a life of radical poverty: "Holy Father, I will never in any way wish to be absolved from the following of Christ."[28] When the same pope released the Franciscan friars from the obligation of pastoral care of the women's community, Clare objected so pointedly (by refusing all foods as a protest over the withdrawal of spiritual food) that the pope speedily reimposed this obligation on the friars.

Conflicts also become visible with Francis, if one does not take a hagiographic or gender-specific script of female dependence and submission as the defining axiom of what can be told and how. There are hints that Francis did not simply believe but had to be convinced that women were capable of living the kind of radicality he envisioned for his *fraternitas*. Once convinced, Francis, together with the local bishop, nevertheless intervened critically in Clare's practice of food renunciation. Later, he made her assume the title of "abbess" in her community, thereby causing Clare to adopt an older Benedictine style of monastic governance that he himself had always resisted for the mendicant men. At another point, Francis forced a novice on Clare whom she considered not appropriate (and who left the community within a year). The saintly tellings of Clare's story stress her humility and obedience in all these conflicts, but a closer look at the texts themselves suggests that she shaped her "obedience" in particular ways, thereby subverting direct compliance. The way in which she chose, for example, to exercise governance of her community and that she never self-identified as "abbess" point to the rather complex ways in which Clare actually practiced her "obedience."

Third, Clare knew when she needed to claim power and she used privileges of her elite education (such as her ability to read and write Latin) without hesitation. Thus, she wrote the first female Rule, that is, canonical legislation for a religious community, which received ecclesial approval. Clare is one of the many women who had to be "firsts" in their fields (if we ever sought a patron saint for "firsts," Clare qualifies more convincingly than she does for the patronage of television). And as is often the case for women who have to be firsts, she was not the first to have tried. Agnes of Prague had written a Rule before Clare and, despite her privileged status as the daughter of the king of Bohemia, had not received papal approval. Clare, like many of us, stood on the shoulders of another woman who tried to chart a new path and who was not able to see it through. Clare does seem to have been a first, without a female failure, or male success having preceded, in relation to the so-called Privilege of Poverty, a papal privilege granting Clare and her community the right to live in radical poverty and to refuse all forms of property.

Finally, Clare lived in women-identified communities all her life and found such communal living life-giving. There were, to begin with, the women of the Offreduccio household, who shaped the first eighteen years of Clare's life with their practices of piety. A significant number of these women later became members of the monastic community around Clare at San Damiano: her mother, Ortulana, her sisters Agnes and Beatrice, and her relatives Pacifica, Amata, and Balvina. Within the San Damiano community thrived a clear and explicit vision of women's flourishing. The stories of Clare's profound care for her sisters, including the healings she performed within and for her community, are ample illustration of this vision:

> Frequently, in the cold of night, she covered them [the sisters] with her own hands while they were sleeping. She wished that those whom she perceived unable to observe the common rigor be content to govern themselves with gentleness. If a temptation disturbed someone, if sadness took hold of someone, as is natural, she called her in secret and consoled her with tears. Sometimes, she would place herself at the feet of the depressed [sister] so that she might relieve the force of [her] sadness with her motherly caress.[29]

Those of us working and living in male-dominated environments—and who among us doesn't?—can surely appreciate such stories of explicit concern for women's flourishing, even if those stories follow a thirteenth-century monastic script. As Caroline Walker Bynum has said forcefully: "If we have confidence in the righteousness of our own rage and in the diagnosis of our own oppression, how can we deny the power of female communities and female visions that, different from our own, are nonetheless our heritage?"[30]

Here, then, are the contours of a Clare who can make meaning with women who co-inhabit a world with the daughters of Clairol. This Clare does not—starkly and ineffectively—call us to boycott Clairol and to shave our heads instead. The latter would hardly be a revolutionary gesture for women today, anyway. This Clare instead challenges and invites us to place faith in the possibility that women's lives can, indeed, be radiant. Where and how this radiance can best shine forth in the twenty-first century and for women who instead of living a cloistered life of radical poverty have to find time in their weekly schedule for the grocery store, these are all questions Saint Clare will not answer for us. We ourselves are called to chart these paths in the twenty-first century.

Grazie, Chiara!

As night came on this Feast of Saint Clare, I knew that I had, for the first time in my life, walked through this day with Clare as a companion. True to her own story, she had to wait for many years until she could move out of the shadows of traditional hagiography that had shaped my childhood imagination. And true to herself, she seemed unafraid to be a conflictual presence in my life. But at the end of the day, Clare had inserted herself into the sacred calendar I kept in my heart, and she was there to stay. As I lay awake, a prayer began to form:

> Holy Clare, blessed stranger to my own life,
> you rendered yourself present today
> in the midst of the quotidian struggles of women's lives.
> Stay with me as I struggle to keep faith
> that women's lives can, indeed, be radiant.

Darkness grew around me as I entrusted to the night the language of my childhood prayers: *Sancta Clara, ora pro me.*

The next morning, sipping a cup of dark, rich coffee, I caught sight of the early sun reflected high up in the crowns of the ancient pines around the back porch. I thought I heard Clare laughing softly. Radiance is yours this morning, she seemed to say. And I silently vowed to take more time to give my life the strength to shine, this brilliant morning after the Feast of Saint Clare, and in all the days to come.— *Grazie, Chiara!*

Post scriptum

I have never used Clairol in my life and have no intention to begin using it now. In a world where—according to a Clairol poll—"fifty percent of women believe that their beauty is something they created on their own,"[31] I share the faith of Clare. All radiance that is ours ultimately reflects that uncreated radiance which the Christian tradition has known as *lux perpetua,* eternal light—be it the radiance of sunlight on ancient pines, be it luxurious golden hair or the lives of shorn women saints.

The Nativity of Mary (September 8)

Every Mother Is a Daughter

THE NATIVITY OF MARY, or the Feast of the Birth of the Virgin Mary as it is now called, probably passes most of us by. September 8 simply is not a feast that evokes our imagination and devotion any more. Popular religious traditions have privileged other Marian feasts, such as the Feast of the Assumption or the Feast of the Immaculate Conception. The latter, of course, is closely related to the Nativity of Mary and is celebrated nine months prior, on December 8. But the Feast of the Nativity of Mary on September 8 actually is one of the oldest Marian feasts in the liturgical calendar. The feast's origins date back at least to the fifth century, when a church was dedicated in Jerusalem at the site of what was assumed to be Mary's parental home and the place of her birth. The Eastern churches to this day claim the Feast of the Nativity of Mary as one of the twelve most solemn feasts in their liturgical calendar. Its elaborate title speaks to its importance: "The Nativity of our most Holy Lady, the God-Bearer and Ever-Virgin Mary." But even for the Western church, the Nativity of Mary is not without significance. The Western liturgical calendar knows only two other feasts that commemorate nativities: the birth of Jesus (December 25) and the birth of John the Baptist (June 24).

The ancient origins of the Feast of the Nativity of Mary and its prominence in the Eastern churches, however, are not the only reasons for this feast claiming our attention today. The feast captures a profound truth of our faith in quite distinct ways. The Nativity of Mary reminds us that every mother, including the mother of God, is a daughter. To put this truth in more biblical language: The woman who bore our redeemer was herself "born of a woman" (see Gal. 4:4). The Feast of the Nativity of Mary invites us to celebrate the fact that the mother of God is also a daughter, born of a woman who herself was born of a woman, born of a woman. In this feast, then, we ultimately glimpse the wisdom and grace of a God who renders Godself present within the fullness of human families, including the intricate web of ancestral, and particularly matrilineal relations. The Feast of the Nativity of Mary reminds us that God does not only have a mother, God has foremothers.

The Scriptures: Jesus has Foremothers

The gospels themselves tell us nothing about Mary's birth or her parents, except to presuppose, by the sheer fact of Mary's life, that she had both. The gospel reading for the Feast of the Nativity of Mary, however, is wisely chosen. The appointed reading comes from the beginning of the Gospel of Matthew, the genealogy and birth of Jesus (Matt. 1:1–16, 18–23).[1] Granted, genealogies are not the most exciting reading.

> Abraham was the father of Isaac, and Isaac the father of Jacob, and Jacob the father of Judah and his brothers, and Judah the father of Perez and Zerah by Tamar, and Perez the father of Hezron, and Hezron the father of Aram, and Aram the father of Aminadab, and Aminadab the father of Nashon, and Nashon the father of Salmon, and Salmon the father of Boaz by Rahab, and Boaz the father of Obed by Ruth, and Obed the father of Jesse, and Jesse the father of King David.[2]

And that is only the beginning of the genealogy of Jesus in the Gospel of Matthew. On the Feast of the Nativity of Mary, however, we do well to listen carefully to this genealogy. The long list of Jesus' ancestors allows us a glimpse of a profound truth of our faith. In Jesus Christ, God became part of the whole fabric of a human family through time. God has ancestors, an unbroken line going back to Abraham and Sarah, and beyond them into the very beginnings of the human family itself. Granted, the genealogy in the Gospel of Matthew does not go back that far. Matthew wants to make clear that Jesus comes as the culmination of God's covenant with Israel and as the son of David. The genealogy of Jesus in the Gospel of Luke, on the other hand, does trace Jesus' ancestors back to Adam (Luke 3:23–38). In claiming for Jesus a human family with all its ancestors, Luke emphasizes how God has ultimately become part of the human family as such.

It is the particular beauty of the Feast of the Nativity of Mary that it lets us glimpse a part of this truth that is occluded in the two gospel genealogies. The genealogies in Luke and Matthew, after all, focus on the fathers and the sons: so-and-so was the son of so-and-so, who was the son of so-and-so, and so on and so forth. Such patrilineal genealogies of Jesus are actually quite odd, and that for two reasons. The first is that Jesus was the "son of Joseph" in a rather complicated way only. The Gospel of Luke thus has to begin Jesus' genealogy with a disclaimer: "He . . . was the son (as was thought) of Joseph son of Heli" (Luke 3:23). Second, according to Jewish law, a child was Jewish if the mother was Jewish (paternity being hard to prove until quite recently). Despite these two problems with patrilineal genealogies, the Gospels of Matthew and Luke nevertheless trace Jesus' ancestral lineage through the fathers—and thereby make themselves witnesses of the power of "patriarchal hegemony over the past" (Laura Barefield). Happily, the Feast of the Nativity of Mary enables us to see the *other* truth of Jesus' ancestral line, by encouraging us to focus on the mothers and the daughters: Jesus was born of Mary who was born of Anna. Sadly enough, the names of many of the other foremothers of Jesus are lost, although the Gospel of Matthew, in a surprise move, does include four women in its genealogy and ends with a fifth, namely "Mary, of whom Jesus was born" (Matt. 1:16). At its culmination, then, the patrilineal ancestral story of Jesus in the Gospel of Matthew breaks down. Jesus' most immediate ancestor was a woman, and a woman only.

But why would Matthew introduce breaks in the patrilineal story even before he comes to Mary? The four women explicitly named in Jesus' genealogy are all women from the Hebrew Scriptures with rather complicated stories of their own in the history of salvation. Tamar resourcefully ensures the ancestral line by tricking her father-in-law into fathering a child with her (Gen. 38). Rahab, a Canaanite prostitute living in Jericho, rescues Israelite spies and in turn is herself rescued and integrated into Israel (Josh. 2; 6). Ruth, a Moabite, inserts herself into Israel's story through loyalty to Naomi and a rather risky maneuver with Boaz (Book of Ruth). Bathsheba, whom the writer of Matthew leaves nameless as "the wife of Uriah," becomes King David's wife through adultery and through David's arranging Uriah's death in battle (2 Sam. 11–12). The Gospel of Matthew, in highlighting these four women, each of whom in one way or another is "out of order" in the history of Israel, prepares for the story of Mary's pregnancy out of wedlock. Mary thus comes to stand in a tradition of other unconventional foremothers of Jesus.

What a pity that the gospel writer tells us about only four of these foremothers of Jesus. Would that we had a fuller matrilineal genealogy of Jesus! The gospel writers could, after all, have included other women among Jesus' ancestors. The Hebrew Scriptures give us some of their names: Sarah, the mother of Isaac, Rebecca, the mother of Jacob, and Leah, the mother of Judah, to name just three. Granted, the names of most of the other foremothers have been lost. This includes the name of the mother of Mary—that is, if we look only at the biblical witness. Fortunately, soon after the biblical witness emerged, readers wanted to know more about Jesus' ancestors than the two genealogies in Matthew and Luke provide. The popular stories that emerged in response give us not only a name for Mary's mother but also detailed accounts of Mary's conception and birth.

Anna: "The Barren One Gives Birth to the God-Bearer"

We learn the name of Mary's mother, Anna, not from the biblical witness but from slightly later writings that lovingly and generously continue to retell the biblical stories, often adding their own truths to the Scriptures. By the mid-second century, the so-called *Protevangelium of James* tells of the circumstances surrounding Mary's conception and birth in such loving and generous detail. Mary's parents, Joachim and Anna, are childless. Analogously to the Hannah of the Old Testament (1 Sam. 1–2), Anna miraculously conceives in old age and promises the child to God. Here is how this second-century text describes Anna giving birth to her baby girl:

> And so her pregnancy came to term; and in the ninth month Anna gave birth. And she said to the midwife, "Is it a boy or a girl?" And the midwife said, "A girl." And Anna said, "I have been greatly honored this day." Then the midwife put the child to bed. When, however, the prescribed days were completed, Anna cleansed herself of the flow of blood. And she offered her breast to the infant and gave her the name Mary.[3]

Not surprisingly, this second-century text describing the birth of Mary came to be read on the Feast of the Nativity of Mary, at least in Eastern Churches.[4] Four centuries later, the wonder of Anna giving birth to Mary is expressed beautifully by Saint Romanos Melodos: "The barren one gives birth to the God-bearer."[5] The paintings and images of the birth of Mary actually might capture the wisdom of this feast better than any written text. Although these images borrow motifs from Jesus' birth, they often in contradistinction show an all-female cast of characters. Gone are the shepherds and the magi. Instead, Anna and her baby daughter are surrounded by female attendants, servants, and visitors. Anna's husband, Joachim, might peek around a corner or even appear to the side, but mostly Anna's birth of Mary is a women-identified celebration. There are some images, in fact, that show three holy mothers and their children: Anna, Elizabeth, and Mary. And there are the many representations of *Anne Trinitaire,* an image of Anna with Mary, who often sits in Anna's lap and in turn holds the Christ child in her own. Clearly, Mary here figures both as daughter and as mother. The "trinity" of Anna, Mary, and Jesus hinges on this *both* of Mary, who is daughter of Anna *and* mother of Jesus.

Finally, there are the many images of the "tree of Jesse," usually in the form of a family tree that begins with Jesse, father of David, or with Adam and ends with Mary and Christ. This motif also is central to the beautiful fifteenth-century Advent hymn "Lo, How a Rose E'er Blooming" (even if most people do not realize this):

> Lo, how a Rose e'er blooming
> From tender stem hath sprung!
> Of Jesse's lineage coming,
> As those of old have sung . . .
> Isaiah 'twas foretold it,
> the Rose I have in mind;
> with Mary we behold it,
> the Virgin Mother kind.

Even if only a few of the representations of the tree of Jesse include Anna, the ancestral line of Jesus clearly is unthinkable without his mother herself having been "born of a woman." The Feast of the Nativity of Mary reminds us of this truth.

The Feast Today: Mending the Broken Fabric of All Human Relations

As a woman who happens to be both a mother and a daughter, I have grown to love the Feast of the Nativity of Mary. The feast reminds me that the mother of our redeemer was a daughter. But this feast is not only a treasure for women—or even more narrowly, for those women who also are mothers and daughters. This feast, as all feasts of Mary, ultimately speaks a truth about Jesus, and with that a truth about God that can nurture the faith and hope of all. In celebrating the fact that the mother of God herself was born of a woman, who was born of a woman, who was born of a woman, we celebrate that God rendered Godself present in the intricate web of human relations through time. This very presence of God in the web of human relations is a sign of profound hope, because human relations are no innocent and unbroken fabric. Human relations always have been and continue to be broken in a multitude of ways, as all of us who live in human families surely know. We ourselves are a part of that brokenness. By assuming, very concretely, human relations in a long line of ancestors going back to the beginnings of time, God mends with God's own presence our always-incomplete ancestral fabric of life. There is no better pointer to this brokenness and the way God assumes this brokenness than the five women named in Jesus' genealogy in the Gospel of Matthew. Tamar, Rahab, Ruth, Bathsheba, and Mary all were woven into God's story with humankind somewhat "out of order." Theirs are no unbroken, neat, nice, and easy stories. As women, seemingly out of order in the patrilineal genealogy of Jesus, these foremothers point to what God's presence at the heart of our ancestral fabric of life can do: mend the brokenness and weave it into God's ever-redeeming and ever-hopeful presence in all of life. God redeems not idealized and glamorized versions of human family, but real families. These families include many stories of brokenness that we ourselves are powerless to heal—the alcoholic aunt, the grandfather who committed suicide, the many children who died in infancy. I, for one, need God's mending of the fabric of life for myself and my family, my ancestors, and all future generations. I cannot redeem the lives of my foremothers, nor is it in my power to make whole the lives within my family. Both their moments of brokenness and of radiance, of holiness and of treachery are beyond my reach. But that is precisely why I celebrate with deep hope the Feast of the Nativity of Mary. The feast tells me that God has rendered Godself present in the fragile fabric of ancestral relations. And as always, God's very presence is the promise of wholeness.

A Day in Extra-Ordinary Time

September 11, 2001

In the year 2001, on the brilliantly clear morning of Tuesday, September 11, I saw the divine presence.

She was squatting in the midst of billowing smoke and raging fire, of mountains of twisted steel and broken glass. An apocalypse of destruction and terror engulfed her. Her face, bearing the serene features of an indigenous woman of this continent, was covered with a thick layer of ash. But the ashen face seemed strangely glistening. The divine presence wept.

And then I saw: in her strong brown arms she was gathering the remains of her beautiful creation, all the maimed and the burnt, the dying and the dead, the unborn, the orphaned, the lost, and those who inflicted loss. I saw her gather, passionately and gently, the lives of all. With tears trickling down her ashen face, she caught in her arms those who jumped from great heights, and she cradled in the palm of her hand a dying priest.

And the divine presence whispered, Holy, holy, holy is every human life. Heaven and earth and the very heart of God mourn when death so violently overcomes life. Then I said, Woe is me! Why do my eyes have to see the divine presence mourning, gathering her torn creation in her arms? Why can I not see God sitting on a throne, high and lofty, with the train of his garment filling the temple and seraphs in attendance above him, each with six wings? I am lost.

Then one of the living dead came to me and touched my eyes. Look again, he said. And I saw the divine presence, groaning, crouched amid the heaps of rubble, her belly large and full of life. And I saw that she was a woman in travail, desperate to birth new life, a child of peace. And as every mother, the divine presence, too, birthed with the rhythm of billowing pain and the fear of futility.

Then I heard the voice of the divine presence saying, Who will labor with me, and who will be midwife to life? Here I am, I said, I want to birth life with you. And the divine presence said, Come, take your place beside me.

In the year 2001, on the brilliantly clear morning of Tuesday, September 11 . . .

Yes, I did see the divine presence. But was it really on September 11? It took days before I was able to see anything resembling a divine presence. On the brilliantly clear morning of September 11, I saw only billowing smoke and raging fire, mountains of twisted steel and broken glass, an apocalypse of destruction and terror. The images were everywhere, stark and powerful, replayed again and again, within ourselves and all around us. Soon, another powerful icon appeared, superimposing itself on the rubble of the Twin Towers: the American flag, raised over the rubble, then swiftly transubstantiating itself into lapel pins on business suits, T-shirts of all imaginable sizes, bumper stickers on both Jaguars and pick-up trucks, and, with the beginning of November(!), patriotic Christmas tree ornaments, "premiering at only $9.99 each." The icon became a totalizing presence, holding captive our eyes.

Where is there space to see this culture's complicity with the roots of the hatred behind September 11? Where is there room to remember the thirty thousand children who died of hunger and hunger-related causes on September 11, and the thirty thousand more who died on September 12, and every day since then? Who will fill national cathedrals for them and their loved ones? What is the meaning of our daily indifference?

United we stand? I have no desire to. Broken, I want to kneel.

I Saw the Divine Presence

Like Hagar in the desert, I yearn to see and to name God, and to live. Instead, the towers, and the flag. And then the words, endlessly . . . those of the reporters and of the politicians, and, above all, a sudden multitude of experts. Heaps of words on heaps of rubble. The religious leaders also are in high demand, the archbishops and rabbis on CNN, and even a theologian on Oprah. It will not last.

Who will help us see the face of God? As a deer longs for flowing streams, so my soul longs to see the Word of Life stand against all idols of death. My soul thirsts for the profound silence of the Unnamable. When shall I come and see the face of God? I am tired of the fine-tuning of words: Will this be the beginning of a war, a just war, an armed intervention, or plain murder? What are the prerequisites for a just war? The carefully crafted theological arguments of the professional theologians—of whom I am one—do not seem to reach the depth of my soul. Deep calls to deep. I yearn to see the face of God and live.

The Divine Presence Wept

Where are the seers and the sages, the visionaries and the wise, the ones who have learned to see the face of God in billowing smoke and raging fire?

Maybe we can learn from the people of Chile. Their September 11 came in 1973. The pictures from Santiago on September 11, 1973, no longer look "foreign"—billowing smoke and raging fire, an apocalypse of destruction and terror, airplanes overhead attacking the Moneda, the symbol of Chilean democracy. And after the airplanes and the fire and the destruction came the disappearances and the tortures, the disbelief and the despair. The unspeakable:

> And then, they took our children —
> And they took their scissors —
> And then they took the hands of our children . . .[1]

Maybe we can learn from the everyday terror in women's lives, from a survivor of rape who wrestles with a psalm:[2]

> **do not give me over to the will of my tormentors**
> You already did.
>
> maybe you cried too . . .

Maybe we can learn from the Palestinian women in Bethlehem:

> Even now as we write this, tank shells are exploding around the Bethlehem area and a young girl and a young woman in Beit Jala have just been killed. . . . There is no time to feel, to weep, death comes upon death, destruction follows destruction. As the shelling becomes louder and nearer, as we listen to the wailing of the ambulance sirens going nearby, we urge you not to leave us "orphans." Do not forget us in our time of trial . . .[3]

Yes, all "thought must be interrupted by the great counter experiences of suffering,"[4] and "theology begins with God's heartache."[5] I long to see God's real presence, but only if it can be a presence for and with the abused, the tortured, and the dead. I cannot imagine God's presence without the gift of tears. Why would the giver of all gifts not claim this one as God's very own?

Holy, Holy, Holy Is Every Human Life

Are there words that sustain, after all? Are there God-sustained words? I am barely able to entrust myself to the shortest of prayers, two or three words. *Kyrie eleison*. Sustain the dying. Deliver us from evil. Comfort those who mourn. *Dona nobis pacem*. Be Thou my vision. *Holy, holy, holy is every human life, every human life.*

Fragments of a theological tradition emerge from deep within which have nurtured faith in the past. None but the briefest ones remain. *Gloria Dei vivens homo*. "God is the beyond in the midst of life." *Solo Dios basta*. I repeat them to myself as if they are confessions of faith. They are. "Just to be is a blessing, just to live is holy."

I Saw Her Gather, Passionately and Gently, the Lives of All

"We have gathered here as Americans, and as Christians." The priest opens the liturgy with these words. I turn to leave. My citizenship is from another continent. As I turn, I suddenly see. In the midst of this liturgy that does not speak to me, I see: *in her strong brown arms she was gathering the remains of her beautiful creation, all the maimed and the burnt, the dying and the dead, the unborn, the orphaned, the lost, and those who inflicted loss. I saw her gather, passionately and gently, the lives of all.* The liturgy continues, but within me, finally, there is only silence, the brilliant eloquence of silence.[6] I see. She gathers the lives of all.

She Cradled in the Palm of Her Hand a Dying Priest

The vision of another man superimposes itself over that of the priest dying among the New York firefighters, a man who also died within the rubble of a world violently crashing all around him. Dietrich Bonhoeffer was hanged in Flossenbürg concentration camp on April 9, 1945, just days before the end of the Second World War. He knew that he was being walked to the gallows when he entrusted these words to a fellow prisoner: "This is the end, for me the beginning of life." Bonhoeffer must have seen what I saw on the brilliantly clear morning of Tuesday, September 11, when Fr. Mychal Judge, OFM, died in the rubble of the WTC: a Life beyond all Life opening up in his ending, ready to cradle him in the palm of Her hand.

Still, the fragmentation of lives ended by violence remains real. For Bonhoeffer, the fragmentation itself became a pointer to an ultimate wholeness that we cannot give but only receive as gift: "there are some fragments . . . whose importance lasts for centuries, because their completion can only be a matter for God, and so they are fragments that must be fragments."[7] With Fr. Mychal, who in his own words had "always wanted to be a priest and a fireman,"[8] there seems to be nothing but perfect meaning in the final fragmentation of his life, since this fragmentation also embodied a final fusion of his disparate passions: the blending of the dying of a priest with the dying firefighters of whom he was one. Would that all our dyings held such clarity and wholeness, in the very midst of the violent fragmentations all around us.

And I Saw the Divine Presence, Groaning, Crouched amid the Heaps of Rubble

The brilliance of these sun-drenched days is real, almost too real. I kneel in front of a golden tabernacle knowing that it holds pure life. Or does it hold a broken body, for a fragmented world? Or is it the one only because it dared to become the other? What do I do with my deep yearning for wholeness, for redemption, for life abundant, for bread *and* roses? My hunger for life only increases with every piece of broken bread I eat and every sip of wine I taste.

In the end, the questions dissolve in the golden brilliance of the tabernacle. There is silence, and in the silence, presence, real presence. I open my eyes to see.

And I Saw That She Was a Woman in Travail, Desperate to Birth New Life, a Child of Peace

Yes, I did see. But I knew, deep down in my heart, that this one would be stillborn. The womb would become a tomb for this child, peace. No matter how many protective symbols I sewed onto the birth-shirt, the "child-eater" would ravish this one, for sure.[9] What was more painful? That simple knowledge, or the knowledge that I could not pretend to be an uncompromising midwife of peace, anyway? Ever since the birth of my child, I had known that I would defend this vulnerable life entrusted to my care, and I would defend it violently if necessary. This realization was painful—more painful than the marks of violence my child's long and hard birth had imprinted on my body for the rest of my life.

I Want to Birth Life with You

Since I bear on my body the marks of having given birth amidst violence, maybe I can learn to midwife amidst heaps of rubble? How can I be anything but midwife—"with-woman"—to one in travail, desperate to birth new life?

A theologian as midwife? I need to learn from Shiphrah and Puah, the Hebrew midwives who defied Pharaoh, how to conspire and co-labor in bringing forth new life.[10] I need to learn with feminist theologians how to engage in the mending of creation.[11] I do know how to recycle my household trash, sign petitions protesting the treatment of Afghan women, and stand in silent antiwar protest on a street corner. But what about the richest country on earth relentlessly bombing the (almost) poorest one, and that for weeks without end? I thought there were no targets. And then the cluster bombs have the same color and size as the food aid packages, and Afghan children pick up both. I desperately need to learn more about the Jewish notion of *tikkun olam*, the repairing of the world. I do not know how to repair a world in which hungry children pick up unexploded cluster bombs instead of food. Does God?

Come, Take Your Place beside Me

There is no other way: I will have to learn to practice midwifery crouched amidst heaps of rubble.

> I pledge allegiance to this vision of the divine presence
> and to the vision of the world for which it stands
> one world
> in which violence and fragmentation are real
> yet in which God labors to bring forth life.
> I am called to kneel beside Her
> in Her labor.

Hildegard of Bingen (September 17)

A Saint in Search of Her Feast Day

IT IS HARD TO BELIEVE: Hildegard of Bingen, the great twelfth-century visionary, monastic leader, writer, composer, and preacher, was never officially canonized. Nor does Hildegard have a place in the liturgical calendar of saints (except for the regional German calendar). On September 17—the anniversary of Hildegard's death in 1179—the Catholic Church in the United States celebrates the memory of a post-tridentine theologian, Robert Bellarmine, SJ (1542–1621). Franciscans mark September 17 as the day on which, in 1224, Saint Francis received the stigmata. Both of these memorials have their own importance, but what about the memory of the "brilliantly original woman"[1] known to us as Hildegard of Bingen?

> Hildegard was the only woman of her age to be accepted as an authoritative voice on Christian doctrine; the first woman who received express permission from a pope to write theological books; the only medieval woman who preached openly, before mixed audiences of clergy and laity, with the full approval of church authorities; the author of the first known morality play and the only twelfth-century playwright who is not anonymous; the only composer of her era (not to mention the only medieval woman) known both by name and by a large corpus of surviving music; the first scientific writer to discuss sexuality and gynecology from a female perspective; and the first saint whose official biography includes a first-person memoir.[2]

So much praise for Hildegard's brilliant originality, from one of the leading contemporary Hildegard scholars. The one word that deserves a question mark in this description of Hildegard's profound importance in church history is the term "saint." Even though a process for her canonization was begun soon after her death, Hildegard has never been officially canonized. In what follows, I trace Hildegard's story— that is, not so much the story of her life, about which much has been written, but the story of her "afterlife," or reception history. Of this reception history, we ourselves become a part every September 17 by

Hildegard of Bingen, by Robert Lentz

either ignoring or laying claim to her story. This examination of Hildegard's story concludes with a liturgy for September 17, honoring her visionary life and writings. This liturgy "performs" what the canonization process (that is, its failure) prevented. It marks September 17 as the feast day of Saint Hildegard.

Hildegard's World: Of *Viriditas* and Visions

I *am* prejudiced when it comes to Hildegard of Bingen since she was one of the towering saints in the geography of my childhood memory. I knew nothing about the failure of the medieval process of her canonization then. The sites of the monastic houses Hildegard founded were only an hour away from my home; and every time I traveled up the Rhine valley, the neo-Romanesque Abbey of Saint Hildegard rose high above the landscape, visible from afar. Etched in my memory is the lush and fertile valley that the Rhine River forms around Bingen, a land blessed with abundant sunlight and covered with vineyards since the Roman era. For much of the year, hundreds of shades of brilliant green dominate the steep slopes of this valley, interrupted only by the majestic blue-gray river below. No wonder the term *viriditas*—variously translated into English as vitality, freshness, greenness, fecundity, or fruitfulness—plays a vital role in Hildegard's writings.[3] No wonder also that Hildegard encountered God again and again as *lux vivens,* Living Light. She describes her foundational vision and calling in terms of this light:

> It happened that, in the eleven hundred and forty-first year of the Incarnation of the Son of God, Jesus Christ, when I was forty-two years and seven months old, Heaven was opened and a fiery light of exceeding brilliance came and permeated my whole brain, and inflamed my whole heart and my whole breast, not like a burning but like a warming flame. . . . I heard a voice from Heaven saying, "I am the Living Light, Who illuminates the darkness. . . . O human, who receives these things meant to manifest what is hidden not in the disquiet of deception but in the purity of simplicity, write, therefore, the things you see and hear."[4]

Even for those whose childhood memory does not include the lure of Hildegard's locality, this twelfth-century woman easily appeals. The breadth of interest in her, so evident particularly in the last few decades, has inspired a Hildegard renaissance well beyond the confines of the Catholic Church. Historians of women's lives, musicians, New Age adherents, proponents of natural medicine, creators of feminist rituals, icons, holy cards, cookbooks, and growers of herb gardens—Hildegard inspires them all. In some ways, this current interest mirrors Hildegard's own breadth of interests: from her theological writings and musical compositions to her consideration of gems and herbs, from her healing practices to her creation of an imaginary language. Compared with most women of her time, Hildegard led a very long life that spanned much of the twelfth century (1098–1179). This period witnessed a profound struggle between imperial and papal powers, ecclesial reform movements, crusading visions, and persecutions of both heretics and Jews. Hildegard's life, although cloistered, could not but intersect with all of these.

A Life in the (Living) Light

Hildegard was born in 1098 to a family of the Rhenish nobility. As a tenth child (and therefore a "tithe" child), she was vowed to God at an early age and then given into the care of the recluse Jutta of Sponheim. Jutta, a noblewoman only six years older than Hildegard, was enclosed with her younger charge in a hermitage joined to the Benedictine monastery of Disibodenberg, located above the confluence of the rivers Glan and Nahe. There Jutta spent her years in prayer, devotion, and rigorous ascetic renunciation. Eventually a small community of women gathered around the hermitage. In 1136, upon Jutta's death at age forty-four, Hildegard was elected the new leader, that is, the *magistra,* of this community. A visionary since childhood (or more precisely, since the time in her mother's womb),[5] Hildegard felt called after her election to write down her visions and reflections. Pope Eugene III himself acknowledged and approved Hildegard's writings (the as-yet incomplete *Scivias*) in 1147–48 at a synod in nearby Treves. Around 1150, Hildegard and her growing number of nuns, all of them noblewomen, left Disibodenberg for her newly founded monastery at Rupertsberg, across from Bingen, where the river Nahe flows into the Rhine. The nuns' leave-taking was not without conflict with the male monastic superiors, especially in relation to the nuns' autonomy of governance and their right to their endowments. In addition to establishing monastic life at Rupertsberg (during which time she wrote liturgical music for her nuns),[6] Hildegard was increasingly present to ecclesial politics. In hundreds of letters (of which four hundred survive), she counseled monastic superiors, bishops, the pope, and the emperor. She prophetically denounced clerical and imperial abuses, traveled, and preached in such important cities as Mainz, Würzburg, Treves, and Cologne. She also

continued her extensive writings. With her community of nuns growing, Hildegard founded a second convent in 1165, on the other side of
the Rhine valley at Eibingen, a convent she visited twice weekly, crossing the river by boat. In 1178, an ecclesial interdict was imposed on
Hildegard's community after she refused to disinter a nobleman buried
on convent grounds. While the question of the man's excommunication
and reconciliation was argued, the nuns were prohibited from singing
the Divine Office, ringing the bells, and receiving communion. The
interdict was lifted only shortly before Hildegard's death at Rupertsberg
on September 17, 1179, at the age of eighty-one. Immediately following
her death, the Rhine valley was said to have been illumined by a flaming light—the result of two rainbows crossing in the sky.

The (Un-)Making of a Holy Woman

Why on earth was this brilliantly original twelfth-century visionary
and monastic leader never canonized? The answer lies in a complex historical process at the end of which stands a woman who—although one
of the towering female figures in the tradition of the church—continues today in search of her feast day.

During Hildegard's lifetime, people from surrounding areas came to
her convent seeking the life-giving wisdom and powers of its abbess.
Hildegard's fame also spread among other monastic houses, such as
Gembloux, Echternach, St. Eucharius in Treves, and Villers in Bel-
gium. Not surprisingly, the first part of her *vita* was drafted during her
lifetime by her secretary, Godfrey of Disibodenberg. It is possible that
Hildegard herself wrote or dictated some autobiographical notes for an
earlier secretary and confidant, Volmar (d. 1173), who had begun a collection of her correspondence. But Godfrey himself also died unexpectedly before the subject of his narrative. In response to a request by
the archbishop of Cologne, Guibert of Gembloux began a *vita* of his
own in the year Hildegard died (1179). This narrative, too, never saw
completion. After Hildegard's death, the monk Theoderic of Echternach was commissioned to complete Godfrey's earlier attempt at a
vita. Theoderic did so by privileging autobiographical materials drawn
up by Hildegard herself, which he complemented with his own awed
running commentary. The result of these various attempts to narrate
Hildegard's life is a both fragmented and fascinating piece of medieval
hagiography.[7] In the late twelfth century, a summarized narrative of
Hildegard's life was composed in the monastery of Gembloux.[8] The
narrative was divided for liturgical reading for the Feast of Saint Hilde-

gard—a clear sign of veneration a hundred years after her death. In fact, early in 1228, Pope Gregory IX responded positively to a request by the convent of Rupertsberg to inquire into Hildegard's life with a view toward canonization.[9] However, the men charged with the task of gathering the necessary materials, especially the accounts of witnesses, failed miserably. Late in 1233, they finally dispatched a report to Rome, but it lacked fundamental details for a canonization process, such as the names of witnesses to Hildegard's miracles, as well as precise dates and locations. In 1237, Gregory (the pope who canonized both Francis of Assisi and Elizabeth of Thuringia) appointed three different men to gather the missing information. These men failed even more grandiosely by, apparently, simply doing nothing. In 1243, after a papal inquiry, a commission finally provided the necessary details to the initial report. To this day, however, it remains unclear whether the report ever reached Rome. What *is* clear is that even though by the early thirteenth century Hildegard came to be depicted with a halo, she was never officially canonized. The documentation for her canonization simply vanished somewhere between the Rhine valley and Rome.

This did not, of course, stop devotion to Hildegard, especially in the convents touched by her life and work.[10] Throughout the Middle Ages, there were ecclesial writers who referred to Hildegard with the title "saint," and even indulgences were granted in her name. In 1489, Hildegard's tomb was opened in the hope of finding not only saintly relics (which were there), but also the bull of canonization (which never existed).[11] By the end of the sixteenth century, Hildegard's name had been recorded in the Roman Martyrology, that is, the calendric listing of saints' names and short *vitae*.

These clear indications of a continuing veneration of Hildegard cannot, however, undo other indicators of the profound silence surrounding her life and writings. Not only did the canonization process end somewhere between the Rhine and Rome, but Hildegard's writings, in the century after her death, came to be excerpted, read (and contested) primarily as prognostic-prophetic oracles.[12] Not surprisingly, the great theologians of the thirteenth and fourteenth centuries—Albert the Great, Thomas Aquinas, Bonaventure, William of Occam, and others—seem to know nothing of Hildegard. In a recent essay on the subject, Hans-Joachim Schmidt has argued that as universities emerged as new sites of knowledge production, Hildegard's visionary knowledge, which followed a different logic than that produced by scholastic theology, was pushed to the margins.[13] Her writings do not seem to have had a rich reception history even in the areas where one might expect—

the homiletic tradition of the time or the writings of women mystics in the following centuries.[14]

It was not until the nineteenth century that devotion to Hildegard of Bingen began to flourish as part of a larger restoration that marked German Catholicism at that time. Devotion to Hildegard also began to spread beyond the convent culture into the local dioceses around Disibodenberg, Bingen, and Eibingen. In the second half of the twentieth century, interest in Hildegard of Bingen finally began to thrive. In 1978, the German bishops even petitioned Rome to have the honorary title *doctor ecclesiae* conferred on Hildegard. The Vatican's response was clear: Such an honor could only be conferred upon those properly canonized by Rome in the first place.[15] But by the late 1970s, the cultural production of "icons" was no longer closely wedded to ecclesial processes of canonization anyway, and so Hildegard's triumphal advance into contemporary consciousness proceeded without Vatican help. At the beginning of the twenty-first century, Hildegard's reception history has grown broad indeed. Unfortunately, some of it (especially in New-Age, alternative-medicine, and esoteric circles) has clearly left behind not only the depth of scholarly work on Hildegard, but also any faith-centered questions about the meaning of venerating this particular woman.

The (Re-)Making of a Saint: A Feast Day Liturgy

There are two developments in the reception history of Hildegard of Bingen that deserve to be unmade by an act of feminist liturgical invention. One is the fact that while Hildegard is included in the Roman Martyrology, she is not included in the official liturgical calendar of saints. As a result, there is no liturgy for September 17 as the feast day of Saint Hildegard of Bingen. The second development that deserves unmaking is the construction of Hildegard as a champion of causes she herself would not have recognized. The liturgy that follows both "makes" September 17 the feast day of Saint Hildegard, and at the same time unmakes an image of Hildegard that is not true to Hildegard's own writings. The latter unmaking is achieved primarily by drawing heavily on Hildegard's own words, visions, images, and biblical reflections, in order to render her visible precisely as a woman who lived a life of holiness within the twelfth-century church. It is only as such that women in the church of the twenty-first century can claim her as their own *magistra*.

A Liturgy for the Feast Day
of Hildegard of Bingen, September 17

Preparation

Create a liturgical center on the floor or on a low table in the middle of the gathering space. Decorate the center with herbs, flowers, grapes, candles, incense, symbols of the four elements (air, fire, water, earth), and—if available—copies of some illustrations of Hildegard's Scivias.[16] *Be sure to have water and roses present, which will be needed for the concluding blessing. At the center, set an image of Hildegard (preferably the one by Robert Lentz).*[17]

Welcome and Invitation to Form a Circle of Life

When all have gathered in a circle around this center, a presider welcomes everyone and invites each individual to introduce herself by name and to light a candle for someone they wish to bring into the circle with them (e.g., "My name is Teresa. I light this candle in honor of my favorite aunt, Hildegard. I wish to bring her into this sacred circle with me.")

Song [ALL]: "Circle of Wisdom"[18]

Circle of Wisdom

L. Collingridge

2. Circle of wisdom, circle of love.
   Turning and returning, in passionate embrace.
   As we weave our way, we hear your voice,
   calling us eternally home.

3. Circle of wisdom, circle Divine.
   Mysterious and hidden, beyond human tongues.
   Wheeling through the cosmos, ever present, ever veiled.
   Turn our minds to thoughts of wonder.

A Presider:

Let us together invite Hildegard of Bingen into this sacred circle, the woman in whose honor we have gathered here today. Although she was never officially canonized, we claim Hildegard as someone whose life inspires us and challenges us to live with clarity, holiness, and beauty. As a visionary, writer, composer, preacher, and healer, she helped to shape a whole century and the witness of the church in her times. Even though for many centuries her memory was faint, she has recaptured the imagination of countless women and men in our time. We are a part of this movement as we honor Hildegard's memory today. We now invite her presence among us.

The presider lights a large candle in front of the image of Hildegard, saying "Be present with us, sister of wisdom." Then she says:

Let us now listen to Hildegard herself, who in a letter written late in her life, described her visionary calling with the following words.

A Reading from Hildegard of Bingen:

I am now more than seventy years old. But even in my infancy, before my bones, muscles, and veins had reached their full strength, I was possessed of this visionary gift in my soul, and it abides with me still up to the present day. In these visions, my spirit rises, as God wills, to the heights of heaven and into the shifting winds, and it ranges among various peoples, even those very far away. And since I see in such a fashion, my perception of things depends on the shifting of the clouds and other elements of creation. . . . The light that I see is not local and confined. It is far brighter than a lucent cloud through which the sun shines. And I can discern neither its height nor its length nor its breadth. This light I have named "the shadow of the Living Light," . . . And sometimes, though not often, I see another light in that light, and this I have called "the Living Light." But I am even less able to explain how I see this light than I am the other one. Suffice it to say that when I do see it, all my sorrow and pain vanish from my memory and I become more like a young girl than an old woman.[19]

These are the words of Hildegard of Bingen.

Response [ALL]: "Thanks be to you, sister of vision."

Psalm 18

Antiphon:[20]   I love you, God my strength,
                    my rock, my shelter, my stronghold.

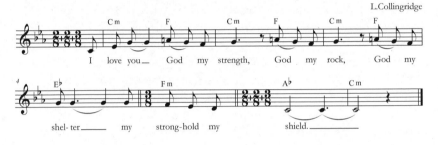

My God, I lean on you, my shield, my rock, my champion,
    my defense.
When I call for help, I am safe from my enemies.
Praise the Lord!

Antiphon: I love you, God my strength, God my rock,
                God my shelter, my stronghold, my shield.

Death had me in its grip, the current swept me away;
Sheol was closing in, I felt the hand of death.
From the depths I cried out, my plea reached the heavens.
God heard me.

Antiphon: I love you, God my strength, God my rock,
                God my shelter, my stronghold, my shield.

The Lord lives!
[B]lessed be my rock, the God who saves me,
the God who avenges, who makes the nations submit.
You humble my foes, from the violent you rescue me.

Antiphon: I love you, God my strength, God my rock,
                   God my shelter, my stronghold, my shield.

Among the nations I praise you, sing your power and name.
You give great victory to your anointed king,
You are faithful for all time
to the house of David.

Antiphon: I love you, God my strength, God my rock,
                   God my shelter, my stronghold, my shield.

A Presider:

From the time she was enclosed to lead a life of prayer and devotion with the noblewoman Jutta of Sponheim, Hildegard was steeped in the psalms. Reciting the psalms was a daily practice for these women; it is no wonder that reflections on various psalms are woven into a number of Hildegard's writings. Hildegard stresses that with her crucial vision at age forty-two came a new understanding of different parts of the Scriptures, and she lists the Psalter first, before other biblical writings.[21]

Here is Hildegard's reflection on the opening verses of Psalm 18:

A Reading from Hildegard of Bingen:

This means that my God, through whom I was created and through whom I live and to whom I reach out . . . and from whom I ask for all good things because I know that he is my God and that I ought to serve him since I have knowledge through him, is my helper in all good things since I accomplish my good works through him. I also place my hope in him because his grace clothes me like a garment. And so he is my defender since he protects me from evil when my evil conscience stings me. He gives me counsel so that I do not do evil works. But God is the horn of the salvation of my soul since he teaches me the law through the Holy Spirit. In the law I walk on his paths and take the food of life that is given to those who truly believe. I will have taken this food by the time God receives me into the highest blessedness after I have been sanctified and chosen through all these things. And he will take me to His bosom.[22]

These are the words of Hildegard of Bingen.

Response [ALL]: "Thanks be to you, sister of blessedness."

Gospel Reading: Luke 15:3, 8–10

So he told them this parable: . . . "What woman having ten silver coins, if she loses one of them, does not light a lamp, sweep the house, and search carefully until she finds it? When she has found it, she calls together her friends and neighbors, saying, 'Rejoice with me, for I have found the coin that I had lost.' Just so, I tell you, there is joy in the presence of the angels of God over one sinner who repents." [NRSV]

A Presider:

Hildegard was not only a visionary but also a gifted interpreter of Scripture, regularly commenting on the sacred writings for her nuns. Fifty-eight of Hildegard's homilies, which she preached to her community, have been collected, but reflections on the Scriptures are woven into all of Hildegard's writings. Here is her interpretation of the passage from Luke we have just heard.

A Reading from Hildegard of Bingen

The Holy Divinity had ten coins, namely ten orders of the heavenly hierarchy, including the chosen angels, and [Humanity]. It lost one coin when [Humanity] fell into death by following the Devil's temptations instead of the divine precepts. Hence the Divinity kindled a burning lamp, namely Christ, Who was true God and true Man and the splendid Sun of Justice; and with Him He swept the house, . . . and found His coin, [Humanity], whom He had lost. Then He called together His friends, namely earthly deeds of justice, and His neighbors, namely spiritual virtues, and said, "Rejoice with Me in praise and joy, and build the celestial Jerusalem with living stones, for I have found [Humanity], who had perished by the deception of the Devil."[23]

These are the words of Hildegard of Bingen.

Response [ALL]: "Thanks be to you, sister of the Sun."

Meditative Silence

A Presider:

Let us now invite Hildegard, the composer, into our circle. Hildegard created chants for her monastic choir of sisters to sing and late in life had many of these compositions transcribed by musical experts from a nearby monastery. One of Hildegard's songs is *"Caritas habundat,"* her antiphon for Divine Love.[24] The first version of this song occurs in a manuscript that was probably prepared during Hildegard's lifetime in her own scriptorium. In this manuscript, the antiphon has a most unusual ending, a note which is not the prescribed final. Might Hildegard have meant this chant not to come to completion, just as Divine Love continues to follow human beings even to the deepest depths of the dreaded land of shades?

Caritas Habundat

Hildegard of Bingen

Divine Love

L. Collingridge

(keyboard)

1. I burn in the sun, I shine in the wa- ters _____ I flame high a - bove _____ the beau-ty of earth _____ I qui-cken cre - a - tion _____ sus-tain-ing all life. _____

2. The deepest of depths,
   bitter Sheol,
   must open to me,
   as I seek out the lost,
   and bring peace
   to those who revere me.

3. Though I may be hidden,
   the breath of my reason
   moves in all creatures.
   I penetrate deeply
   those who invite me,
   I am love Divine.

Meditative Silence

A Litany in Honor of Saint Hildegard

The communal response after each petition is: "Walk with us, sister of courage."

For all women called to visionary clarity, . . .
For all women who nurture the faith of their sisters, . . .

For all women who speak truth to power, . . .
For all women who write words of wisdom, beauty, and life, . . .
For all women gifted with melodies and song, . . .
For all women who heal, . . .
For all women who cherish creation and discern in it the ways of
  the Creator, . . .
For all women whose names and lives are forgotten when we call
  on the saints, . . .
For each of us here and for all those we have brought into the
  circle with us, . . .

Concluding Reading: Hildegard's Death

After the holy mother had completed, with devotion, many distressful
battles, she grew tired of the present life . . . in the eighty-second year of
her life, on September 17 [1179], in a holy death she went to her heavenly bridegroom. Her daughters, whose joy and consolation she had
been, shed bitter tears at the home-going of their beloved Mother. . . .
God, however, clearly indicated at her departure the reward that she
would have from him. At early twilight on that Sunday, two very bright
arcs of various colors appeared in the heavens over the chamber in
which the holy virgin returned her happy soul to God . . . and they
enveloped the entire mount in brilliant light. We have to believe that by
these signs God revealed the fullness of light with which he had glorified
his beloved in heaven.[25]

Response [ALL]: "We give thanks for your life and death, beloved of the
Living Light."

Blessing

From Hildegard's *vita*, we know that she once blessed a child
with river water, scooping up water from the Rhine in her left
hand and blessing it with her right hand, before touching and
healing the child. Another tradition has it that Hildegard used a
rose to sprinkle water in blessing.

You are now invited to bless each other, using words of Hildegard herself, from a letter to an unnamed prioress, who had
sought solace from her. Hildegard ended the letter to the dis-

traught prioress, saying: "May God make you the temple of life."[26]

The participants take a rose each and bless each other, saying, "May God make you the temple of life."

Closing Song: "Circle of Wisdom"

Saint Teresa of Ávila (October 15)

Teacher of the Church

ONE OF THE PROMISES the liturgical calendar holds for women comes with its invitation to celebrate women of faith who have gone before. As the year progresses, the sanctoral cycle weaves the feast days of a colorful communion of women saints into our daily lives. As with most of the church's liturgical life in relation to women, however, the sanctoral cycle and its women saints are not without problems. To begin with, the process of canonization throughout history has clearly been male-dominated, which is one of the reasons for the underrepresentation of women in the sanctoral cycle even today. Additionally, many of the women who are included in the calendar conform to a certain stereotypical depiction of female sanctity. Their piety centers, on the one hand, on obedience and submission to the church and, on the other hand, on stark practices of renunciation, especially sexual and food renunciations. It is no wonder, then, that a disproportionately high number of women saints lived ascetic lives, typically in religious communities. It is also no wonder that women were not recognized by the church for their teaching authority and given the honorific title "teacher of the church"—that is, until Saint Teresa of Ávila was named a *doctor ecclesiae* by Pope Paul VI in 1970. Since then, two other women saints, Catherine of Siena and Thérèse de Lisieux, have joined Teresa (but together they are still outnumbered ten to one by their male colleagues as teachers of the church).

Women and Worship

For women today, honoring these mothers in the faith who also are recognized for their teaching authority holds great promise—not least of all the promise of a vision of a liturgy in which women can flourish. What follows is an attempt to connect with one of these women teachers of the church: Saint Teresa of Ávila. As the first woman to be so recognized, Teresa has much to teach us. Here, however, I am most concerned with whether she can also teach us something about liturgy and will thus reread Teresa's life and writings in light of that question.

Communities of religious women for almost fifteen hundred years have provided a specific interplay between women and worship, and a reflection on that interplay. In the past, many convents were privileged sites of female literacy, mostly because religious women were enjoined to recite the Divine Office. Teresa of Ávila is one example of the many religious women who not only lived lives of daily liturgical prayer but also wrote on fundamentals of this practice, and whose writings, moreover, are not only extant but also accessible today (countless religious women's writings remain in manuscript form in archives). Teresa thus stands in a long tradition of praying and writing women. But she was also on the cusp of new developments. Her lifetime saw the final breakup of western Christendom in the Reformation, the conquest of the Americas, the global expansion of Christian mission, and the formation of Tridentine Catholicism, which shaped the Roman Catholic Church well into the twentieth century.

Teresa Sánchez de Cepeda y Ahumada

Who is this woman? Teresa was born in Ávila , Castile, in 1515, as one of twelve children. Her family, which counted itself among the minor nobility, was wealthy but vulnerable in its social position: Teresa's paternal grandfather had been Jewish and had converted to the Christian faith under pressure from the Inquisition. Teresa grew up with a vivid religious imagination, nourished by the reading of saints' lives. The story of her pursuit of martyrdom at age seven is often recounted: Teresa left home with her brother to die for the faith in the land of the "Moors." When, as an adolescent girl, Teresa turned to the finer things of life (including romantic fiction, clothes, and jewelry), her father boarded her with Augustinian nuns. Teresa fell ill and left the convent, only to join a Carmelite convent four years later, against her father's wishes. Plagued by illness, she struggled with monastic life and prayer practices that left her dissatisfied. After eighteen years in the convent, Teresa had a profound experience of conversion, in front of a statue of the suffering Christ. During her forties, her mystical experiences flourished. So did her vision to reform the Carmelite order by bringing it back to its simple and austere beginnings. In 1562, Teresa founded the first reformed Carmelite convent, Saint Joseph in Ávila. More than a dozen other houses followed all over Spain. This period of her life also witnessed Teresa's sustained literary activity. She wrote an autobiographical account of her life and prayer practices (*Book of Her Life*), a theology of prayer (*Way of Perfection*), *Meditations on the Song of Songs*, and *The Interior Castle*, among others. Teresa also maintained a vast correspondence and wrote poems and carols. Her contemplative life was a very active one indeed. Teresa continued her Carmelite reforms against strong civil and ecclesial forces of opposition. On one of her extensive travels dedicated to her reforms, she was overcome by her final sickness. Teresa died in the evening hours of October 4, 1582, at the age of sixty-seven.

Judging from her life, this woman obviously can teach us a lot about tenacity, determination, and courage in following God's call in her life against all ecclesial opposition. She also has rightly been acclaimed a teacher of the ways of prayer. Does this woman have anything to teach us about the practice of prayer embodied in liturgy?

"It's Not for Women"

In Teresa's writings, liturgy is no subject matter of its own. As a woman of the sixteenth century (and as a Christian of Jewish descent), Teresa was in no position to intervene in liturgical developments, champion liturgical reforms, or shape liturgical laws and practices—at least not beyond the confines of her own convents. Nevertheless, as a monastic reformer responsible for the lives of her sisters and as a woman writing on the life of prayer, Teresa does afford us glimpses into how liturgy shaped her life and that of her communities. Teresa's world offered her a conflictual context for her reflections. Religious renewal movements at the time advocated interior prayer and mystic contemplation, and a critical indifference toward liturgical forms, vocal prayer, and popular devotional practices. Women experimented with new forms of living and praying, while elite women exercised profound influence on religious life through patronage,[1] and writing women flourished.[2] Not surprisingly, many of these trends attracted the sustained suspicion of the Spanish Inquisition. Teresa lived and wrote in this context.[3]

With male confessors and the Inquisition looking over her shoulder, and with male clerics and theologians insisting that contemplative prayer was dangerous, particularly for women, Teresa knew well the objections to her chosen lifestyle: "it's not for women, for they will be susceptible to illusions"; "it's better they stick to their sewing"; "the

Our Father and the Hail Mary are sufficient" (*Way of Perfection* 21:2).[4] Teresa herself did not deny the importance of formal liturgical prayer (although that prayer came in a language, Latin, in which she most likely was only phonetically literate). In fact, Teresa insistently wove formal liturgical and contemplative prayer together by depicting formal prayer as open to, indeed as embedded within, contemplative prayer. At the same time, however, Teresa acknowledged her (early) lack of interest and skill in liturgical and musical practice, as well as her disinterest in the more extravagant popular devotions, which she depicted as particularly attractive to women (*Book of Her Life* 31:23; 6:6).

At one point, Teresa even included the recitation of the Divine Office in a list of monastic trials and tribulations (*Way of Perfection* 12:1). Her description of the recitation of the Divine Office in the convent in Villanueva de la Jara provides a good illustration of these trials. Only one of the sisters was able to read well, and the sisters used different breviaries, including old Roman ones handed down to them from clergy. As Teresa put it, "God must have accepted their good intention and effort, for they must have said little that was correct" (*Book of Her Foundations* 28:42). Teresa also recounted the devil tempting her to be satisfied with the recitation of the Divine Office, as all the other nuns were, and not to aspire to deeper ways of praying (*Book of Her Life* 19:10). Not surprisingly, in her *Constitutions*, Teresa asserts that, on non-feast days, the four offices of Prime, Terce, Sext, and None were to be recited together, as one office, at six o'clock in the morning. Moreover, the offices and daily Mass were to be spoken, not chanted. Teresa claimed efficiency as her reason(!), namely, that the sisters would have more time to earn their livelihood.

On the other hand, Teresa's writings are filled with references to frequent confessions, to devotion to the saints, feast days, penances, novenas, and all the other forms of devotion to be expected from a sixteenth-century nun. She wrote poems and songs for liturgical occasions and urged her sisters not to neglect the Divine Office, since it rendered the sisters available to hear God's call (*Way of Perfection* 18:4). According to Teresa, aspirants for the novitiate should be not only healthy and intelligent but also "able to recite the Divine Office and assist in choir" (*Constitutions* 21). And there is at least one passage in Teresa's writings that conveys a clear sense of pleasure in the description of a liturgical event: a procession with the Blessed Sacrament into the church of a new convent (*Book of Her Foundations* 28:37).

Furthermore, Teresa developed her theology of prayer through an interpretation of formal prayer, namely, the Lord's Prayer (*Way of Perfection* 27–42)—after insisting, with strategic humility, that she only reflected on minor details of the life of prayer and left a real theology of prayer to learned men.[5] Teresa's spirituality was also deeply material: devotional objects, images, statues of the suffering Christ, the crucifix, the rosary, holy water, the sign of the cross—these all had their place in her spirituality. Moreover, there are numerous passages in Teresa's writings that link formal prayer or liturgical moments with mystical experiences. Teresa's first ecstatic experience occurred when intoning the hymn "Veni Creator Spiritus" (*Book of Her Life* 24:5–7). Praying the rosary brought her to the heights of mystical experience, and, while reciting the Office, she heard the Lord audibly speak to her (*Book of Her Life* 38:1; 19:7). During a festive Mass she received a vision of redeemed humanity; during another Mass, an ecstatic experience of being clothed in a white vestment—an experience that rendered her unable to see the elevation of the Host or follow the rest of the liturgy (*Book of Her Life* 33:14). The Virgin Mary appeared to Teresa in choir after compline, and Teresa had visions during funeral services and during matins (*Book of Her Life* 36:24; 38:24ff.; 40:14). Worship also figured repeatedly as an entry point for Teresa's experiences with the demonic. One All Souls' Night, for example, Teresa struggled with the devil alighting on her prayer book to prevent her from finishing her prayers (*Book of Her Life* 31:10, cf. 38:23).

Of all liturgical moments, receiving communion was especially important to Teresa. God's presence became tangible as nowhere else, and Teresa described an almost unspeakable desire to receive the Eucharist (*Book of Her Life* 39:22). Quite a number of her mystical experiences occurred at this point. Going to communion on the Feast of Saint Clare, for instance, Teresa had a vision of the Franciscan saint who promised to support her (*Book of Her Life* 33:13). The reservation of the Blessed Sacrament held special importance for Teresa and was one of the key reasons for her horror at the "Lutherans" (*Book of Her Foundations* 3:10).

"The Lord Walks among the Pots and Pans"

In summary, one can say that Teresa lived, and thus reflected, an oscillating liturgical spirituality. Clearly, the liturgy was a fundamental part of her daily life. It is equally clear that liturgical celebrations were often the gateway for Teresa's mystical experiences. But these mystical experiences could transcend any liturgical event or be connected with events other than liturgical celebrations. What then can we learn about liturgy from women such as Teresa of Ávila ? I suggest the following: although Teresa accepted the liturgy as a site of encounter with the Holy One, she also relativized that site. As a woman of her time, she could only intervene in the construction and performance of liturgical life within her own limited sphere. Teresa was aware of some of these limitations. She hinted at not having the freedom, as a woman, to preach and hear confession, but instead had to be satisfied with decorating images (*Book of Her Life* 30:20ff.)—a stark analysis of gendered liturgical power relations! Yet from Teresa's marginalized subject position grows a particular insight: the insistence that the ultimate point of liturgy lies beyond liturgy is a crucial corrective to a tradition that strongly linked grace to the performance of particular rites. Ultimately, Teresa reassigned the place of the liturgy in the lives of women by locating it within broader possibilities of the mediation of divine presence: "the Lord walks among the pots and pans" (*Book of Foundations* 5:8). That is, God is also present in the menial domestic work usually assigned to women. The everyday lives of women, so often trivialized, and the liturgical practices of the church are both sites of encounter with God.

On that account alone, Teresa continues to have much to teach us about the relationship between liturgy and women's lives, and we do well to celebrate her life and testimony every year on October 15. For it was no accident that made Teresa of Ávila the first woman "teacher of the church."

Blessed Mother Teresa (October 19)

Woman Scripts: "Saint," "Satin," or "Stain"?

"CHAMPAGNE SATIN GOWN with black velvet trim: $328," read the tiny script at the bottom of the full-page ad in the Sunday *New York Times*. The ad showed the image of a tall, slender woman in a floor-length glittering gown. The satin gown was sleeveless, its plunging neckline accentuated by a dark velvet trim. The woman gazed intently at the viewer, her body curved, her high-heeled sandals and a tiny handbag silently speaking extravagance. "Razzle dazzle" proclaimed the large script of the ad loudly, the letters running across the woman's body precisely at the level of her pubis.

It was Sunday, October 19, 2003. In Rome, the pope was beatifying a woman who, in a quite different way, had dazzled the world. Oddly enough, she too was identified by a peculiarly trimmed gown, with matching sandals. And her body postures were recognized by millions around the globe: the diminutive nun kneeling and embracing one of the wretched of the earth; her hands clasping a rosary in prayer; her deeply wrinkled face smiling broadly. On the day of her official beatification, not only the Vatican's Web site but also the *New York Times* ran photos and a story about her. In the *Times,* the photos and story appeared on the opposite side of the "Razzle Dazzle" woman in a satin gown trimmed with velvet. The gown of the woman now called "Blessed," however, was a simple and coarse Indian sari, the trademark blue trim its only distinguishing feature; the woman's sandals were worn. In all of this, she resembled women's lives around the globe much more closely than Ms. Razzle Dazzle ever would (or would ever want to). What distinguished the wrinkled old woman from most other women around the globe—even if she shared with them her distance from a "satin" life—was the way in which she embodied the life of a saint.

Woman: "Saint" or "Satin," the double page of the Sunday paper seemed to ask on October 19, 2003. One does not need to have read *The Da Vinci Code* to detect an anagram in this antithesis or to realize that the same five letters could be rearranged in yet another, third way.

The only question is, does this anagram, this scrambling of letters to form three very different words, hold any meaning—beyond the interesting tastes of the *New York Times* graphic designers on this day of the beatification of Mother Teresa?

In what follows, I offer one possible answer to this question. I take the anagram—"saint," "satin," "stain"—as a pointer to a recurring theme at the intersection of women's lives and lived faith. This recurring theme is the complex relationship between three different woman scripts: those of femininity ("satin"), of female sanctity ("saint"), and of its opposite other ("stain"). I will suggest that the anagram might inadvertently point to a deeper truth about how women's holiness is made. Although the three anagrammatic words suggest very different scripts for women's lives, the basic building blocks, that is, the letters themselves, are identical for all three words. The letters are merely arranged differently. That, indeed, is the point of an anagram. Might not a holy life be made in similar ways? The basics of a particular woman script are not simply left behind, but are rather rearranged to create something dazzlingly different. And, contrary to what one might expect, such "mere" rearranging does not leave intact, but fundamentally destabilizes the original script. To stay with the layout of the *New York Times* on October 19, 2003: The very meaning of a "satin" woman script is profoundly challenged when its basics can be seen also to make a "saint." Thus, Blessed Mother Teresa, appearing next to a woman in a dazzling satin gown, renders this woman visible in ways nothing else could: as a deeply un-real and inadequate script for women's lives, focused as it is on glitter, extravagance, and a highly sexualized body image. In the face of an old woman embracing the wretched of the earth, the "satin" woman seems disturbingly removed from lived life. It is precisely the "saint" next to the "satin" that renders visible the possibility of "satin" morphing into "stain." To put this very differently: Meaning is never fixed, whether it is in scripts of femininity, of sanctity, or of sinfulness.

One Is Not Born, but Becomes, a Saint

A more detailed look at how constructions of femininity and of sanctity have always intertwined can add contours to these observations. Simone de Beauvoir's groundbreaking insight—"One is not born, but becomes, a woman"—might also be taken to describe the making of a holy life: One is not born, but becomes, a saint. This is to

say: Saints are made of human beings—who cannot escape having gendered, sexed bodies (even if they seem to relate to these bodies primarily through sexual renunciation[1]). Given the inescapable togetherness
of sainted and sexed bodies, sanctity both is shaped by and itself shapes
performances of gender and symbolic meanings associated with femininity and masculinity. To put it differently, the hagiographic tradition can be read as the result not only of holy lives, but also of cultural
forces, power relations, the privileging of certain voices over others,
and constructions of femininity and masculinity.

Gendered Holiness

Long before contemporary scholarly work on gender and hagiography had begun, there were multiple indications that sanctity never was
gender-neutral in the first place. To begin with, there is a clear numer-
ical asymmetry between men and women who have come to be recognized as saints. The sanctoral cycle privileges male versions of the holy
life.[2] Given this representation of holy lives as dominantly male, are we
to assume that men generally lived more convincing lives of holiness
than women? The answer to this question surely has to be *no.* Other
factors than men's greater holiness will have to account for the numer-
ical imbalance in canonizations. Gendered asymmetries of power are
among these factors.

Gender asymmetry also marks the ranking of days in the sanctoral
cycle, if one brackets out devotion to Mary, the Mother of God, for a
moment. The highest rank in the liturgical calendar that any woman
(other than the Blessed Virgin) has achieved is that of memorial. There
are no feasts or solemnities associated with a female saint. At stake here
obviously is not only the ranking but also the richness or poverty of
liturgical texts and readings related to the different ranks.

A third indicator of how the hagiographic tradition has always been
gendered is the uneven descriptors for saints in the liturgical calendar.
The prevalence of the descriptor "virgin" for women and its lack as a
descriptor for men are a case in point.[3] The liturgical calendar, to put
it sharply, regularly seems to tie female sanctity to gynecology or,
more precisely, to an "intact" virginal female body. Even Blessed
Mother Teresa of Calcutta officially is identified first as a "virgin"
before being described as the founder of her order, the Missionaries of
Charity. Interestingly, Pope John Paul II highlighted a quite different
characteristic of this woman in his address to pilgrims after her beatifi-

cation. The pope described Blessed Mother Teresa as *"[f]irst and fore-most a missionary: . . . one of the greatest missionaries of the 20th century."*[4] This descriptor is refreshingly a-typical when it comes to women saints. On the whole, women have come to be heralded for stereotypically feminine virtues, such as service, humility, self-denial, compassion, interiority, bodily suffering, and obedience. Not surprisingly, Mother Teresa's missionary identity comes to be interpreted as related some-how to the *"noblest qualities of her femininity,"*[5] and, moreover, clearly distinguished from "preaching." As the pope goes on to emphasize in his address:

> The Lord made this simple woman who came from one of Europe's poorest regions a chosen instrument (cf. Acts 9:15) to proclaim the Gospel to the entire world, *not by preaching but by daily acts of love towards the poorest of the poor.*[6]

The "feminine" virtues of service, self-effacement, compassion, and virginal purity are not the only way in which gender constructions and sanctity interrelate. There are a host of other peculiar tensions around women's bodies, sexualities, and reproductive functions inscribed into the hagiographic tradition. I will name but a few of these here. The understanding of Saint Maria Goretti's resistance to a rape as a heroic battle for her purity, rather than as a girl's desperate struggle against sex-ualized violence, betrays an understanding of rape that many women today find deeply troubling.[7] Similarly, women's silent endurance of battering by their husbands is not convincing as a sign of their sanctity for women today who struggle against the pervasive presence of domestic violence.[8] Finally, the official communion of saints did not include a married couple (canonized as such) until Pope John Paul II beatified Luigi and Maria Beltrame Quattrochi in 2001. The pope made the remarkable decision that the feast day of the couple in the liturgi-cal calendar would be their wedding anniversary, rather than the respective dates of their deaths. On the other hand, the Quattrochis clearly lived a quite unrepresentative version of married life. Three of their four children chose religious life, and the fourth never married; the parents lived a life of sexual abstinence for many years. Will this particular model of married life strengthen the real lived lives of cou-ples into the twenty-first century?

A fourth indicator of how the hagiographic tradition has always been gendered is found in the very formation of this tradition. Women usually are not the authors of authenticating narratives of holiness, such as the *vitae* of the saints. Almost exclusively, these *vitae* are male-authored texts, even when they concern women saints. The "male gaze," in other words, controls the textualization of women's lives of holiness.[9] Rare is the life of holiness in which a female "voice" can actually be heard, at least until modern times.

There is a fifth indicator of how the hagiographic tradition has always been gendered. Gender is clearly inscribed into liturgical patronage and devotion to the saints. There are, for example, powerful saints who come to be invoked particularly in relation to women's bodies and reproductive functions, especially fertility and childbirth. Clearly these saints, such as Margaret of Antioch, were invoked primarily by women. In addition, there are women-specific forms of devotion, even when a male saint is the object of this devotion. Women's particular attraction to Saint Jude, the patron saint of hopeless causes, is a case in point.[10] There are, moreover, devotional objects related to the specifics of women's lives: the robe and cincture of the Virgin Mary venerated in Constantinople, the Virgin's veil, and her breast milk are examples of women-specific (secondary) relics. And Mary's birthing shirt and the swaddling clothes of baby Jesus, venerated in the Romanesque Cathedral of Treves, presumably had an immediacy of relevance for women that they did not have for men.

"Nothing So Clearly Divided the Ranks of the Saints as Gender"

With such a rich tapestry of interwoven threads, it is no wonder that the complicated intersection of gender constructions, women's lives of holiness, and lived devotion to the saints has received marked attention in the last quarter of a century. The study of hagiography came to a peculiarly fertile moment with the beginning of the 1980s. The richness of the moment was created by the confluence of diverse disciplines into a transdisciplinary interest in hagiography. The vibrancy of feminist scholarship quickly brought questions of gendered identity to the foreground in this emerging transdisciplinary scholarship. Gender, a previously undertheorized marker of the hagiographic tradition, now received striking attention, as the following quote from *Saints and Society* shows:

> [N]othing so clearly divided the ranks of the saints as gender. . . . the path
> to the holy life was markedly different for girls and for boys. This diver-

gence widened rather than narrowed as aspiring boys and girls became holy men and women.[11]

Soon, this scholarly inquiry was rendered complex and divergent, not least of all because theories of gender became refined and contested. The "linguistic turn" in intellectual knowledge production, with its focus on representation, also impacted this scholarship. The genre of hagiography, after all, with its complex relation to historicity, is fertile ground for questions of representation. Both ecclesial and secular historians have contributed much to the richness of the field, with detailed studies of particular figures, time periods, regions, and groups of saints (such as virgin martyrs or holy mothers). Feminist theologians such as Elizabeth Stuart and Elizabeth A. Johnson also have attended to the communion of saints.[12] Obviously, all these lines of inquiry provide a rich, and sometimes divergent, tapestry of materials. What might be said to stand out?

Where "Saint" and "Satin" Meet: Femininity and/as Sanctity

First and foremost, scholarship at the intersection of gender constructions and hagiography has made clear that narratives of holy lives *are* marked by gender, even if the scholarly inquiry into precisely *how* gender marks hagiography continues. There are distinct ways of theorizing this *how*, often shaped by distinct gender theories. One line of inquiry, for example, has focused on the differences between representations of male and female holy lives, arguing that male saints are much more likely to have a story of sudden conversion and renunciation of power, status, and sexuality than female saints. This line of argument is supported by studies of how historically men simply had more power to determine the shape of their own lives than women (who often controlled neither property nor their own sexuality). Differing scripts of sanctity, then, can be seen as the result of different possibilities to exercise agency. Caroline Walker Bynum has put this succinctly for medieval scripts of holy lives: "each gender renounced and distributed what it most effectively controlled: men gave up money, property, and progeny; women gave up food."[13]

Second, scholarship at the intersection of gender constructions and hagiography has shown that differing scripts of sanctity can be located also in details other than gendered asymmetries of agency. There is, for example, the importance of voluntary suffering in the stories about women saints or of eucharistic devotion in their spirituality. Living by eucharistic bread alone is a peculiarly women-identified practice.[14] Hagiographic narratives of women also show a greater interest in the interior lives of these women. Gendered identity thus marks not only the larger life narratives of the saints but also the details of their telling.

Third, scholarship at the intersection of gender constructions and hagiography has shown how underlying the gendered scripts of sanctity are broader cultural and religious constructions of femininity and masculinity. For much of Christian history, "woman" was seen as the weaker sex, and her body coded as "lack" in comparison with the male body. For the hagiographic tradition, this meant that women's lives of holiness deserved special praise, because women had to overcome a weaker, more sensual, and less rational nature than did their male counterparts. The peculiar difficulty for women to live holy lives, however, also meant that "woman" could come to stand for fallen humanity par excellence (Eve!), and that the turning of a woman into a saint stood for the astounding power of divine grace as nothing else could. The repentant prostitute and the holy woman who transcends her femininity into an honorary maleness thus are recurring themes in hagiography.[15]

Recent scholarship at the intersection of gender constructions and hagiography has pointed out a fourth characteristic. Women's bodies come to be marked in the hagiographic tradition as peculiar sites of the struggle for holiness. This is not surprising in a Christian tradition that defines the sexed body as a privileged locus of renunciation and, moreover, evidences a marked ambiguity in relation to women's bodies (as not made in the image of God,[16] or as deeply "stained"). Whether it is bleeding, illness, hair, wounds, stigmata, scars, or extraordinary bodily postures—swooning, swelling, levitating, and "seeing"—women saints simply do significantly more of these than their male counterparts. The body thus appears as a crucial site of female sanctity in ways that it is not for male saints.[17] Even where the body becomes a site of holy struggle for both male and female saints, this struggle takes different forms. Saint Francis of Assisi, for example, renounced the world by undressing in broad daylight and in public, confronting his audience with his nakedness. Saint Clare of Assisi renounced the world by having her hair shorn by Francis in the darkness of night, in a little chapel at the outskirts of the city.

Fifth, as scholarly inquiry has covered more and more historical ground, it has become obvious that representations of female sanctity shift significantly through the centuries (as does the number of canon-izations of women). These shifts can be traced in relation to changing gender constructions and cultural expectations around femininity, as well as in relation to changing ecclesial practices. Not only do different ideals of female holiness develop over time, but women saints also come to be read and reread differently throughout the centuries.[18] Contemporary examples for the ever-evolving reception history of women saints might be the feminist appropriation of Teresa of Ávila, Hildegard of Bingen, or even Thérèse de Lisieux. The richest example for the ever-evolving reception history of a holy woman surely is Mary of Magdala, who made it from a biblical witness to the resurrection to a repentant prostitute and back.

A sixth insight at the intersection of gender constructions and hagiography is the following. Constructions of sanctity obviously depend in part on what is considered "not holy" (i.e., sinful, or "stained") and on what has to be given up and left behind in the strug-gle for a holy life. Here, too, the scripts for women are not identical to those of men, since they both regularly depend on differing cultural constructions of femininity and masculinity. Suffice it here to give but one example, from an examination of conscience in preparation for the sacrament of confession in the prayerbook I used as a young woman. In this examination of conscience, men were asked to reflect on whether the good looks of their wives were overly important to them, while women were asked to think about their husband's career as a source of sinful pride. I refrain from further comment, except to say that it seemed quite obvious to me, even as a young woman, that there were many women with careers to be proud of, and at least some men with good looks.

Seventh, the difficult subject of the differences between women saints' own voices and the representation by their male interpreters has received marked attention. The studies in *Gendered Voices* suggest that women saints have a more active and assertive self-understanding of their calling than their male interpreters do. The same studies also sug-gest that male interpreters typically code saintly women as mystical and mysterious (more so than the women themselves do), and that the same men tend to employ nuptial imagery in their discussions of holy women even when the women themselves do not invoke this imagery.[19] The latter point reminds one of Pope John Paul's homily at the beatification of Mother Teresa and his insistence on "the delicacy of her spousal love" which (somehow) revealed the *"noblest qualities of her femininity."*[20]

Lastly, it is important to note that the grammar of sanctity can also be a powerful challenge to established gender identities and their cultural codes. In fact, "[s]ainthood often works by breaking with normal social values, and gendered identity may be amongst these: constructing one's gender identity differently may be a marker of holiness."[21] The hagiographic tradition knows and appreciates forms of gender bending, gender crossing, and gender slippage: from the transvestite saints to Raymond of Capua seeing the face of Catherine of Siena becoming the face of God, from male writers imaging their souls as brides of Christ to men who submit to the spiritual power of holy women. Hagiographic narratives, with all their traditionally gendered scripts, also embody their own profound challenges to the living of gendered identity.

Saints: Women of Power, or Pious Little Dolls?

When Mother Teresa appeared before the United Nations General Assembly in 1985, the Secretary General introduced her as "the most powerful woman on earth."[22] Granted, she embodied a potent cultural woman script, namely, the compassionate, maternal, comforting female presence. But she also transgressed many dominant cultural constructions of femininity; the "satin" woman script of the *New York Times* ad on October 19, 2003, is a case in point. Even where women saints seem to be nothing but quintessentially feminine, their very sanctity holds the power to subvert conventional scripts. The saint after whom Blessed Mother Teresa was named, Thérèse de Lisieux, qualifies as such a quintessentially feminine yet subversive woman. Thérèse, the Little Flower, might seem to be "just a mute pious little doll in the imaginations of a lot of sentimental old women."[23] But as Thomas Merton, who initially thought her thus, discovered to his surprise: "not only was she a saint, but a great saint, one of the greatest: tremendous!"[24] Merton's surprise at this woman's profound holiness was coupled with his acknowledgment that Thérèse did not, in fact, shed a conventional woman script on her road to sanctity. She "kept everything that was *bourgeois* about her"—and what a stereotypically feminine bourgeois description Merton's is: "her taste for utterly oversweet art, and for little candy angels and pastel saints playing with lambs so soft and fuzzy that they literally give people like me the creeps."[25] Despite all this, Thérèse de Lisieux and Thomas Merton become joined in a holy friendship that he describes thus:

The discovery of a new saint is a tremendous experience: . . . the saints are not mere inanimate objects of contemplation. They become our friends, and they share our friendship and reciprocate it and give us unmistakable tokens of their love for us by the graces that we receive through them.[26]

Saints, indeed, are much more than "mere inanimate objects of contemplation." Contrary to the dazzling "satin" woman in the *New York Times*, women saints can be befriended and, indeed, called upon. It will be interesting to see in the years to come how Blessed Mother Teresa of Calcutta responds to the women and men who call upon her as they struggle to live their own lives of holiness, beyond both "stain" and "satin."

All Souls (November 2)

Wild Strawberries on a Mother's Grave

ALL SOULS CAME EARLY THIS YEAR. It was around the summer sol-stice that I visited my mother's grave and prayed for her soul. My mother's grave is a magic place. In the summer, especially, it seems enchanted. The whole place is lush and green and overgrown. There are more roses than eyes can behold, almost too much for one grave, but we let them grow as wild as they want. It is hard to believe that we brought my mother to this place in the depth of winter. Snow covered the earth and we buried her in frozen ground.

Maybe that is why I love visiting my mother's grave in the height of summer. Life is everywhere around her dead body. It is easy to prac-tice resurrection. This summer, however, I drew near to my mother's grave with trepidation. I knew that the grave would have sunk in by now. It was that time since her death. I remembered my father's grave sinking in, some time after we had buried him, and I felt again the star-tled pain that vision had caused.

This time, I was ready to claim the pain as part of my love for this woman. I was more than willing to embrace the grief: that the body who was my first home on this earth was so clearly no more. I remem-bered how I continued to treasure my mother's physical presence even while she was living her own last way of the cross, which came in the form of senile dementia. I treasured the ability to caress her old and frail body and to make the sign of the cross on her forehead as she had done a million times as I grew up, and beyond. I would place my hand on her body, on her womb, and whisper in her (surprisingly big) ears: I call myself blessed because I am the fruit of your womb.

Now this woman who had given birth to my life was dead. She had become all soul. Her body, slowly turning into the earth in which we laid it, witnessed to the starkness of her ending. As I made my way to her grave on that beautiful summer day, the sense of loss, once again, irrupted.

The grave was as I had imagined it, visibly sunken in, yet as lush and overgrown as ever. There seemed to be no incongruence here. I knelt to tend the flowers and the ground, when something caught my attention. On the grave, a little strawberry plant had managed to grow, of the kind that littered our garden when I was a child. My mother would give us bowls and send us into the garden to pick these strawberries. The harvest was precious, since the wild strawberries were tiny and it took time to fill our bowls. With pure delight I now picked the strawberries on my mother's grave and put them into my mouth. They tasted as sweet as ever.

Only then did I realize that the little strawberry plant had grown on the very spot where I knew my mother's body to be, the part of the grave that had now so visibly sunken in. The revelation dawned on me that I had just been nurtured by the very body whose passing I was grieving. All Souls, yes; and also a mother's body that nurtures beyond the grave. I was almost certain that I could hear the Spirit, and my mother, laugh softly together. And I knew to pray that my own child would find me life-giving even when I will have died.

I spent the afternoon tending my mother's grave, removing some of the weeds and cutting those roses that had withered. But I was careful not to touch the wild strawberry plant that had grown so precisely on my mother's body. The next day, I brought my little son to my mother's grave. We ate strawberries together. I still hear the litany of my son's questions: Mama, will I have to die, too? Mama, will you have to die? Will you go to the same God that I go to? Can we do it together? Mama, when can I go back into your womb? Or maybe when I die I will go back into God's womb?

Yes, beloved. And when I die, may wild strawberries grow on my grave for you.

Our Lady of Guadalupe (December 12)

A Vision of Roses in Winter

MARY OF NAZARETH APPEARING on an Aztec holy mountain, in the middle of the greatest genocide in human history? The Mother of God, bearing the features of an indigenous woman of this continent and speaking Nahuatl? The Queen of Heaven imprinting her image on a peasant's maguey-fiber cloak? Roses in winter? A virgin's womb carrying a child? Paradoxes are written large into many Marian feasts, but into none more so than the Feast of Our Lady of Guadalupe, on December 12. Ever since this Lady made her appearance in the ancient lands of *Abya Yala*[1] five centuries ago, Mexicans in particular, and Latinos/as in general, have been devoted to *Nuestra Señora de Guadalupe*. But the celebration of Our Lady of Guadalupe, Patroness of the Americas, now also is a feast in all dioceses in the United States.

What *is* this feast celebrated throughout the hemisphere on December 12? And how does it speak to women's lives as lived on this continent? To answer these questions, one needs to go back in time—and much farther than five hundred years, as will become clear. One also needs to enter the world of paradox, and especially the meaning of roses in winter. I begin with history, or in this case truly: herstory.

The "Grandmother" of La Guadalupana: An Iberian Mary

The story of Our Lady of Guadalupe can be told in myriad ways. Behind them all is the story of an encounter (involving much violence and suffering)[2] between two different cultural contexts and distinct religious traditions. *Nuestra Señora de Guadalupe* is heir to both: she embodies the *mestizaje*, the hybridity that is a characteristic part of the encounter between *Abya Yala* and the Iberian culture brought to this continent in 1492. The hybridity embodied in *Nuestra Señora de Guadalupe* has become a symbol far beyond the confines of the Catholic Church. Her image graces not only Catholic churches and homes, but taxis, revolutionary banners, restaurants, and gang members' backs—not to mention T-shirts, jackets, key chains, and the like. Devotion to the "goddess of the Americas" runs deep and wide, from the agnostic Jew to the secular feminist, from the gay performance artist to the Latina poet.[3] Her feast day on December 12 is not only a liturgical celebration but also a cultural "event." Roses upon roses overwhelm even the largest images of Our Lady of Guadalupe on that day.

The roots of Guadalupe's powerful allure go back deep into history. One of the two "grandmothers" of the Virgin of Guadalupe is the medieval Iberian devotion to Mary, which came to *Abya Yala* in 1492 onboard a flagship named *Santa María,* no less. This devotion to the Mother of God was centuries old and ran particularly deep and wide in Spain even by late-medieval Catholic standards.[4] There were not only magnificent Spanish cathedrals dedicated to the Virgin and exquisite statues such as the smiling *Virgen Blanca* of Toledo. There were also all kinds of popular devotions, Marian poetry and plays in the vernacular, flamboyant processions with images, flowers, dances, fireworks, and bull fights in the Virgin's honor. Not surprisingly, Mary played a part in the *reconquista,* the wresting of Iberian lands out of the hands of "infidels" (Muslims and Jews). Mosques of Muslim city-states such as Córdoba and Sevilla became churches dedicated to Mary, when "reconquered." The creation of one sanctuary in particular is linked with this history of conquest, the shrine of Our Lady of Guadalupe in the mountains of Estremadura. In 1340, a church was built at Guadalupe after an unexpected victory against the Moors. The site for the new church was indicated by an apparition of Mary and a statue of the Virgin found there by a peasant. The statue, so the story goes, had been hidden by Christians fleeing the Moors. The Virgin commanded a peasant to go to the priests and tell them to build a church on the spot. Soon, Guadalupe in Estremadura became an important place of pilgrimage. When Iberian culture and faith sailed westward in 1492, devotion to the Virgin of Guadalupe was onboard ship, especially since several of the conquistadors had links to Estremadura, among them Colón, Cortés, Pizarro, and de Soto.

The Other Grandmother: Tonantzin

Just as every woman has two grandmothers, so too *La Guadalupana.* If Iberian devotion to the Estremaduran Virgin of Guadalupe was one grandmother, the other one was closer to home—even if much harder to fathom. Long before 1492, the mountain that became home to *Nuestra Señora de Guadalupe* in the Americas was a sacred space. It was dedicated to an indigenous feminine representation of the divine revered by many different names and under various forms. Most commonly, Mount Tepeyac was known as the shrine of *Tonantzin* ("Our Mother"). A recent description of her puts it well:

> *Tonantzin* . . . was a complex, multiform symbol representing in its feminine aspect the ultimate dimension of reality as understood by the ancient Mexicans. She was, at once, *Tonantzin* (Our Mother), *Toci* (Our Grandmother), *Cihuacóatl* (Woman of the Snake), Tlazoltéot (Goddess of Carnal Things), and *Coatlicue* (Woman with the Serpent Skirt). . . . Our Mother was a powerful figure.[5]

Pilgrims came to Mount Tepeyac from as far south as what is now Guatemala—that is, until the Aztec capital Tenochtitlán fell to the Spaniards in 1521. With the fall of the once powerful Aztec empire, its capital became the early center of colonial "New Spain." Franciscans soon began evangelizing the indigenous peoples, but initially, this evangelization bore little fruit. By the middle of the sixteenth century, however, so a later chronicler tells us, Christian pilgrims had begun to flock to Mount Tepeyac. They wanted to pay homage to a new feminine figure known as Our Lady of Guadalupe. Two very different grandmothers, it seems, had put their heads together on Mount Tepeyac—or was it their hearts?

A Granddaughter: Our Lady of Guadalupe at Tepeyac

The story of what happened is quickly told, if one follows the traditional way of narrating the events.[6] In 1531, the Virgin appeared to a baptized, Nahuatl-speaking native, Juan Diego, at Mount Tepeyac. She appeared four times between December 9 and 12 and requested to have a sanctuary built. A miracle of roses, growing in the midst of deep winter, authenticated her message. The Spanish bishop, who initially refused Juan Diego's request, was convinced of its truth when Juan Diego unfolded his *tilma* (a maguey-fiber cloak) to show the roses he had picked: Miraculously imprinted on the cloak was an image of the Virgin. A sanctuary was built on the site of the appearance of the Virgin. A Franciscan priest and early historian of New Spain, Toribio Motolinía, wrote a few years later that some nine million Aztecs had become Christian in response. Today, the Basilica of Guadalupe is one of the most visited shrines in the world; Our Lady of Guadalupe is

Juan Diego, by Robert Lentz

Patroness of the Americas; and Juan Diego in 2002 became the first (official) indigenous saint of this hemisphere.

Thus far her story, but what about the meaning of the symbol, especially for women's lives? What about the promise of roses in winter? How do we encounter *Nuestra Señora de Guadalupe* in the winter of our own lives?

Roses in Winter:
Encountering Our Lady of Guadalupe

He went to the top of the hill, and he saw a lady who was standing and who was calling him to come closer to her side. When he arrived in her presence, he marveled at her prefect beauty. Her clothing appeared like the sun, and it gave forth rays. And the rock and the cliffs where she was standing, upon receiving the rays like arrows of light, appeared like precious emeralds, appeared like jewels; the earth glowed with the splendors of the rainbow.[7]

> Grace-ful mother
> perfect beauty
> wrapped in this flowing mantle of indescribable color
> green-blue, emerald-like
> with golden stars
> that are supposed to repeat the precise constellation of stars
> on that December dawn when you appeared
> in 1531
> at Tepeyac
>
> Standing on the moon
> and engulfed in blazing rays of sunlight
> slender and enigmatic
> you have captured the imagination of peoples and of cultures,
> of countless women
> > who claim you as one of their own
> > > even if you did not choose one of us as your messenger
> > > Why, Mother?
> > Why did you not call on one of your most abandoned
> > daughters?

"Know and be certain in your heart, my most abandoned son, that I am the Ever-Virgin Holy Mary, Mother of the God of Great Truth, Téotl, of the One through Whom We Live, the Creator of Persons, the Owner of What Is Near and Together, of the Lord of Heaven and Earth." [7f]

You have captured me
even if I am not one of your native children
even if I am not one of your sons, but a daughter
Mother of this continent
and its peoples and cultures
       mother of its women
       who come to you
       many on their knees

"Am I not here, your mother? Are you not under my shadow and my protection? Am I not your source of life? Are you not in the hollow of my mantle where I cross my arms? Who else do you need? Let nothing trouble you or cause you sorrow." [14f]

Source of Life
Shadow and protection
Rose in winter
what woman does not know that dream
or is not drawn to your magic?
You have taken up in your embrace *Tonantzin,*
Divine presence among the Aztecs,
and all the women since then
who have come to you,
bringing you roses
even in winter

He bowed before her, heard her thought and word, which were exceedingly re-creative, very ennobling, alluring, producing love. [7]

Your presence is powerful
alluring
far beyond the confines of your church.
I have seen you grace taxis,
and revolutionary banners,
and gang members' bodies.
I have seen you on the wall of a shack
in a slum
next to a playboy centerfold
       powerful silent beauty that you are
I have seen you on the front of a priest's liturgical vestment
       gracing his male torso
with the Aztec symbol of pregnancy

He unfolded his white mantle, the mantle in whose hollow he had gathered the flowers he had cut, and at that instant the different flowers from Castile fell to the ground. In that very moment she painted herself: the precious image of the Ever-Virgin Holy Mary, Mother of the God Téotl, appeared suddenly, just as she is today and is kept in her precious home, in her hermitage of Tepeyac, which is called Guadalupe. [20]

I will admit
I have seen more exquisite images of you,
Blessed Mother:
La Virgen Blanca in the Cathedral of Toledo,
Or the *Schutzmantelmadonna* in Saint Stephen's, Vienna,
       but none more mysterious or more powerful
       than the image you imprinted
       on the *tilma* of Juan Diego.

Mother of the Americas
can you unfurl this green-blue mantle of yours
and wrap it around me?
Can you hold me in your embrace?
Can you make roses in my winter?

"Listen and hear well in your heart: that which scares and troubles you is nothing. Do not let your countenance and heart be troubled; do not fear." [14]

Roses in winter
       and God becoming human in your womb
who cannot understand
or is not drawn to your magic?

December 17 to December 23

The O-Antiphons and the Production of (Women's) Desire

BEGINNING WITH THE 17TH OF DECEMBER, the liturgical tradition marks each day until Christmas Eve with an ancient and mysterious text, one of the so-called O-Antiphons. Meanwhile, the world we inhabit—and in which the liturgical tradition has to be lived for it to be real—counts the shopping days left before Christmas. Women in particular balance the tensions of these differing yet tightly intertwined ways of marking time. It is to women's lives, then, that I turn for insight into how to live these days. I begin with the O-Antiphons themselves, going back to the terse Latin text and its literal translation, in order then to speak afresh the deepest longing of these texts. Next I turn to the lived lives of women in the days before Christmas and reflect on the cultural production of (women's) desires that surrounds us. My guiding question is whether the crisscrossing of the desire voiced in the O-Antiphons with the desires of the material world can illumine a God who comes to be born among us.

The O-Antiphons

The O-Antiphons are among the most magnificent and ancient compositions of the Roman liturgy.[1] Dating back to at least the seventh century, they are antiphons for the Magnificat, chanted at Vespers on the days before Christmas Eve.[2] They are named "O" after their introductory exclamation of longing. The number of O-Antiphons has varied over the course of the centuries, sometimes to as many as twelve, but the norm now is seven.

The O-Antiphons give voice to the deepest longing of Advent, the coming of the Redeemer. Each daily antiphon takes a different image from the Hebrew Scriptures—Wisdom, Lord of Israel, Root of Jesse, Key of David, Dawn, King of Nations, Emmanuel—to plead for the coming of Christ. Together, these antiphons move toward Christ's birth, celebrated the day after the last of them has been chanted, an event that is the answer to the pleading for the coming of the Redeemer. In English-speaking contexts, the well-known hymn "O Come, O Come, Emmanuel" has popularized these O-Antiphons far beyond the confines of ecclesial tradition.

December 17

O Sapientia, quae ex ore Altissimi prodisti, attingens a fine usque ad finem, fortiter suaviterque disponens omnia: veni ad docendum nos viam pruden-tiae.

O Wisdom, who proceeded from the mouth of the Most High, reaching from one end to the other and ordering all things powerfully and gen-tly: come to teach us the way of prudence.

> **O Holy Wisdom,**
> **how I long for you!**
> **You are the Word of Life**
> **whispered by the Divine Presence.**
> **With fierce tenderness**
> **you reach to touch the ends of the galaxy**
> **and the edges of the universe,**
> **inviting all creation to flourish.**
> **Come, Holy Wisdom,**
> **show us wisdom's ways.**

December 17, and eight more shopping days until Christmas. It is futile to pretend that our religious world and our commercial culture are not intimately joined (probably much more stably than most mar-riages). As Leigh Eric Schmidt has shown in his book *Consumer Rites,* religious people embraced and shaped the emerging consumer culture, their high holy days providing cultural legitimization and authoriza-tion for consumption. This is particularly true for Christmas. Christ-mas gift giving today is worth billions of dollars to the U.S. economy. Continuing "lament over the blitz and glitz of Christmas"[3] is now a Christmas tradition itself because it too has been subsumed under com-mercialization—witness the irony of the slogan "Put Christ Back into Christmas" on a variety of commodities from bumper stickers to sweatshirts.[4] At the same time, other "discordant systems of meaning" have become visible around Christmas, embodied, for example, in holiday crisis hotlines, the commercialization of Kwaanza, menorahs in public places, and holiday escapes to the Caribbean, to name but a few.[5]

No wonder then, that Christmas renders visible deep ambiguities in our culture: tensions between "asceticism and indulgence, simplicity and affluence, piety and spectacle, religion and consumerism, Christ and culture."[6] Women live out these ambiguities in particular ways. They, after all, are the ones who orchestrate and choreograph much of the domesticity of Christmas. They are responsible for much of the nurturance of relationships at Christmas, from hosting Christmas parties to writing cards to family and friends to Christmas gift giving (and the attendant labor of choosing, buying, wrapping, decorating, and often transporting or sending the gifts). Moreover, consumer research has shown that in America, women are not only the primary shoppers, but they also do the majority of holiday shopping. Women actually start shopping for the holidays earlier than men, but finish just as late. Women also bear most of the burden of other additional holiday preparations: from baking the cookies to getting the kids ready (practicing holiday songs for school concerts, decorating the Christmas tree with children, and making sure that that cooperation harms neither the ornaments nor the children, etc.). The holiday season, then, makes women "nothing if not extremely busy."[7]

Can the O-Antiphons be anything but antithetical to these activities, yet one more insistence that Christ be put back into Christmas? The O-Antiphons seek to shape our desire toward that midnight hour between the 24th and the 25th of December when, two millennia ago, God was born in human form. One would think that the desire to witness anew God becoming human in our midst would not need to be awakened, that this desire is, indeed, the deepest longing of our whole existence. The O-Antiphons would then simply call our attention to and speak this deepest longing. As the first of the O-Antiphons puts it: How I long for you, Holy Wisdom, show us wisdom's ways! Calling on Wisdom, that ancient feminine embodiment of the divine presence, could be a particularly compelling vocative for women to begin to speak their desires and deepest longings. "Come, Holy Wisdom," is, however, by no means the only vocative we hear during this season. In fact, long before the O-Antiphons ever have a chance to shape our desires toward Holy Wisdom, desires have already been constructed for us in myriad ways that even the most astute of us find hard to acknowledge. And the well-meaning Advent sermons that challenge us to resist conspicuous consumption seem to assume that the problem arises at the moment of decision when we come face to face with a particularly seductive product: to consume or to resist consuming. In reality (and it is the reality particularly of women's lives in these days before Christmas), the problem emerges much, much earlier. The crucial moment, I would argue, is the construction of our desires, which—if effective—actually disables us from the very choice that many Advent sermons invite us to make. We are beyond choice at the point identified in these Advent sermons, since long before we are confronted with a product, our desires have already been shaped in ways that make that product seem vital to our well-being and flourishing.

Imagine, then, a product such as the following in the peculiar temple of (women's) desires that is Bed Bath & Beyond. This company, with over five hundred "superstores" nationwide, prides itself on "a constantly evolving shopping environment that has proven to be both fun and exciting for customers,"[8] especially women, one might assume from the name of the chain. At Bed Bath & Beyond, the O-Antiphon for December 17 meets its match when it comes to voicing desire. Holy Wisdom, meet the Luminous Ledges Relaxation Fountain! The latter comes with its own construction of women's desires, and the whispering of its own words of life: "Take a break from everyday stress with this relaxing fountain. You'll create a tranquil and soothing atmosphere in any room you place it. The sounds of bubbling water will bring you the peace of mind you seek." It surely helps that the fountain promises "adjustable flow settings," is perfect "for home and office," and assembles in minutes. Eight days before Christmas, a "relaxation fountain" for women will not so much evoke conspicuous consumption as sheer survival.

But what to do with these promises of flourishing? Do I turn to Holy Wisdom and away from the promises of Bed Bath & Beyond? Do I make my own the "piety of protest" (Schmidt) that calls me to resist the lures of Christmas advertising? Or might I just find Holy Wisdom in the soothing tranquility of the Luminous Ledges Relaxation Fountain? There are six more O-Antiphons and seven more shopping days to ponder these questions.

December 18

O Adonai et dux domus Israel, qui Moysi in igne flammae rubi apparuisti, et ei in Sina legem dedisti: veni ad redimendum nos in bracchio extento.

O Adonai, and leader of the house of Israel, who appeared to Moses in the fire of the flaming bush and on Sinai gave him the law, come to redeem us with an outstretched arm.

> **O Holy One with the unnamable name,**
> **how I long for you!**
> **You are a warrior god,**
> **a fiery presence.**
> **You defend without end the people you claimed**
>   **as your own.**
> **Come, O powerful redeemer,**
> **open wide your arms in our defense.**

December 18, and seven more shopping days until Christmas. The O-Antiphon conjures up God's fiery presence in a burning bush. Bed Bath & Beyond advertises a Feng Shui Candle Gift Set. The candles "follow in the tradition of feng shui—a way of living harmoniously with the natural environment." The burning bush, on the other hand, seems quite destructive of the harmony of the natural environment, even if it did not actually consume the bush. From the description of the gift set, I learn that each Feng Shui candle "represents one of the elements believed to affect one's fortune according to Ancient Chinese legend." I assume that the burning bush is an "Ancient Hebrew legend" that would not help sales of anything much this Christmas season. The Feng Shui Candle Gift Set, on the other hand, comes with "instructions on finding your element and even what direction to face your candle while burning it"—all for $14.99.

Come, warrior god, fiery presence, powerful redeemer, open your arms wide to defend me. But against what? The Feng Shui Candle Gift Set cannot possibly be the enemy. What, then, is? There are five more O-Antiphons and six more shopping days to ponder these questions.

December 19

O radix Iesse, qui stas in signum populorum, super quem continebunt reges os suum, quem gentes deprecabuntur: veni ad liberandum nos, iam noli tardare.

O Root of Jesse, who stands as a sign for the people, before whom rulers will keep silent (but) to whom the people will cry out: come to free us, delay no longer.

> O God of all generations,
> divine life hidden deep within all ancestral roots,
> how I long for you!
> From the depth of barrenness
> you suddenly call forth new flowering,
> a sign of life for all.
> Human power is nothing in your presence.
> Come, life-giver,
> free us to flourish,
> come now.

December 19, and six more shopping days until Christmas. Today's O-Antiphon calls forth God's creative power—new life and promise out of the root of an ancient tree. Bed Bath & Beyond advertises a Bamboo Wall Shelf Set, "designed to simulate a lucky garden" and to give any room "instant style." The set includes "four faux bamboo stalks and a bag of polished river stones." Here is a moment where the O-Antiphon can easily triumph over the cultural production of desire for the day. There is no way "faux bamboo stalks" can be any match for the radical vision of the prophet Isaiah that is at the heart of today's O-Antiphon: "A shoot shall come out of the stump of Jesse, and a branch shall grow out of its roots. The spirit of the Lord shall rest on him, the spirit of wisdom and understanding, the spirit of counsel and might, the spirit of knowledge and the fear of the Lord. . . . On that day, the root of Jesse shall stand as a signal to the peoples; the nations shall inquire of him, and his dwelling shall be glorious" (Isa. 11:1f.,10 NRSV).

Pondering Isaiah's promise, I suddenly realize that I do have a set of two little bamboo stalks (real ones, fortunately), an unexpected gift, on an otherwise very ordinary day. I take pleasure in these stalks and their shoots. Thus, although the Bed Bath & Beyond offer of a faux Bamboo Wall Shelf Set evokes scorn when juxtaposed with the Root of Jesse, the meaning of these bamboo stalks is by no means stable. They can, after all, become a sign of a generous giving of self. I cannot so easily dismiss them.

There are four more O-Antiphons and five more shopping days to ponder the complex relationship between real and faux, O-Antiphons and the cultural productions of desire.

December 20

O clavis David, et sceptrum domus Israel; qui aperis, et nemo claudit; claudis, et nemo aperit: veni et educ vinctum de domo carceris, sedentem in tenebris et umbra mortis.

O Key of David, and scepter of the house of Israel: You open and no one closes, you close and no one opens. Come, and from the house of bondage lead forth the prisoner and those sitting in darkness and the shadow of death.

**O God of the magic keys,
how I long for you!
Yours alone is the royal gateway to freedom,
and the sovereign power to open wide its doors;
both opening and closure are in your hands.
Come and unlock our prison doors,
dissolve the shadows of death
in the light of your presence.**

December 20, and five more shopping days until Christmas. I am confronted with the specter of a Princess Pop-Up Castle Tent. This castle, however, comes with neither royal keys nor a scepter that would help me imagine the ancient symbols of power invoked in today's O-Antiphon. Instead: "The lovely combination of lilac and pink will coordinate perfectly with the matching princess bedding." The castle does feature "door and mesh windows," but primarily "for extra ventilation." There is nothing in this castle that helps me understand the O-Antiphon's powerful imagery of opening and closing doors through the royal power of the keys. Could it be the gender of the imagined castle owner that removes this Princess Pop-Up Castle Tent from the symbolic world of power and sovereignty? As a woman contemplating the ancient symbol of the power of keys in royal hands, I am dissatisfied. Stereotypical gender constructions are nothing if not part of the house of bondage we live in. But this gendered house of bondage is as real in the world of faith as it is in the world of Bed Bath & Beyond. The O-Antiphon for today, after all, images God as sovereign; but hardly anyone praying this text will conjure up the vision of a queen who wisely wields her sovereign power. Maybe this is where Bed Bath & Beyond can assist the religious imagination, so caught in its own gendered world: Do we really have to continue to link divine power with masculinity? Why not imagine the magic keys in the hands of a divine presence that is powerful yet not male? What if God were Queen of heaven?[9]

There are three more O-Antiphons and four more shopping days to ponder the tensions I live with.

December 21

O Oriens, splendor lucis aeternae et sol justitiae: veni et illumina sedentes in tenebris et umbra mortis.

O Dawn, splendor of eternal light and sun of justice, come and shine on those sitting in darkness and the shadow of death.

> **O Radiant Dawn on the day of the winter solstice,**
> **morning star in anthracite sky,**
> **how I long for you!**
> **You are the brilliant promise of light.**
> **Your justice is luminous and clear.**
> **Come and dawn on us.**

December 21, and four more shopping days until Christmas. I awaken knowing that *Oriens* beckons, the powerful O-Antiphon on the day of the winter solstice. It is the shortest day and the longest night of the year. I bundle up and step into the darkness outside to witness what the O-Antiphon invokes: in the east, the morning star is in sharp relief against the anthracite sky. Slowly, the promise of a radiant dawn emerges; I only have to be, and to see, and to witness the transformation. A few hours later, a similar dawning is repeated: the silver paten and chalice on the altar are bathed in brilliant sunlight as the young priest stretches out his hands over them. When he lifts the host high above his head, it is not hard to see a morning star in his hands, a brilliant promise of light, a radiant dawn on the day of the winter solstice. I only have to be, and to see, and to witness the transformation.

Nothing at Bed Bath & Beyond can capture my imagination today. There is only so much radiance and brilliant promise of light one needs on this longest night of the year.

Two more O-Antiphons and three more shopping days until Christmas Eve. But I have already seen the morning star in the anthracite sky.

December 22

O Rex gentium et desideratus earum, lapisque angularis, qui facis utraque unum: veni et salva hominem, quem de limo formasti.

O King of all peoples and their desire, corner stone that makes two sides one: come and save humanity that you formed from mud.

> **O Sovereign One**
> **beyond all sovereignties**
> **final fulfillment of all human desiring,**
> **how I long for you!**
> **In you alone**
> **earth and heaven become one.**
> **Come and bring heaven to earth,**
> **to that earth from which you formed humanity.**

December 22, and three more shopping days until Christmas. I am beginning to get tired of Bed Bath & Beyond. One piece does capture my attention, however, if only because its name reminds me of a theme in today's O-Antiphon. Earth Therapeutics Moisturizing Gloves and Socks promise to "help relieve dry hands and feet simply and afford- ably." The "simply" includes an overnight procedure: "*Simply* apply your favorite lotion to the affected area before bedtime and put gloves or socks on. Leave on overnight for optimal results." What *is* truly sim- ple is that one size fits all. I am unable to see what is "Earth Therapeu- tic" about all this, but I am struck with the O-Antiphon's sense that the final fulfillment of all human desiring is to weave heaven and earth into one. Maybe the Earth Therapeutics Moisturizing Gloves and Socks reflect a faint memory of the depth of this human desiring? Only one more O-Antiphon and two more shopping days left to ponder such questions.

December 23

O Emmanuel, rex et legifer noster, exspectatio gentium et salvator earum: veni ad salvandum nos, Domine Deus noster.

O Emmanuel, our king and lawgiver, the longing of nations and their redeemer: come to save us, Lord our God.

O God with us,
our sovereign desire,
our redemption,
how I long for you!
Come,
be forever
our beyond
even in the midst of life.

December 23, and the last of the seven antiphons. Our desire, our redemption will soon "materialize." The retail industry, on the other hand, reports that their hopes are *not* materializing since consumers have failed to meet the expectation of the industry.

What happens, then, when one crisscrosses the production of desire in the O-Antiphons with the productions of Bed Bath & Beyond? On the surface, they both seem to speak of desire, linked to a "beyond." But other than that, there is nothing more than an "open mesh of possibilities, gaps, overlaps, dissonances and resonances, lapses and excesses of meaning."[10] Maybe this is precisely the point, however. Against a homogenized version of Christmas, this crisscrossing reveals a profound dissonance that itself is a clue to what Christmas is about: the defining moment two thousand years ago when the separate identities of human and divine, heaven and earth, became one. Christmas, in other words, spells dissonance: the holy and the human, God and materiality, the O-Antiphons and Bed Bath & Beyond. It is time to acknowledge afresh the complexity of that dissonance—and what its dissolution might mean. At Bethlehem, God became material reality, the ultimate beyond in the midst of our life.[11] Ever since then, our faith cannot but include all material realities, its beds, baths, and minor "beyonds." But Bethlehem is not only about embracing material realities. It also sharpens our eyes to see the exclusions produced by our world. Many human beings, after all, continue to live without either "bed" or "bath." So did God. God's bed, after all, ended up being a trough. Ultimate dissonance is the heart of Christmas. If crisscrossing the O-Antiphons with Bed Bath & Beyond reveals this dissonance, it accomplishes much.

Fourth Sunday of Advent

Elizabeth: Glimpses of Grace

O N THE FOURTH SUNDAY OF ADVENT, a woman of advanced maternal age regularly takes center stage. She provides quite a contrast to the young mother and child who represent the heart of Christmas. This woman is Elizabeth, mother of John the Baptist and—according to the Gospel of Luke—a relative of Mary, the mother of Jesus. The Advent reading from Luke in which Elizabeth appears focuses not on her maternal role, however, but rather on her prophetic witness. This is what Luke writes:

> Mary set out and traveled to the hill country in haste to a town of Judah, where she entered the house of Zechariah and greeted Elizabeth. When Elizabeth heard Mary's greeting, the infant leaped in her womb, and Elizabeth, filled with the holy Spirit, cried out in a loud voice and said, "Most blessed are you among women, and blessed is the fruit of your womb. And how does this happen to me, that the mother of my Lord should come to me? For at the moment the sound of your greeting reached my ears, the infant in my womb leaped for joy. Blessed are you who believed that what was spoken to you by the Lord would be fulfilled." (Luke 1:39–45 NAB)[1]

At first sight, this gospel seems an odd choice for the Fourth Sunday of Advent, given its close proximity to the feast of Christ's birth. This story, after all, forces us back in time, nine whole months to be precise, to the very beginning of Mary's pregnancy. According to Luke, Mary had just been told by an angel that she would conceive a child. The angel had pointed out Elizabeth's pregnancy as an authentication of Mary's own: "behold, Elizabeth, your relative, has also conceived a son in her old age; and this is the sixth month for her who was called barren; for nothing will be impossible for God" (Luke 1:36f.). Not surprisingly, Mary hurried to see Elizabeth. But why this particular gospel reading when we are so close to celebrating the birth of Jesus? Why look back in time, when all we want to do is look forward?

The answer to this question, I suggest, lies with the "other" woman in this gospel story. It is Elizabeth's prophetic witness to Christ—even before his birth—that is the central motif of this reading for the Fourth Sunday of Advent. Who, then, was this woman who stands as the very first witness to Christ, the Lord?

Elizabeth: From Barrenness to Birth, and Beyond

Elizabeth appears in the New Testament only at the beginning of the Gospel of Luke, but Luke describes her in quite some detail. Elizabeth is a woman of priestly descent, that is, from the lineage of Aaron. She is married to a priest, Zechariah. Both of them are devout; they are "righteous in the eyes of God" (Luke 1:6). But Zechariah and Elizabeth are childless, "because Elizabeth was barren" (Luke 1:7). The couple is of advanced age, that is, past the years of childbearing. When God finally surprises this old, childless couple with the promise of a son, Elizabeth and Zechariah react in distinctly different ways. Zechariah doubts the angel's message that Elizabeth will bear a son and promptly loses his voice. Elizabeth, who apparently has not received an angelic message but discerns in her own body the promise of new life, simply embraces the miracle of her pregnancy and in this *finds* her voice. She breaks out in praise: "So has the Lord done for me at a time when he has seen fit to take away my disgrace before others" (Luke 1:25). As a barren woman who conceives, Elizabeth stands in a line of notable women in the Hebrew Scriptures who faced the same "disgrace," among them Sarah, Rachel, and Hanna, the mother of Samuel. While Elizabeth's pregnancy includes her in the lineage of Hebrew foremothers to whom God granted children, her trust in the miracle of new life within her contrasts sharply with Zechariah's distrust. Continuing that contrast, Elizabeth—rather than Zechariah—is the one who names her newborn son; she defiantly rejects the suggestion that the child should bear his father's name: "No. He will be called John" (Luke 1:60). The still speechless Zechariah writes on a tablet "John is his name," supporting Elizabeth's voice—and in doing so regains his own (Luke 1:63f.). Elizabeth's clear "no" is one of the most beautiful words of women in the entire Bible: Between her "yes" to God for the new life within her and this "no" when naming this life in defiance of patrilineal tradition, Elizabeth has much to say to women today.

Not surprisingly, though, it was not that defiant "no" to patrilineal tradition for which Elizabeth's story was prized in the Christian tradition. Later accounts of her life concentrate on her as the mother of

John the Baptist. The second-century *Protevangelium of James* has Elizabeth fleeing to the hill country with her baby boy during the Bethlehem massacre, and she is said to have died in the desert during the holy
family's flight to Egypt. The medieval stories surrounding Elizabeth
concentrate on her relationship and encounter with Mary, and this, of
course, is also the focus of the reading from Luke for the Fourth Sunday of Advent. Some Latin manuscripts, in fact, put the Magnificat in
the mouth of Elizabeth rather than Mary. And in a beautiful and imaginative retelling of the encounter between these two pregnant women,
a well is said to have sprung up where they met. Some stories continue
the intimacy of that encounter to the birth of John the Baptist by
insisting that Mary served as Elizabeth's midwife. Behind all of these
later developments in the story of the encounter between Elizabeth
and Mary, however, stands the text of the Gospel of Luke, and central
to that story is Elizabeth not only as a mother, but also as a prophet.

Elizabeth: A Pregnant Prophet

The angel had told Mary that Elizabeth's pregnancy would be a sign
for her own God-sustained pregnancy, and so the two women, pregnant with God's future, meet. This encounter has been told and retold,
sung and painted throughout Christian history; it surely is one of the
most moving stories of our faith. But the depth of this story is not
exhausted by the emotional appeal of two pregnant women embracing
and supporting each other, beautiful as that is. In the encounter
between Elizabeth and Mary something quite astonishing happens.
Long before the angels sing Jesus' birth, and shepherds come to gaze
curiously, and wise men bring gifts, Elizabeth is the one who witnesses
to the presence of God that is Mary's unborn child. She discerns the
very beginning of Emmanuel, God-with-us, and she responds like the
prophets of old: "Elizabeth, filled with the holy Spirit, cried out in a
loud voice" (Luke 1:41ff.). Quite appropriately, Elizabeth's prophetic
greeting, "Blessed are you among women, and blessed is the fruit of
your womb," has become one of the most quoted biblical texts ever.
This greeting, after all, continues to be repeated in every single Hail
Mary ever prayed, making Elizabeth in all likelihood the most quoted
woman in the history of our faith.

There is something else that is startling about Elizabeth, the pregnant prophet. With Elizabeth's witness, Luke puts the first confession
of Christ the Lord in a woman's mouth. Such a confession is extra-

ordinary for two reasons. First, women were not considered reliable witnesses under Jewish law, yet Luke entrusts the crucial first witness to Christ to Elizabeth. Second, this confession of faith regards someone barely conceived, namely, Jesus, in Mary's womb in the earliest stages of her pregnancy.

I keep an ultrasound picture that was taken of my own son in the first few weeks of my own pregnancy. Pondering the story of Elizabeth's witness to the unborn Jesus, I took the photo and measured the tiny white blur that was my son. He measured barely one-third of an inch. Going back to the story of Elizabeth's prophetic witness, I realized that Elizabeth would not have seen a very pregnant Mary, although many later images of the encounter depict two women with bellies full of life. But Luke himself makes quite clear that Elizabeth saw with eyes of *faith*. Her insight was prophetic, she "was filled with the holy Spirit," as were the prophets of old. Elizabeth herself insists that she received some help from her own unborn child who "leaped for joy" at the sound of Mary's voice. There is nothing intrinsically miraculous about such a "leaping" of an unborn in the womb. It was, after all, the sixth month of Elizabeth's pregnancy and like most mothers, she would have felt her child moving within her quite vigorously by that time. The miracle of this pregnant prophet's insight lies elsewhere. Elizabeth witnessed to what could only be discerned with eyes of faith.

Elizabeth: A Pregnant Prophet as Midwife

It is precisely Elizabeth's prophetic insight into the presence of God where there was only the tiniest physical evidence that makes her so important. Elizabeth discerned God's presence, even when this presence was hidden in the womb, perhaps only one-third of an inch in length. Granted, Elizabeth had practice. She had discerned in her own womb the graciousness of God and God's gift of new life. But in the encounter with Mary, all she could rely on were the eyes of faith. There was as yet nothing much to see. It is precisely at this point—this seeing with the eyes of faith where there is nothing much to see—that Elizabeth becomes so important for us and for our faith. We are, after all, no Mary, no Joseph, no shepherds, and certainly no angels. We are no wise men (even if there are some very wise women among us). We cannot see in person the Christ Child. Like Elizabeth, we can only discern with eyes of faith what are tiny glimpses of God's presence in our lives: an unborn child, the gift of new life, moments of true encounter and wondrous friendship, the joy of proclaiming good news, light in the darkness, a piece of bread and a sip of wine, the hope of God's coming into our world in all its profound midnight hours. This discerning of God's presence in the tiny things, in mere glimpses of the coming of the Lord, is what Elizabeth can teach us so well. She can be midwife, "woman-with," to our faith, to our ability to catch glimpses of grace.

On the Fourth Sunday of Advent, and in such close proximity to Christmas, may we say with Elizabeth: blessed is every glimpse of clarity amid all the ambiguity that surrounds Christmas—its hectic activity, its overabundance, and our own inescapable melancholy at the elusiveness of the promise of peace. Blessed is even the smallest glimpse of the coming of God. And blessed is this pregnant prophet, Elizabeth, who is woman-with-us, as we struggle to glimpse Emmanuel: God-with-us.

Christmas

"And Became Hu/man"

EVERY TIME I RECITE THE CREED, but never more urgently than at Christmas, I confess that God became "human." The two letters *h* and *u* usually bring me slightly out of sync with the rhythm of the congregation, which continues to confess simply that God became "man." Such a confession is not an option for me. I cannot bear to render the succinct beauty of the Creed's *et homo factus est* with the English "and became man." The Latin *homo*—as distinct from the Latin term for a male (*vir*)— means human, after all. The same is true for the original Greek in which the Nicene Creed was crafted. The root of the term *enanthrōpēsanta,* "and became human," is the Greek word *anthrōpos,* "human being." Any translation of *enanthrōpēsanta* should capture this truth at the heart of our confession of faith: The Word took human form in the incarnation, rather than maleness only. The maleness of the Incarnate Word seems to be of no interest to the Nicene Creed. Maybe this strikes me as so obvious because in my mother tongue, rendering the Creed appropriately never was a problem in the first place. German, my first language, knows two quite different terms—*Mann,* meaning "male," and *Mensch,* meaning "human being." The translation of the Creed into the vernacular of my childhood was unequivocal: und *ist Mensch geworden.* God became *human.* The English language, unfortunately, used the same term, "man," to mean both the "male" and "human." Because of this linguistic particularity, our confession of faith in English has been rendered ambiguous. Especially on Christmas Day, the confession of the deepest meaning of what happened at Bethlehem deserves more clarity than the words "and became man" are able to yield.

There is no need to deny, of course, that in Jesus of Nazareth, God became human *and* a male, or, more precisely, God became human in the gendered particularity of maleness. Why, then, do I insist on confessing that God became "human" when all around me people opt for the shorter confession of God becoming "man"? Why might it be important to distinguish the two, after all?

The Incarnation: Of Redemption and of Chromosomal Particularity

The first reason for distinguishing between God becoming human and God becoming male is a theological one. The words of the Creed were carefully crafted, and we do well to attend to the Creed's choice of words, if only out of reverence for and faithfulness to the inspiring meticulousness of our tradition. But it is not simply a matter of faithfulness to the original words of the Creed. These words also safeguard a profound truth of our faith. In insisting that God became human, the Creed stresses that what is life-giving for humanity in the incarnation is that God assumed the human, not the male, condition. God redeemed humanity by becoming one of us. The chromosomal particularity of the incarnation is a contingent reality, as was Jesus' height, or the color of his eyes, or the size of his feet.

A second reason for distinguishing between God becoming human and God becoming male is the fact that the gendered particularity of the incarnation is much less clear-cut today than it ever was. Many of us by now accept the fact that "maleness" and "femaleness" largely are socially constructed categories. What, then, does it mean to emphasize the "maleness" of the redeemer? Even if we went with something as seemingly basic as chromosomal identity, biological research tells us that humans exist in more than two chromosomal patterns. There are not only the male XY and the female XX patterns, but there are also XXX, XXY, XYY, XO, and occasional XXXX forms. In fact, almost six million human beings today live with chromosomal patterns other than the two dominant male and female ones.[1] What exactly do we claim, then, when we confess that God became "male"? I am afraid the answer to that question often involves an argument about external genitalia. The much emphasized "natural resemblance,"[2] for example, that supposedly needs to exist between Christ and a priest is never linked to Jesus' height, or the color of his eyes, or the size of his feet. Neither does it seem to have anything to do with beards, or with Jesus being circumcised. What is left as the crux for "natural resemblance," then, is what (mercifully?) is least visible in priestly functions.

The wording of our confession of faith, on the other hand, is very clear: God became human; external genitalia simply are not the point. The particularities of Jesus' earthly life were a necessary part of the incarnation, but they are not what redeem. Karl Rahner puts this well: "Why do we have to accept the mediator [between God and humankind] to be a man and not a woman? Our answer will surely be that the maleness of the mediator is ultimately irrelevant for his universal significance as Savior of us all. Maleness is simply part of the contingent particularity . . . which the eternal Word of God had to take upon itself."[3]

A third reason for insisting on the distinction between Jesus' humanity and Jesus' maleness lies in the realm of language—more precisely, current North American developments and changes in the English language. It might have been appropriate to confess that God became man when "man" was still in common usage as a generic term for humanity (although even then this terminology was risky, since it occluded the distinction between maleness and humanness). The time is gone, however, when "man" could safely be assumed to refer also to women, at least in North American English. The church, in pretending that the older generic use of "man" can still function in the liturgy, alienates people, especially women who linguistically have entered the twenty-first century. But there is yet a deeper problem. In insisting on the highly ambiguous term "man," the church occludes the truth the Creed spoke so clearly for its own time and language, namely, that the salvific importance of the incarnation lies with God assuming humanity, not maleness.

An interesting light is thrown on this whole problem by a closer look at the Christian tradition and its ways of interpreting gender as integral to the incarnation. From among the wealth of possible themes, I wish to highlight but one—female images for christological truths. These images, I suggest, hold an important corrective for those to whom the maleness of the redeemer seems to be of such utmost importance.

The Breadth of the Tradition:
Jesus as Breast Milk, and Other Impossibilities

The Holy Scriptures and the Christian tradition offer a wide variety of images for God. Among these images are several that are feminine. Jesus himself expressed his love for Jerusalem in maternal images: "Jerusalem, Jerusalem. . . . How often have I desired to gather your children together as a hen gathers her brood under her wings" (Matt. 23:37 NRSV). Along similar lines, some of the earliest Christian communities shaped their christological reflections by imaging Jesus as the prophet of Wisdom, a feminine personification of God's presence witnessed to in the Hebrew Scriptures.[4] A marked lack of concern about questions of christological gender representation surfaces again and again in the Christian tradition. This lack of concern with the narrow confines of Jesus' maleness leads to a sense of ease with feminine images for the presence of God and to the acknowledgment that women, too, stand *in persona Christi*. Here are some examples of these often overlooked elements within the Christian tradition.

In the late second century, in one of the accounts of martyrdom that came to be collected, persecuted Christians from Lugdunum in Gaul told of seeing a crucified woman as an image of their crucified Savior. The fact that it was a woman who was martyred "cruciformly" for her faith only intensified her Christlikeness, because for the witnesses, the martyrdom of the supposedly weaker sex held special power. Here is what these Christians reported:

> Blandina was hung on a post and exposed as food for the wild beasts let loose in the arena. She looked as if she was hanging in the form of a cross, and through her ardent prayers she stimulated great enthusiasm in those undergoing their ordeal, who in their agony saw with their outward eyes in the person of their sister the One who was crucified for them. . . .[5]

For the other martyrs, the cruciform Blandina rendered visible the crucified Christ, and this not in some metaphorical sense but for "their outward eyes." Blandina's cruciform body imaged Christ's body on the cross. Cruciformity thus was the locus of natural resemblance, not the genitalia or gender of the one hanging on the cross.

The metaphor of the Eucharist as mother's milk and of Christ as the nursing breasts of God takes us in the opposite direction, namely, the representation of christological truths in feminine images. In this particular case, the very celebration of the Eucharist itself encouraged a feminine-maternal image of God or was influenced by such an image. A liturgical pointer to this influence can be found in those early Christian communities that blessed and served a chalice containing milk and honey along with bread and wine to the newly baptized at Easter and Pentecost. The patristic scholar Johannes Betz, who first brought to light the importance of these early eucharistic images and practices, wrote: "The metaphor [of the Eucharist as milk and of Christ as the breasts of the Father] was attractive to Christians whose image of God encompassed maternal aspects."[6] The image of the Eucharist as nursing is not limited to early Christian communities, however. The motif is present also in the visions of the fourteenth-century anchoress Julian of Norwich, for example:

> But our true Mother Jesus . . . must needs nourish us, for the precious love of motherhood has made him our debtor. The mother can give her child to suck of her milk, but our precious Mother Jesus can feed us with himself, and does, most courteously and most tenderly, with the blessed sacrament, which is the precious food of true life.[7]

The "Jesus-our-mother" motif on which Julian meditates is among the best known feminine christological images of our tradition. But Julian is not alone. Three hundred years before Julian, Anselm of Canterbury (ca. 1033–1109) meditated:

> And you, Jesus, are you not also a mother?
> Are you not the mother who, like a hen,
> gathers her chickens under her wings?
> Truly, Lord, you are a mother; . . .
> It is by your death that they have been born,
> for if you had not been in labor,
> you could not have borne death; . . .
> So you, Lord God, are the great mother.[8]

Feminine christological motifs are much more widespread than Anselm's and Julian's writings alone suggest. Female images for Christ are found in medieval devotional literature most noticeably in three areas.[9] First, the sacrificial death of Jesus on the cross is described as a birth, that is to say, the Crucified is seen as a woman in the travail of childbirth. This image of Jesus' death as maternal labor is present, for example, in the meditations of the thirteenth-century Carthusian mystic, Marguerite d'Oingt (d. 1310). She writes:

> Are you not my mother and more than mother? . . . Oh, Sweet Lord Jesus Christ, who ever saw any mother suffer such a birth! But when the hour of the birth came you were placed on the hard bed of the cross where you could not move or turn around or stretch your limbs as someone who suffers such great pain should be able to do; . . . And surely it was no wonder that your veins were broken when you gave birth to the world all in one day.[10]

The thought of Jesus' death as a form of birthing is not that far-fetched, I would suggest. Jesus himself evoked the image of a woman in childbirth on the night before he died: "When a woman is in labor, she has pain, because her hour has come. But when her child is born, she no longer remembers the anguish . . ." (John 16:21). More poignantly, Jesus died with the psalm on his lips that images God as a midwife. Psalm 22, which begins with the haunting "My God, my God, why have you forsaken me?" sharpens the sense of betrayal by reminding God of the midwifery God practiced at the psalmist's birth:

> Yet it was you who took me from the womb;
> You kept me safe on my mother's breast.
> On you I was cast from my birth,
> And since my mother bore me you have been my God. (Ps. 22:9ff.)

Jesus' dying psalm thus links death and birth in concrete ways. Some of the medieval devotional writers emphasized that link in imaging Jesus' dying as maternal labor.

A second example of feminine images of Jesus in the devotional literature of the Middle Ages is provided by the motif of Jesus as mother. Anselm of Canterbury and Julian of Norwich are two of the best-known exponents of this motif. Almost three hundred years after Anselm wrote his moving meditation on "Christ, my mother,"[11] the anchoress and visionary Julian of Norwich (c. 1342–after 1413) meditates:

> So Jesus Christ, who opposes good to evil, is our true Mother. We have our being from him, where the foundation of motherhood begins, with all the sweet protection of love which endlessly follows. As truly as God is our Father, so truly is God our Mother.[12]

Third, Christ's self-sacrifice in the eucharistic meal is imaged as breast-feeding; that is to say, Christ is seen as a mother who feeds her children at her breast. As we have seen, the image of the Eucharist as God's mother milk is already present in the early church and among medieval writers, but it also, for example, finds an echo in the writings of the sixteenth-century lay theologian and reformer Katharina Schütz Zell. Meditating on the passion, Zell writes:

> [Christ] gives the analogy of bitter labor and says: "A woman when she bears a child has anguish and sorrow" [John 16:21] and He applies all of this to His suffering, in which He so hard and bitterly bore us, nourished us and made us alive, gave us to drink from His breast and side with water and blood, as a mother nurses her child.[13]

In a contemporary of Zell, the monastic reformer and mystic Teresa of Ávila , this image of breast-feeding is applied to the heights of mystical experiences:

> it seems to the soul it is left suspended in those divine arms, leaning on that sacred side and those divine breasts. It doesn't know how to do anything more than rejoice, sustained by the divine milk with which its Spouse is nourishing it. . . . An infant doesn't understand how it grows nor does it know how it gets its milk, for without its sucking or doing anything, often the milk is put into its mouth. Likewise, here, the soul is completely ignorant. . . . It doesn't know what to compare His grace to, unless to the great love a mother has for her child in nourishing and caressing it.[14]

The image of a woman on the cross also resurfaces in the Middle Ages. A Dominican friend of Lukardis of Oberweimar (ca. 1274–1309) had a vision of a crucifixion in which he saw Lukardis hanging on a cross. A voice, self-identifying as the voice of God, indicated that the woman on the cross was Lukardis, who came to be identified with the Crucified Christ because she suffered so much.[15] Lukardis of Oberweimar also was one of the women who received the stigmata and so carried signs of the crucifixion on her very body (the phenomenon to this day is rare among men).

The fluidity in gender representations to which all these examples witness also is present in other areas than that of Christology. Representations of the Virgin Mary and other holy women dressed in liturgical vestments are a case in point. Here too, typical gender stereotypes are reversed, in that women—at least in the religious imaginary—take over functions at the time reserved for men. This is the case, for example, in the visions of Saint Juliana of Cornillon, who appeared as an altar server; in a vision of Blessed Benevenuta, who saw Mary as the celebrant of the Mass; in a vision of Saint Mechthild of Magdeburg, who experienced Mary as choreographing the celebration of the Mass; and in an ecstatic vision of Blessed Ida of Leuwen, who saw herself dressed in liturgical vestments and so received the Eucharist.[16] Mary, above all, was easily coded as "priestly," since she was the one who first gave humanity Jesus' body and blood.

Many other examples of the fluidity in gender representations from within the Christian tradition could be mentioned. The examples make clear what historians and scholars in gender studies frequently stress, namely, that gender representations were surprisingly fluid at least until the dawn of modernity. That is to say, while images might use male or female representations, gender was not necessarily the central focus of the images. That which we today decode as a highly charged gender image might not have had gender as its primary focus at all. Thus, female images could be used in devotion to Christ and in christological reflection, and male images could be used in Marian piety.

Christmas as Real Presence

So much for a look at the tradition of the church, which clearly is richer in gender representations than most people suspect. Given this richness of the Catholic tradition when it comes to gender representations, it becomes ever more problematic to emphasize the *maleness* of the Redeemer in the Creed. Not only is such a confession untrue to the original language of the Creed, but it also betrays the English language as spoken in the twenty-first century. The confession of Jesus as "man," moreover, occludes the fundamental truth of the incarnation, namely, that God saves humanity by rendering Godself present in human form. Last but not least, the confession that God became "man" leaves little space for the imaginative richness and fluidity of confessions of Jesus as "our mother," as the breast-milk of the Father, and as the One in labor on the cross, birthing new life in death.

On Christmas day, as on no other day of the liturgical year, our faith's answer to life's deepest questions seems to be simply this: *et homo factus est.* When we wonder how on earth God redeems, really redeems concrete human lives, the answer of Christmas is clear. God redeems through rendering Godself present in the midst of concrete human lives. There is nothing peculiarly "male" about this redemption, just as there is nothing spectacular or glamorous about it. There is just presence, real presence. Whatever we know of redemption is either in that kind of real presence, or it simply is not real.

Christmastime

Mothering Redemption

"Going My Way" during the Octave of Christmas

O N ONE OF THE EVENINGS between Christmas and the New Year, when life had slowed down just a bit, I watched an old movie. *Going My Way*, a 1944 Paramount movie with Bing Crosby, had won seven Academy Awards including Best Picture, Best Actor, and Best Supporting Actor. Although sixty years have passed since *Going My Way* was first released, the movie continues to be powerfully present in contemporary culture. *Going My Way* was invoked, for example, by Maureen Dowd in the *New York Times* during the clergy sexual abuse crisis. Dowd described the church as "arrested in its psychosexual development" and wondered whether the "last happy, hetero, celibate parish was run by Barry Fitzgerald and Bing Crosby. (Or was it?)"[1] Kenneth L. Woodward even titled his reflections on the clergy sexual abuse crisis in *Newsweek* with "Bing Crosby had it right."[2] *The Complete Idiot's Guide to Understanding Catholicism* highlights Fr. Bing as a "magical version of priestliness."[3] Catholic writer Mary Gordon ponders the power of the film (and its sequel, *The Bells of St. Mary's*) which shaped the Catholic culture of her childhood.[4] Perhaps most startling among all contemporary references to the film, its theme song "Going My Way" is a subtext in Hans Küng's memoirs, *My Struggle for Freedom*. Küng first saw the film when it was shown to seminarians at the Gregorian in Rome in the 1950s.[5]

What might account for the continuing allure of the film and its almost iconic cultural power? The story in and of itself seems simple enough. Its central character is young Father O'Malley (Bing Crosby), who is sent to Saint Dominic's Parish to help the elderly Father Fitzgibbon. Father Fitzgibbon had built Saint Dominic's forty-five years earlier and ministered in the parish for almost half a century. But he was growing old now, the parish was debt-ridden, and the young people were being lost to gang life. At the end of the film, however,

Father Bing has organized the gang into a nationally renowned boys' choir, the parish is able to rebuild even after a devastating fire, and the old priest has found new hope.

The Maternal and the Redemptive

There is nothing particularly startling or mysterious about the movie's story, if told in this way. It is simply one of innumerable Hollywood productions working toward its own version of a "happy ending." As I watched this movie between Christmas and the New Year, however, something else appeared, beyond the simple story. Maybe it was because I saw *Going My Way* during the days defined by the liturgical calendar as "the Octave of Christmas." This octave, that is, eight-day celebration, ends with the Solemnity of Mary, Mother of God, on January 1. The maternal, thus, is written into the very fabric of these days. The maternal, interestingly, also is written deeply into the fabric of *Going My Way,* and it is this subtext that might just account for the movie's cultural staying power. However that may be, this subtext certainly does shed light on something written deep into Christmas itself. There is a link, in what is celebrated at Christmas, between mothering, on the one hand, and redemption, on the other hand, or—to stay more closely with the film—between priestly ministry and mothering.

A caveat is necessary before exploring this link further. Obviously, watching *Going My Way* in the twenty-first century, one cannot but cringe at the film's running commentary on the position of women in the church. For the clerical culture of the time, women's appearance was all too predictable. Women in *Going My Way* function within the range of a narrow repertoire. They are mothers of priests, ugly matrons, priests' housekeepers, young independent flirtatious lost girls (who "convert" to marriage), and, last but not least, the ones a priest has to leave behind for the sake of his vocation. Despite this stereotyping of women's roles, the image of priestly ministry as a form of mothering is unmistakable in the movie. To begin with, Father Bing's only overtly religious act in *Going My Way* is his lighting two candles in front of a statue of Mary with child. More centrally, there is the startling scene of Father Bing himself assuming a maternal role in relation to the old priest. When Father Fitzgibbon returns home after having "run away" from his parish, Father Bing brings the old priest to bed and sings him to sleep with a childhood lullaby. The scene is watched over by a picture of Father Fitzgibbon's real mother (who continues to provide comfort for her son by sending a bottle of whiskey every year). The very end of the film sees this old mother (re-)appear, gently embracing her son: The old priest can entrust himself to real mothering, once again. The presence of this real mother also signals the end of Father Bing's ministry of "mothering" at Saint Dominic's. When the real mother appears and, without a word, takes her son, old Father Fitzgibbon, in her arms, Father Bing's task is complete. He leaves. The End.

There is a lot of tenderness (in the 1940s still coded as "feminine") in the ways the priests relate to each other in this movie. The local bishop and Father Bing slowly ease the old priest into facing the demise of his ministry. The old priest gently falls in line with the bishop in the conversation with him. Father Bing sings to sleep Father Fitzgibbon with a lullaby. The two young priests "help" the old priest along on the golf course. The transformation at Saint Dominic's is thus accompanied throughout by images and practices of mothering. And when a real mother finally appears, the film can come to its "heartwarming" end (as the description on the back of the video has it). Strikingly, given this deeply maternal coding of priestly ministry, Father Bing himself appears "mother-less." He hints at having lost his mother when he was very young. There certainly is no one who mothers *him* in the film. With all his practices of mothering, the young priest himself is firmly in power, not vulnerable or in need of nurture. He mothers, but is not mothered himself. Even with this caveat, the overlaying of priestly ministry with maternal images in *Going My Way* remains telling. As Christmas makes so very clear, the maternal and that which redeems are, indeed, linked in the Christian tradition.

How Does God Redeem—in 1944?

But what did all this powerful invoking of the maternal mean in 1944? One can only assume that it suggested a way of speaking meaning amidst much ambiguity. With the Second World War still not over, this was a Christmas when people did not see clear-cut signs of victory-over-evil that everyone wished for (the cultural imagery of the "white" Christmas). Christmas was celebrated in gray that year, amidst all the profound ambiguities of war. How on earth does God redeem, then and now? In one sense, *Going My Way* with its fusion of images of mothering and of redemption offers one possible, powerful retelling of the Christmas story itself. Christmas, after all, is the story of God entrusting God's own life to mothering, in all its human ambiguity. And both the birth at Bethlehem and the "signs" promised to the shepherds by the angel announcing redemption ("a savior has been born for you") are nothing if not ambiguous: "this will be a sign for you: you will find an infant wrapped in swaddling clothes and lying in a manger." The signs of redemption at Bethlehem are most basic: a young woman becoming a mother, a newborn in all his powerlessness and dependence (wrapped in swaddling clothes), and marked as having been birthed "out-of-order" (lying in an animal troth).

God's Presence, Real in Basic Ambiguity

Going My Way is telling in its own rendition of this motif of God being present amidst the most basic and ambiguous of human realities. There is, of course, an ecclesial message in the film. One might say, in short, that here is a Vatican II priest in the Catholicism of 1944. Here is a priest whose ministry is lived not only amidst but through the very material realities that are the lives of ordinary people. Instead of Father Bing celebrating the Eucharist, reading his breviary, hearing confessions, saying the rosary, and administering what was then called last rites, we witness a priest whose tools of the trade are a baseball cap, golf clubs, fishing rods, and a piano. He engages the real lives of people, not with pious platitudes or sour moralizing, but with practical ways of being present and changing things for the better. Not surprisingly, Father Bing is styled as "progressive" by his bishop (watching the movie in the twenty-first century, Father Bing looks more like an outdated poster child for the 1960s version of priestly ministry).

Interestingly, the precise calling of Father Bing to priestly ministry is left unclear. His actions in the parish are depicted as priestly, even if not so under more traditional configurations of Catholic priesthood. But he initially evades questions about his priestly identity (i.e., the repeated "How did you become a priest?"). Later in the film, it becomes clear that Father Bing had made a choice between music (and a woman singer) and the priesthood. "Going My Way," Father Bing's theme song, suggests that the "my way" is not an individualistic Sinatra-like affirmation—as in "I Did It My Way"—but rather the embrace, with all its ambiguity, of a life lived for others. That is precisely how the old priest summarizes Father Bing's ministry at Saint Dominic's just before the ultimate cultural symbol of "for others," namely, a mother, makes her appearance. Father Bing himself had sent for the mother of the old priest. She enters the church to the tune of the Irish lullaby now hummed by the former-gang-turned-choir.

For the Christmas of 1944, this movie with its fusion of images of mothering and of redemption might have been a convincing translation of the story of Bethlehem. God redeems by rendering Godself present amidst the basics of human lives: a newborn in swaddling clothes, a priest with a baseball cap and golf clubs, the maternal face of self-giving, the grayness of war. Certainly, in our own time, we have to translate yet again the meaning of Christmas, and there are a myriad ways of doing so. But the link between mothering and redemption is a subtext within the Christmas story that should not be lost in translation. God knows, part of the power of Christmas is precisely this link.

New Year's Eve
Of Mass and of Mending

I saw Orion in the sapphire sky
this New Year's Eve,
   and fireworks on earth
I had champagne,
   and eucharistic wine
I made up a bedtime story for my son
about a firefly
who came to Mass on New Year's Eve
and found it the perfect place to be:
all the lights and the glitter
the firefly decided to stay and celebrate
Earlier at the New Year's Eve Mass
I had been lector and altar server all in one
   since none of the young altar servers had showed up

I suddenly remembered
the old parish priest at St. Elizabeth
   who never allowed a girl to serve at the altar
   when I grew up
   I had to wait until my mid-forties
to help with the eucharistic dishes
   and then only because some youngsters had better things to do

I glimpse God in fragments
   this New Year's Eve Mass
   standing behind the altar
I was reconciled
with the memory of my childhood
the magic of the Mass is not on this side of the altar, either
may the old parish priest from St. Elizabeth rest in peace

I glimpse God in fragments
  the Hispanic man
  who came after Mass
  with candles in a K-Mart bag
  asking me to bless them
  why did I send him to the priest?

I glimpse God in fragments
Yesterday, I mended
  carefully and tenderly
  the fragments of an old Christmas ornament
that had belonged to my mother

and I caught a glimpse of God
  carefully and tenderly
mending all of creation

May I be a part of Her mending
in this coming New Year
and for ever more

A Day of Prayer for Peace in the World
W/riting Interfaith Prayers

INTERFAITH PRAYERS are a liturgical genre for which the Christian tradition does not hold too many blueprints.[1] As with women's presiding in the liturgy, in interfaith prayers, too, the way is made by walking. One example of how these different paths into new terrain intertwine is embodied in the correspondence that follows below. The focus of the correspondence is the creation of a local interfaith prayer service for peace, to coincide with the 2002 Assisi World Day of Prayer for Peace presided over by Pope John Paul II.

Dear Fr. David:

Thank you for the invitation to be the speaker at the upcoming Interfaith Prayers for Peace. This invitation is a stark challenge. It is also one I have decided to accept.

Here are some quick thoughts on the draft for the worship service, which you sent. First, as with the Muslim–Catholic Prayer Service we held at our church after September 11, this service, too, is heavy on the verbal side. I find this odd, given that words are a particular problem in interfaith worship. Which language do we use for our prayers, how do we name God, what can we actually say together? In light of these problems, why not let representatives from the different faith communities *do* something together? Symbols speak louder than words. Each representative could, for example, light a candle and speak his or her faith community's name. Or let each pour water in a basin as he or she names the faith community they represent. The symbolism of the latter is especially powerful, since the water that is poured ends up being one in the larger basin.

A second thought about the worship service. The draft envisions organ music only. How sad. Is that the best we can do? Why not invite the African American children's choir that sang at our church some months ago? They reconfigured the whole space in one song. I know

142

that music in worship will be an issue with some faith communities, but "interfaith" should not mean that we hide our particularities as best we can. Rather, we open our treasures for each other. In light of that, would it be so impossible to try and sing something together?

Teresa

∽

Dear Teresa:

Your ideas are wonderful. Lighting a candle and speaking a community's name will get everyone involved right from the start. I also like the water ritual. And you are right, we should have some congregational singing, otherwise people become observers.

David

∽

Dear Fr. David:

I assume that for the water ritual you will avoid any reference to our water basin being a baptistery! After a tradition of forced baptisms of Jews and Muslims by Christians, I would try to hide as much as possible that this is a baptismal font. I am racking my brain on other possibilities for a large water basin. . . .

Teresa

P.S. I have some doubts about naming this service a "Peace Summit." It sounds unnecessarily grandiose. Why not simply Interfaith Prayers for Peace?

∽

Dear Fr. David:

I read over the new draft for the worship service and have several suggestions concerning the liturgical "choreography." First, I would not tell the representatives of the different faith communities to bring "small carafes" for the water ritual. Symbols have to be conceived generously. Second, the carafes, once their water has been emptied into the large basin, should remain visible for all to see. Let the water carafes, as now empty vessels, point to having become part of something larger. On a side note: I always find it disturbing at the Easter Vigil when we try to give deep meaning to lighting Easter candles, only for people to blow them out three seconds after use, as if the symbol can simply "be disappeared" like that.

That reminds me of the candles for the interfaith prayers. Could we encourage people to bring the candles from the worship service to the reception afterwards? Since it will be evening and, by the time the prayers end, dark, the candles will help light the way. We can have a bowl full of sand at the reception where the candles can burn to the end.

Also, if I were presiding, I would not "explain" the water ritual. Allow people themselves to make meaning with this ritual. Such meaning making does not need to be controlled by the presider.

Lastly, is there a tension in the draft of the worship service between the "clergy" and the "representatives" of the different faith communities? Who will actually pour the water into the water basin, the clergy or representatives from the congregations? I prefer the latter; official symbol bearers of a tradition often do not handle "non-official" symbols well.

And what would it look like to open the water ritual to "others"? I am thinking of people from other cultures who might bring faith traditions inflected not primarily by differences of "denomination" or "religion," but by geopolitics and ethnicity. Think of the Ugandan Catholic, or the Peruvian Methodist, or the Korean Presbyterian, who will all be coming to this Prayer Service. Where will they find themselves when the different faith communities are named?

One last thought about the active participation of all those present. We could have pieces of paper at the door, and let people write their own prayers for peace as they gather and wait. Then, sometime during the service, all these papers can be collected, brought forward, and, later on, carried to the reception. Maybe some of them can be read there.

Teresa

Dear Fr. David:

I think I need to be in our sanctuary and choreograph this worship service through in that space itself. Can you let me in? As regards the individual prayers for peace to be written by people before or during the worship service: People who want to do this, simply will. I do not think we need to waste a lot of energy motivating them. We could collect the "peace prayers" (and images, if people would rather draw) together with the collection. Alternatively, if it becomes clear that many people are writing, we could gather the texts during the Litany and lift them up at the end as a gathering and concluding prayer gesture. Just dreaming along. . . .

Teresa

୬୨

Dear Teresa:

Your ideas are wonderful. I feel that my liturgical education is taking a Quantum leap.

I am presently looking for a water basin. Our baptistery would be ideal, from one point of view, but having heard your objection, I think not.

At the beginning of the worship service, I envision calling out each faith community's name, e.g., the Presbyterian Community, the Muslim Community, the Jewish Community, etc. Then the representatives of these faith communities (not the clergy person alone) would come forward and pour water into the basin. People from other parts of the world would come forward when their own particular faith community is called.

David

୬୨

Dear Fr. David:

It was good to choreograph this service through in the church. The colorful Bolivian cloth will work beautifully over the baptismal font. A very minor point: if you have not sent the bulletin out yet, you may want to render "thurifer" differently for people not familiar with that terminology. And at the end, talking about the candles at the reception being put into a "container" conjures up the image of a trashcan. Is there not a more imaginative and poetic English word one could use?

Teresa

P.S. Creating these interfaith prayers with you has been nothing short of fascinating, even if a colleague of mine yesterday raised the possibility of "idolatry." I responded that every liturgy faced that danger. Many I have seen, for example, positively embrace an idolatry of masculinity. At least our Interfaith Prayers for Peace will not do that.

୧୨

Dear Fr. David:

Please remember the following:
1. You need to find the beautiful Bolivian cloth, to veil the water basin.
2. We need a sand-filled something at the reception for the candles.
3. Remember the floating candles. The others will sink.

Teresa

୧୨

Dear Teresa:

All seems to be in order.
1. I have the beautiful cloth.
2. I have the sand-filled candleholder for the reception.
3. The candles float.
"All will be well."

୧୨

Dear Teresa:

It was a wonderful service. . . . I believe that everyone present had a blessed experience. And I learned more about liturgy in one night than I have learned all these past forty years of presiding at liturgies.

David

୧୨

Dear Fr. David:

I spent this morning reading through all the peace prayers that were written during the worship service. It was a deeply moving experience. There were many prayer papers with drawings, including one of big eyes with glasses, and the hope to be able "to see differently." There was the hesitant handwriting of an elderly person and the picture drawn by a child. There was much eloquence, and several papers with only one or two words. There was a prayer in Spanish, and a quote from the Quran. There was the personal: "I would like to make peace with my brother. . . . I don't like him, but I love him." There was much that was political. Most prayers were personal and political, all in one. There was the Simon and Garfunkel song, and a quote from the walls of a concentration camp. And there were the many, many visions of a more peaceful world. I have a sense that, as we were "riting" interfaith prayers for peace, people were w/riting theirs.

May God who is ever-faithful and ever-merciful hear all our prayers.

Interfaith Prayers for Peace

A Rite

Preparation

The representatives of the different faith communities gather well before the service. They have been asked to wear their traditional religious vestments, and to bring a carafe, if possible one that is related to the worship life of their faith community. The carafes are filled with water.

As the congregation gathers in the sanctuary, each person is given a worship program, a candle, and a pen or pencil. Within the worship program, there is a piece of paper and an open invitation for people to write, draw, compose or otherwise express their own prayers for peace. A note explains that these prayers will be gathered during the worship service and read during the reception that follows the service.

In the center of the worship space is a large water bowl, on a stand. The stand is covered with a beautiful cloth that flows to the floor. Arranged in a semi-circle around the water bowl and facing the congregation, are seats for the representatives of the different faith communities.

The service begins with an entrance chant, during which the clergy from the different faith communities process into the sanctuary, carrying their full water carafes.

Entrance Chant[2]

Welcome and Call to Prayer

Ritual of Water

Each faith community's name is called. As the representative of the faith community brings the carafe to the large water bowl, other members of that faith community are invited to come forward also. The representative then pours the water into the large bowl and says:

Many rivers, one ocean of peace

An improvisation on the guitar, on the theme of the entrance chant, accompanies the ritual.

Reading: Book of Habakkuk 1:2–3a, 3:17–18

How long already, God, do I cry to you,
and you do not hear me?
I shout to you, "violence," and you do not intervene.
Why do you make me see wrong and gaze upon sorrow?
. . .
For the fig tree does not blossom,
and there is no fruit on the vines,
the produce of the olive tree fails,
and the fields yield no food . . .
Yet I will rejoice in my God,
that is: I will keep the faith.[3]

Reflections

[These reflections were offered during the actual worship service.]

Es ist schwer, für heute abend eine Sprache zu finden, die uns alle einschließt, die unsere unterschiedlichen Glaubenstraditionen und unsere unterschiedlichen Namen für den Frieden, den wir erbeten, nicht nivelliert. Es ist schwer, eine Sprache zu finden, die all unsere unterschiedlichen Sprachen hörbar bleiben läßt, ihnen aber gleichzeitig Heimat bieten kann in der Vision eines letztlich von Gott getragenen Verlangens aller Menschen guten Willens nach Frieden.

Before some of you begin to wonder whether this will be a much stranger gathering than you anticipated, let me reclaim the language most of us here speak (even if that language is not my mother tongue). Is this not what any interfaith prayer for peace has to embrace from the start? We all bring what is ours, willing to open ourselves to that which is not.

What I tried to say in my mother tongue is simply this. Tonight is a difficult night for words, whatever language we use. It is a night in which any single language quickly comes to its limits, because as a particular language, it can never capture the truth of all our languages. Tonight is a difficult night for words because we come from different faith traditions, with distinct languages of their own, and with unique ways of naming the divine presence. We come from different backgrounds, from different parts of town, and, for some of us, from different parts of the globe. To make things even more difficult, we have gathered around a word that is not only compelling and evocative in its simply beauty; it is also a deeply troubling word: "Peace" is as elusive as ever this night.

Why, then, do we gather, and why would someone dare to wrestle with words on a night such as this? I will admit that I, for one, am glad that there are other languages than words with which we can speak tonight. There is the language of water, and the language of light. There are the languages of our writing, and maybe of our art, if we chose to draw our vision for peace. There is the language of music. And there is the language that precedes them all, namely, the language of presence, the simple fact that we have gathered here tonight, as people of faith, to pray for peace.

That fact alone says something important. Wherever we do not claim, with our voices and our bodies, with water and with fire, with our music, and yes, with our words, a place for peace, that void will be filled with the absence of peace, with indifference, with bitterness, and with violence and its empty promises.

Let me take up, then, this impossible task of claiming with words a space for us by reading again the words of an ancient prophet, the prophet Habakkuk. Habakkuk lived 2,600 years ago in a city that is named for "peace," *shalom*—and arguably has known less peace than most other cities on earth, Jerusalem. We have heard read how Habakkuk begins:

> How long already, God, do I cry to you,
> and you do not hear me?
> I shout to you, "violence," and you do not intervene.
> Why do you make me see wrong and gaze upon sorrow?

This lament of the ancient prophet rings true for us today. It is as if Habakkuk has looked over our shoulder for the last four months. Or has Habakkuk been looking over our shoulder for much longer? If we look at our world truthfully, we will have to acknowledge that violence did not enter the world with the tragic events of September 11, 2001.

On September 10 of last year, thirty thousand children had died of hunger-related causes and preventable diseases. Thirty thousand more children died on September 11, and on September 12, and every day since then. No national cathedrals fill in mourning for these children. There were twenty million refugees in the world on September 11, and there are no fewer today. On September 11, close to two million people had already died of AIDS in Africa alone that year. Twenty-one people had been murdered in our city in the first nine months of 2001. Three had been executed by the state. Two more would follow before the year ended.

Our lives are woven into intricate webs of violence. Habakkuk's questions easily span twenty-six hundred years: "How long?" "Why, why do you make me see wrong?" I know that I have asked those questions for as long as I can remember. I was born into a world that could not hide its own violence. My childhood world—Germany after the Second World War—was populated with maimed bodies. So many of the men I saw had only one arm, or one leg, had lost fingers, or toes, or ears. There were buildings in ruin all around me. And there was the day our school closed because children had picked up something from the school playground—the undetonated bomb that exploded in their hands killed several of them. These children, late victims of a murderous regime and a murderous war, were among sixty million human beings who had died: six million Jews, twenty million people in the former Soviet Union, people with disabilities, the women of Ravensbrück Concentration Camp, gypsies, homosexuals. Sixty million human beings—I grew up on the heaps of that carnage.

Maybe this is why I resonate with Habakkuk. In contradistinction to the glorious vision of a fellow prophet, Habakkuk does not claim to see a vision of "swords turned into plowshares and spears into pruning hooks." Habakkuk's vision is much more subdued. It begins with a lament over violence, and it stays there for quite a while.

Praying for peace has to begin where Habakkuk begins, by facing and naming the webs of violence in which we live. Think of the obscenity of dropping both bombs and food packages, in bright yellow colors. Think of the violence of children going hungry and haunting us with their all-knowing, empty eyes. Think of the terrorism of influential CEOs ruining the lives of people who depend on their company, both in this country and around the globe.

The violence that Habakkuk saw and the violence of our world are enough to bring anyone to their knees in despair. It is precisely here that people of faith can bring a profound witness. Yes, we also are brought to our knees, as everyone else who looks with open eyes at the webs of violence in which we live. Our faith, in fact, sharpens our vision of this violence, because as people of faith we have to acknowledge this violence as a violation of the sacredness of all life, a violation of a creation that was meant for something else than carnage. But for people of faith, being on our knees is not only a posture of defeat and despair. It is also a place of prayer, of hope against hope that One is present who sustains the Universe and whose very presence means life and peace. As people of faith, we know peace not only as something we are called to "make," but also as a gift, as something that is beyond human capacity and yet can be pleaded for, prayed for. Tonight, we claim a space for that vision.

I take my clue again from Habakkuk. At the end of his little book, Habakkuk moves in a surprising direction. We might call it an embracing of a "despite," a keeping of faith over and against.

> For the fig tree does not blossom,
> and there is no fruit on the vines,
> the produce of the olive tree fails,
> and the fields yield no food . . .
> *Yet/but/nevertheless/despite:*
> I will rejoice in my God,
> that is: I will keep the faith.

This embracing of a "despite" is not without its sharp edges. By keeping this faith, I deny that the power to save and to make meaning lies elsewhere. I say: No, the nation-state will not save us; neither will military might. No, peace is not made with bombs, and it cannot be sustained with coercion. No, I will not use language that degrades another human being, that depicts him as a rat or as an animal to be smoked out, no matter how much evil this person has done. I will not degrade that vestige of humanity we share, because in degrading that vestige, I degrade myself.

How is such a "despite" possible? What nurtures such a vision? How can it be more than a grandiose "visualizing of world peace," a dreamy, utterly unrealistic pacifier? Here is how. We obviously cannot make violence go away by magic, nor will it be overcome by pious platitudes. Peace is hard labor—something akin to the hard labor of mothering. It is a daily practice of nurturing a fragile life, not a grandiose idea or an abstraction. It is utterly specific, unromantic, and exasperatingly concrete. It is hard labor, indeed.

In comparing peacemaking to mothering, I am drawing on a book by the philosopher Sara Ruddick, *Maternal Thinking*.[4] Ruddick claims that distinctive practices are called forth by the needs and demands of children, and she argues that the skills we learn in mothering are also the skills needed for peacemaking. Ruddick is quick to point out that "mothering" is not only done by mothers, or done only by women, for that matter. Anyone who nurtured life in all its fragility is engaged in maternal practices, the priest and the imam, the minister and the rabbi, preachers, teachers, and nurses. Another caveat is important. Mothering is not a natural quality. There are plenty of mothers with violent responses to their children, who do not at all mother in ways that parallel peacemaking.

That said, Ruddick highlights three practices of mothering that do parallel those of peacemaking. These practices are the resolute commitment to protect a vulnerable being; an inventive nurturing of growth; and a steadfast apprenticing in living. Mothering is the struggle to embody these practices amidst the multitude of temptations and failures that also are a part of mothering. You can probably see how Ruddick conceives of mothering as analogous to the practice of peace. As no human child can survive without people around him or her who engage in mothering, so peace cannot survive without people who practice the "mothering" of peace. For Ruddick, the peacemaker has to be as active, inventive, and angry as an ordinary, harassed, coping mother. As one of these ordinary, harassed, coping mothers, I understand. There is nothing automatic about mothering, or about peacemaking. Both have to be embraced again and again, reinvented in their ever-changing specific commitments.

Maybe this is what tonight is about: a moment of reinventing and recommitting to mothering peace. There is nothing glamorous about this, only great specificity, namely, to stand in the way of violence wherever it occurs. Whether it is on the battlefields or in the bedrooms, in the boardrooms, in our streets, or (maybe most importantly) in our own hearts.

I want to challenge you to give life to this moment tonight, to recommit to a peaceful way of being in our world. Choose something now! The great gift of a gathering of people of faith is this: Between us we should be able to cover the basics. Choose one area in your life tonight where peace, a fragile and vulnerable being indeed, needs to be nurtured and mothered. That one area may be your own heart; it may be your neighborhood, or a relationship, or your work place, or your faith community. Commit yourself to it. Write it down if you want to; draw it if you can; name it in the silence of your heart if nothing else.

There may be those who recommit to a peaceful mothering of their difficult children, and others who recommit to their work with groups such as People of Faith Against the Death Penalty, or the Religious Coalition for a Non-violent Durham. There may be those who commit to praying aloud in their worship services for another faith tradition, and those who commit to gathering to pray again like this for peace. There will be those who commit to protest and to defy the culture of violence that surrounds us. And there will be those who need to commit to confronting, with deadly seriousness, the violence within themselves, the angry fantasies present in all our lives.

Between us, we as people of faith claim space for a small circle of peace that breaks the cycles of violence. What happens here tonight will not make Headline News tomorrow—but, then, what of the patient, exhausting, and exhilarating work of mothering ever does?

Litany for Peace

A sung response (by J. Michael Joncas, "God ever-faithful")[5] follows each petition of this litany:

God ev-er faith-ful,   God ev-er mer-ci-ful,   God of your peo-ple,   hear our prayer.

that spears may be turned into pruning forks and swords into plowshares

God ever-faithful, God ever-merciful, God of your people, hear our prayer

that one nation may not wage war against another

God ever-faithful, God ever-merciful, God of your people, hear our prayer

that the one spirit animating the earth, our mother, may animate us to recognize our oneness in the human family

God ever-faithful, God ever-merciful, God of your people, hear our prayer

for forgiveness of our sins against one another

God ever-faithful, God ever-merciful, God of your people, hear our prayer

for the healing of the nations
God ever-faithful, God ever-merciful, God of your people, hear our prayer

for deeper oneness while respecting diversity
God ever-faithful, God ever-merciful, God of your people, hear our prayer

for an end to racism, ethnic violence, sexism, and homophobia
God ever-faithful, God ever-merciful, God of your people, hear our prayer

for a sharing of this world's goods, that terrorism may find no fertile soil
God ever-faithful, God ever-merciful, God of your people, hear our prayer

that all life might be respected
God ever-faithful, God ever-merciful, God of your people, hear our prayer

for the rising up of peacemakers
God ever-faithful, God ever-merciful, God of your people, hear our prayer

Ritual of Light

As the names of the faith communities gathered are called once again, teens from the different communities come forward. They are each given a candle, as they offer a sentence or two in response to this question: "What are your hopes for peace?" When all have spoken, the teens will take their candles to the other members of the congregation and light the candles everyone had been given at the beginning of the service. The lights in the worship space will be dimmed. Everyone is then asked to come forward and place his or her own prayers for peace in a large and beautiful basket at the foot of the water bowl.

Closing Prayers

Each representative of a faith community will pray a brief prayer for peace from within his or her own tradition. There will be silence after each prayer.

Sending Forth

The congregation is invited to process out together with the representatives of the different faith communities, all carrying their lighted candles into the darkness and on to the place where the reception will be held. A candle stand is prepared there to receive the candles. The entrance chant is sung as the congregation forms its procession.

Ash Wednesday

*Facing Finitude: Between "Now"
and the "Hour of Our Death"*

"REMEMBER, YOU ARE DUST, and to dust you will return." These stark words traditionally accompany the imposition of ashes on Ash Wednesday.[1] The Lenten reminder of human mortality issues a profound challenge for us to face our own finitude. For centuries, all who came forward at the beginning of Lent to receive ashes were addressed with these words: the young and the old, those in good health and those who were dying, those who unbeknownst to anyone would die within the year, and those who had a long life ahead of them. This challenge to acknowledge our earthly limit, so pronounced at the imposition of ashes, continued throughout Lent. The ancient Lenten antiphon "In the midst of life we are encircled by death" (*media vita in morte sumus*) echoed the Ash Wednesday reminder that each human life is finite. Contemplating death, then, was seen not as a task for the last few moments of life, but rather as an ongoing, lifelong challenge—something to practice from "now" until the "hour of our death."

By contrast, the culture we inhabit labors to avoid such intimate reflection on death, especially our own.[2] As avid consumers of all things material, including life itself, we are supposed to have infinite appetites and an infinite capacity to satisfy these appetites. The burgeoning cultural interest (not least of all commercial) in the "silver" or "golden" years rarely focuses on the existential limit of these years. More surprising than the cultural evasion of dying, however, is that contemporary spiritual practices also offer us few opportunities to confront our own end. Certainly, we acknowledge the deaths of others, Jesus' above all, as we journey through Lent toward Good Friday. There are also the memories of the saints and martyrs inscribed in the liturgical calendar, and intimations of the dying and the deceased, from liturgical intercessions to Christian burials. But where do we confront our own death? Who dares to remind us that we are dust and that to dust we will return?

The knowledge of our own end is not something we can ever really

155

forget. Life is fragile. It takes something as ordinary as a drunk driver to bring on that defining moment of our life. But beyond this deep-seated, even if hushed, knowledge of the certainty of our own coming death, there is also the possibility of engaging that death deliberately, with open eyes and an open heart. This is a daunting task in our culture. Reflecting upon death can easily be seen as morbid, or as a condition needing medical attention (recurring thoughts of death, of course, are one of the symptoms of depression), or as an invitation for the thanatologically sensitive expert to advise us on how to "have a nice death."[3] In what follows, I hope to show that it is precisely the contemporary labored and fleeting experiences with finitude that are distinctly odd, not the faith-filled acknowledgment that one's life is finite. If nothing else, the avoidance of this reflection is doomed to fail in each and all of our lives. And what can be odder than ignoring such a large-scale failure?

There is an additional reason for facing finitude in a book that reflects on women's lived lives in relation to the rhythm of the liturgy. As with all other cultural formations, the engagement with mortality is gendered. Statistically, women have more time between "now" and the "hour of death" than men, since we outlive men, at least in the so-called first world (the 2000 U.S. Census reported 20.6 million women who were sixty-five or older, compared to 14.4 million men). Contemplating death, then, is something women in general will spend more time doing than men. What resources do we have for this lifelong task?

Historically, the church has been a place where people learned and practiced together "the art of dying." Even if the medieval practices that constituted this art cannot simply be reclaimed (as if nothing in the world had changed), the Christian faith still offers spiritual wisdom for anticipating death. For many centuries, preparing for death was an important part of the spiritual life.[4] It was something one learned early on, practiced, and taught to children and grandchildren. I seek to befriend this tradition of deliberately anticipating the hour of my death, and Lent is an appropriate time to revive this practice as one response to the ancient challenge embedded in Ash Wednesday: "Remember, you are dust, and to dust you will return."

Facing the Scriptures

The Scriptures are a good place to begin. They are no strangers to facing finitude, and in fact encourage us to do precisely that. The psalmist prays: "Lord, let me know my end, and what is the measure of my days; let me know how fleeting my life is" (Ps. 39:4). For the psalmist, acknowledging mortality engenders not a morbid fascination with death, but rather wisdom for the living of our days: "[T]each us to count our days that we may gain a wise heart" (Ps. 90:12). Jesus tells the parable of a man who lacked precisely such wisdom. This "rich fool" ably planned ahead for his own estate, all the while ignoring the finite state of his own life. He says to himself, "Soul, you have ample goods laid up for many years; relax, eat, drink, be merry." God's response is simple: "You fool! This very night your life is being demanded of you" (Luke 12:19ff.). In a similar vein, the writer of the Letter of James has this frank reminder for his readers:

> Come now, you who say, "Today or tomorrow we will go to such and such a town and spend a year there, doing business and making money." Yet you do not even know what tomorrow will bring. What is your life? For you are a mist that appears for a little while and then vanishes. Instead you ought to say, "If the Lord wishes, we will live and do this or that." (Jas. 4:13–15)

James's admonition gave rise to the Christian practice of literally adding a "Lord willing"—or the more erudite Latin *sub reservatione Jacobea*—after voicing plans for the future. (I wonder what it would do to our vision of a New Year, with all its plans, appointments, and tasks, if we marked our calendars or Palm Pilots with these words).

The Scriptures also include whole prayers for confronting death. Innumerable Christians have died with the words of Psalm 23 on their lips, comforted by the vision of God as a good shepherd even in the valley of the shadow of death. In Psalm 71, the psalmist envisions aging and dying as a continuation of God's caring presence since birth. A contemporary meditation, written by a "middle-aged" woman who looks back to her own birth and ahead toward her own death, renders Psalm 71 thus:

> God, you have been my vision and my hope
> since the very beginnings of my life.
> In my mother's womb, you were with me.
> You were the midwife who eased me into this world,
> You the giver of the gift of life.
> You let me flourish, bloom, and ripen.
> My praise rises towards you continually
> like whiffs of perfume from my body.

In you I trust all the days of my life
my refuge, my shelter, my home.

Now, in the middle of my life,
I look both back and to the future.
Do not forsake me as I grow old,
as my strength begins to lessen.

Those who always envied me your gifts of energy and power
will laugh at me:
You are beginning to look really old!
And they will think:
She is fair game now,
no divine power can save her from old age.

God, shield me
from those who consider me senile and useless.
Let them see your strength and power
even in my frailty and weakness.
Confound those who idolize youth
with your love for both young and old.
Confuse them with your own repeated trust in old women,
women like Sarah, Hannah, and Elizabeth,
whom you called to birth hope in old age.

Since my youth you have taught me
to discern your wisdom and presence in all
and to walk in your strength.
Do not leave me
as I turn old and gray,
as my body begins to show signs of weakness and frailty.
Let women friends be at my side
who want to age with me:
who want to become old and wise,
old and young at heart,
old and rich in lived life.

And at the very end of my life
be midwife for me once more.
Ease me out of this world
back into your own womb.
Until that precious hour
my mouth will speak of your justice and power
every day of my life.

I will glorify your faithfulness with my lute.
I will gladly sing your praise with full lungs,
God of my youth and of my old age.
To my children and my children's children
I will speak of your amazing power
which you pour out on all ages.[5]

Facing the Scriptures and their ancient wisdom about the end of life is one way of facing our own end.

Facing the Light

The wisdom of the Scriptures meets us not only in texts. We encounter this wisdom also in the biblical stories that have been taken up in the liturgy and popular devotions. A case in point is Luke 2:22–38, the story of Jesus' presentation in the temple and the encounter with Simeon and Anna. The Feast of the Presentation of the Lord celebrates these events annually on February 2. At the heart of this feast stands an encounter: God's own new life, in the form of the infant Jesus, dawns on a man and a woman of advanced age, the two prophets Simeon and Anna. God had told Simeon that he would not see death without having seen the Messiah; Anna is eighty-four years old and clearly coming to the end of her life. When they encounter the infant Jesus, both Simeon and Anna understand that their hour has come. Cradling the infant in his arms, Simeon praises God for letting him depart in peace, since the promise that had kept him alive was fulfilled. He had, indeed, seen the light (Luke 2:32).

This encounter between God's own new life and two elderly people gave rise to a particular devotional practice. On February 2, candles were (and in many places still are) blessed in memory of Simeon and Anna seeing the light. The traditional name for the feast witnesses to this custom: Candlemas. There was also a link between this celebration of Candlemas and the hours of death. The devout would keep at home some of the candles blessed on February 2 to light when someone was dying. It is interesting that in our own times, although a bewildering variety of candles is available "for all occasions," dying does not seem to be a part of this "all." Even in traditional Catholic contexts, we are hard-pressed to find mention of blessed candles for the dying.[6] Emergency telephone numbers for medical personnel, living wills, and directives for private bank accounts concern us profoundly, not religious symbols for the hour of death. But why choose between these different practices? They are in no way exclusionary. Blessing candles on Candlemas for those who will encounter their own death within the year in no way precludes having emergency telephone numbers and living wills ready.[7]

Facing the Night

Within the rhythm of liturgical time, Simeon's response to seeing the light (Luke 2:29–32) appears not only at the Feast of the Presentation of the Lord. These words also have their place in the daily rhythm of prayer, since they form the gospel canticle appointed for Night Prayer. We can see this Night Prayer, or Compline (i.e., that which completes the day), as one precious moment each day of contemplating death. Written deep into this prayer is the fusion of two horizons, namely, the coming of the night and the coming of our death.[8] As we confront the closure of the day and our own falling asleep, the horizon opens to our last falling asleep, from which there will be no awakening to this earthly life. Simeon's song, "Lord, now you let your servant go in peace," is one moment in this liturgical fusion.[9] There are others throughout Night Prayer. Some of the traditional Compline hymns expressly hold the night and the hour of our death together. A contemporary rendition of the Compline hymn "*Te lucis ante terminum*" puts it thus: "We praise you, Father, for your gift of dusk and nightfall over earth, foreshadowing the mystery of death that leads to endless day."[10] The concluding Compline prayer also fuses these two horizons: "May the all-powerful Lord grant us a restful night and a peaceful death." If nothing else, making this our prayer every night is one profound way of remembering our own mortality.

Facing the Hour

If facing the night offers a daily reminder of our existential limit, such a moment is also embedded in one of the most traditional and beloved prayers of all times. This prayer is not bound to any specific period, or date, or place, or posture, or need. Millions have prayed it and continue to pray it every day. Whenever this prayer is breathed, it brings the one who prays into direct address with her own mortality: "Holy Mary, Mother of God, pray for us sinners, now and at the hour of our death." It is by no means the "Hail Mary" alone that sounds this theme. The ancient prayer known as "Soul of Christ" also looks to the hour of death and pleads: "At the hour of my death call me. Into your presence lead me, to praise you with all your saints for ever and ever."[11] But naming and claiming the "hour of our death" proceeds from a tradition much broader than the spoken prayer. For centuries, Christians contended with their mortality in a great variety of ways. Some of these practices were harsh, born of a profound denigration of the human body and all things material. In one of Saint Teresa of Ávila's Carmelite monasteries, for example, the skull of a deceased prioress rested on the refectory table to remind the nuns of their own end.

What would it look like to make such moments of prayer more explicit? A prayer group I was a part of many years ago dedicated the last prayer "for the one among us who next will have to confront the hour of death." Initially, this prayer startled and unsettled me. Much later, however, a woman in my faith community was killed in a car accident as she drove home from Sunday Mass. I wished then that we had dared to include such an intercession in our public prayers. Our shock and struggle with this sudden death would have had a different dimension, namely, the consolation that we had prayed for this woman just minutes before she got into her car.

Engaging with death in prayer, especially as we become increasingly aware of the fragility of all life, daunts us. The knowledge that this can be done with more than words might offer solace here. Many Christians have turned to music.[12] The chorales of Johann Sebastian Bach that focus on dying and death are a striking example. The well-known passion hymn "O Sacred Head, Now Wounded" begins with a meditation on Jesus' dying agony and ends with a prayer for one's own death. The words, unfortunately, rarely appear in contemporary hymnals, but they are worth committing to memory: "My Savior, be Thou near me when death is at my door; Then let Thy presence cheer me, forsake me nevermore!"[13] I could mention many other chorales and hymns here, but they share the underlying conviction that our meditations on death might need more than words alone.

Facing Finite Others

Even if I am the only one who will experience that particular death which is mine to die, all of us confront the end. But none of us is alone with this challenge. The Christian tradition offers what we might call "finite others" as companions for this journey. Some of these companions have already been mentioned: biblical authors, the psalmist, Jesus,

Simeon and Anna, and the writers of beloved prayers and hymns. There are many more. The saints and all those who lived and died in exemplary ways are one example. Stories of their dying can still inspire, even if their deaths do not take the traditional form of martyrs' stories or edifying deathbed narratives. Think, for example, of the profoundly "obscure" death of Edith Stein, also known as Sister Theresia Benedicta a Cruce. This Jewish philosopher-turned-Carmelite nun died in the gas chambers of Auschwitz. No one knows exactly when and how. The train that brought Edith Stein to Auschwitz arrived on August 9, 1942. There is no trace of her after that, but, like countless others, she likely died with her body reduced to smoke and ash. The last eyewitnesses who saw Sr. Theresia alive, however, and scraps of paper written by her in transit to Auschwitz, reveal a woman who faced her own murder without blinking. Sustained by prayer, Sr. Theresia entered a profound solidarity-to-death with her own Jewish people. At the same time, she quietly and resolutely cared for others in the transit camps, especially the children. She washed and cleaned, combed and fed, all the while knowingly walking toward her death. Edith Stein offers us a richly textured life to ponder (she was one of the first women to receive a doctorate in philosophy), but the last days of her life inspire, even as the hour of her death is shrouded in genocidal gas and smoke.

In the communion of saints, there are many, like Edith Stein, with the gift of accompanying the dying. There are saints to aid us with a "good death," among them Birgitta of Sweden and Barbara. The latter especially is traditionally invoked against a "sudden death," that is, a death that finds the person unprepared. None of these saints will be in great demand today, especially not the ones invoked against a sudden death. Most people seem to want precisely this kind of death: quick, painless, and, if possible, while asleep, that is, without having to know the dying. Can the patron saints for the dying nevertheless proffer wisdom for today? We may actually need them more than ever, even if not so much for fear of a sudden death. In a culture where most of us will die alone, in hospitals and nursing homes, we may welcome saints who accompany us into the hour of our death when few others will. Maybe these saints can also become companions as we contemplate death throughout our life. They might enable us to (re-)conceive of our dying as something we need never do entirely alone. In the traditional prayers over a deceased person, it is precisely the "saints of God" who are asked to draw near (*subvenite, sancti Dei*), and the angels who are bidden to meet and accompany the departed to paradise.

Other companions for this open-eyed journey are those from among our own family and friends who have died. We do well to remember these dearly departed and to offer them continuing hospitality in our midst. Such hospitality can take many forms. Why not, on the anniversary of a death, place a photo of that family member on the kitchen table and light a candle? Children grasp these simple symbols instinctively. The photo and lit candle often prompt the stories we tell about the one who has died but who continues to be a part of our family. Depending on cultural context, hospitality toward the ancestors can take much more elaborate form. The Hispanic celebration of the Day of the Dead, with its home altars full of photos, memorabilia, food, flowers, and candles, is a case in point.

It is not only the familiar dead who are our companions. Indeed our closest companions may well be our living friends and relatives. As we age together, we face our mortality together. There will be those among us who carry the marks of a terminal illness. There are the elderly, who not only are close to their own death, but who have accompanied others on that road and have wisdom to share. Even our children will ask us out of the blue when we will die, and where we want to be buried. We all encounter our own death within the larger web of relationships that constitute our lives. It is well to attend to the ways this web is subject to its own finite limits.

Lastly, accepting our own body as it ages also means befriending a companion on the journey to the hour of death. Whether it is our wrinkles, our increasingly gray hair, or the changing rhythms of our (female) bodies, we do em-body our own finite state. Why not befriend more willingly this finite body? It will, after all, be (with) us at the hour of our death, even if no one else is. Befriending our body that will die raises one last question about finite friends and companions on the journey. Can our own death be befriended, too?

Facing Sister Death

An often-quoted prayer of Saint Francis of Assisi names death our "sister" for whom we praise God, together with Brother Sun, Sister Moon, Sister Water, Brother Fire, and other siblings. Francis, in this prayer, befriends death by including it in the created order, all of which points and ultimately leads to the Creator: "Praised be You, my Lord, through our Sister Bodily Death. . . . Blessed are those whom death will find in Your most holy will, for the second death shall do them no harm."[14]

Envisioning death as a "sister," however, is only one way in the Christian tradition of naming and confronting the end of life. There are other, more negative ones, from the biblical images of death as the "last enemy" (1 Cor. 15:26) or the "wages of sin" (Rom. 6:23) to the ways we mock death ("Where, O death, is your victory?" 1 Cor. 15:55). The breadth of possibilities suggests that naming death defies an easy either-or choice. Whether we experience death as a "sister" or an "enemy" (or as a sister-turned-enemy for that matter) depends not least of all on when and how we encounter death. Different moments in life will make us see death differently. Someone who has just fallen wildly in love, or birthed a child, or almost completed a book will probably think poorly of having to die. Someone who finds herself alone, having lost her beloved after a long and debilitating disease, might welcome her own death.

Wherever we are in life, confronting death is best done as part of a larger whole, namely, the living of life. It is the vision of this larger whole that gives the Christian approach its particular stamp. Our faith invites us to face our end as part of facing the ultimate source of all life: Godself.

Facing the Source of All Life

This might in fact be the most important gift the Christian tradition offers for those willing to contemplate their own death. Our faith envelops this contemplation within our encounter with the ultimate source of life. We live into our own dying most deeply by each day drawing closer to this source of all life, God. A person of faith, who every day prays the ancient commendation of the soul—"Into your hands I commit my spirit" (Ps. 31:5 NIV)—might not need to do much more in the hour of her death. Jesus himself died with these words on his lips.[15] Our faith arguably was born in that very moment, when the ultimate source of all life, God, faced down finitude in the death and resurrection of Jesus of Nazareth. Our life, including the hour of our death, is in good hands with such a God.

Facing Finitude: A Prayer

Graceful God
Weaver of the Web of Life

Mystery at the Heart of the Universe
Holy Wisdom, Vibrant Spirit

I enter
the space of my own dying,
the holy ground of facing finitude,
my own.
I stand before you with empty hands.

The world of appearances
will fade away.
The performances of authority
and the power of my own life
will lose their defining edge.
I can already sense
the web of my life being unmade.
I stand before you with empty hands.

I pray:
as I face my own dying
as I walk on this holy ground
toward the hour of my death,
become for me, yet again,
Holy Wisdom and Vibrant Spirit,
the Mystery at the heart of my own universe,
the Weaver of the Web of Life, your life within me.

Grant me the grace to hold still
and to sense your Spirit hovering
over the troubled waters of my soul.
Hold me gently in your arms,
when facing my own dying
brings emptiness and agony.
Teach me to yield to my life's unmaking
but also to discern and fight the evils that might surround it.
Sustain me as I try to live
while walking toward my own death.

And when this holy hour of my death comes,
as it so surely will,
when my life is for ever unmade

in that all-defining moment of my life,
let me knowingly yield to you,
Passionate Weaver of the Web of Life,
that you might re-weave my broken web
into the fullness of life that is your own.

Lent

Reconciling Women[1]

But when there is reason for urgency, the penitent should fulfill his own part, by being contrite and confessing to whom he can; and although this person cannot perfect the sacrament, so as to fulfill the part of the priest by giving absolution, yet this defect is supplied by the High Priest. Nevertheless confession made to a layperson, through lack of a priest, is quasi-sacramental. . . .

—Thomas Aquinas, *Summa Theologica Suppl.* 8, 2

And in the sacrament of Reconciliation, could not a lay person be seen by the Church, after prayerful reflection, as the authorised speaker of the forgiveness that comes in reality from God alone? It is not difficult to conceive circumstances in which a female minister could more appropriately than a man be the receiver of the humble confession that opens a soul to hear the glad words of the Lord's forgiveness.[2]

—Bishop Vincent Malone

IT IS A WEEKDAY IN LENT. In the evening, the Lenten Reconciliation Service will take place in the parish. The woman has looked forward to the service, even if she has decidedly mixed feelings about the all-male cast. Her life in the last few years has held enough experiences of brokenness, contradictions, and pain for her to cherish every moment of reconciliation and healing. After a first rather awkward attempt to make the sacrament of reconciliation her own again, the woman has begun to appreciate the Reconciliation Service in her parish deeply. She remembers gratefully priests who were able to speak words of wisdom for her life. She hopes that tonight will offer a similar moment of insight and reconciliation. Earlier in the day, she had taken time to think about her own life and what to name as needing to be healed that night.

In the late afternoon, the woman's youngster surprises her with a sudden high fever. Quickly it becomes clear that she cannot leave her sick child alone. As the woman sits at home, comforting her listless child, she feels an acute sense of loss. Once again, a moment of healing and wholeness for her own life seems mysteriously to escape her grasp.

Struggling to keep back the rising floodwaters of her inner sea of sadness, the woman's thoughts turn to two of her friends. These women not only live next door; they also are members of the parish. The woman knows one of her friends to be at home, recuperating after surgery, and therefore unable to attend the parish's Lenten Reconciliation Service. Her feisty partner had already made clear a while ago that she finds the all-male cast of the Reconciliation Service deeply hurtful and fatally flawed and that, Lent or not, she has no intention to subject herself to the concentrated clerical presence of this liturgy.

The woman suddenly has an idea. She grabs some pieces of paper, pens, matches, and a candle. Having settled her young son on the couch to rest, she briskly walks next door. To her surprised friends, she suggests a simple liturgy of their own: Each of them will write down on a piece of paper what needs healing and wholeness in her life. The papers will then be gathered and burnt. The feisty next door neighbor mutters that her main sin is her deep-seated antipathy to clericalism. The woman laughs, telling her friend that this cannot possibly count as a real sin. In the end, the three women light a candle and settle on the floor to write. In the process of writing, one of them remembers the importance of auricular confession from her childhood catechism. The women decide to change the flow of their confession. They not only write down but also speak openly their shortcomings to each other. After hearing her friends' confessions, one of the women says: "I hope God at least knows how to absolve through women."

The three women friends then burn their pieces of paper together and silently watch the flames reduce their confessions to ashes. At their parish church, the lines have by now begun to form in front of the priests. As the flames die down, the woman rises to embrace her friends, and takes her leave. As she returns to her own house and opens the door, her eyes fall on her child, sleeping peacefully on the couch.

An Examination of Conscience

The Bread of Life in the Land of Fast Food

Sorting Through Life

EVERY TIME I TRY to "examine my conscience"—that is, sort through my lived life—this inevitably leads me to think back. Sorting through one's life, after all, requires re-membering. Sometimes, I think back quite far.

I literally have no recollection whatsoever of my first examination of conscience and my first "confession" (as it was then called). This significant sacramental moment simply left no memories in me, either traumatic, or pleasurable. I know that I am different from many other Catholics at this point. I also have only a couple of memories of my first communion—a significant day in the lives of most Catholics, and one that imprints itself deeply on our memories. I, however, chiefly remember that the tiny, dry piece of bread I received that Sunday tasted of cardboard, disappointingly so because I had expected a mysteriously rich taste of the "bread of life." My culture of origin, after all, knew a wealth of daily, tasteful, nourishing breads. It was a surprise that the real bread of life tasted of so little. But besides this dissonance and a couple of photos of myself in a white communion dress, there are only two memories of my first communion that do stand out. The first memory is of my mother, passing on to me that day a gold cross that her mother had given her at her first communion. The second memory is the presence of my father in church with me. It was the only time I ever saw my father in church. I know that he was not there because he all of a sudden decided that the church was not that bad after all (he never did decide that). He was there simply because he loved me and wanted to be present in my life at that important moment. Gone, for me, are all the other memories: of presents, of food, of beautiful clothes, of the Mass itself, never mind the sermon. I simply have no recollection of any of these. Sorting through the memories of my first confession and Eucharist, what I do remember most clearly is the longing for the bread of life, and two symbols of real presence: my father in church with me, and my mother's gift of a gold cross.

My reminiscences touch on a question of fundamental importance, and one that lies at the heart of any examination of conscience. The question is this: What is lasting in life, what is not? What is worth keeping, what has to be left behind? What is life-giving and continues to speak of moments of love and real presence? What nurtures the experience of life being graced, what is destructive and broken in my life, death-dealing for me and for those around me?

The sacrament of reconciliation and the examination of conscience that precedes it are an invitation to reflect on and to sort lived life, to let that which will endure come to the foreground, and to leave behind—as forgiven—that which hinders life. The immediate question, of course, is how I sort through my lived life. What mechanism helps me distinguish the life-giving from the life-defeating? If I take the analogy of working with a computer, I know that there are a variety of options for sorting through my accumulated files. I can sort my files by name, by date, by type, or by size. The same applies to other areas of life. I only have to think about sorting laundry. I typically divide the piles of laundry by colors, by fabrics, by the temperature of the washing cycle, by what I need most urgently, or by a combination of all of these.

But how do I sort through my life as I approach the sacrament of reconciliation?

Christians through the centuries have used a variety of ways to help them sort through their lives. Among these ways of sorting is reflection on the Ten Commandments, or meditation on the two great commandments, or pondering the traditional catalogue of virtues. Some of us have also grown up with quite elaborate catalogues of questions, conveniently printed in our prayerbooks, to guide our sorting through our lived lives.

For now, I choose a focusing Scripture to guide my sorting through life. I want to listen anew to a gospel story and an image Jesus uses to describe the meaning of his own life. The gospel story is the feeding of the five thousand (John 6) and Jesus' self-identification as the "bread of life." Listening again to these words, I want to sort through my own life with them.

The Bread of Life

The image of Jesus as the "bread of life" appears at an important moment in the Gospel of John. Jesus has just multiplied five barley loaves and two fish and with them nourished a hungry crowd. Not surprisingly, people wonder about Jesus' power to respond to their hunger. Jesus, though, challenges them to distinguish between their daily bread and the bread of life: "Do not labor for the food which perishes, but for that food that endures to eternal life." His hearer's respond with the obvious: "Give us this bread." Jesus then identifies himself: "I am the bread of life; the one who comes to me shall not hunger, and the one who believes in me shall never thirst. . . . I am the living bread which came from heaven; if any one eats of this bread, that person will live forever." Jesus' hearers find those extraordinary claims quite difficult. Many of his disciples no longer follow him from this point onward, according to the Gospel of John. The twelve, however, remain, and Simon Peter responds to Jesus' challenge with this beautiful confession: "You have the words of eternal life; and we have believed, and have come to know, that you are the Holy One of God." So far this story from the Gospel of John. Can it help me sort through my life?

In the Land of Fast Food

The vision of a "bread of life" that satisfies my deepest hunger is beautiful and evocative. It is also far away from the reality in which I now live. In this world of mine, bread no longer simply stands for life, as it did in Jesus' time. On the contrary, where "low carb" dominates the landscape, bread actually is a problem-food, even when marketed as "low fat cholesterol free." Would Jesus speak of the "bread of life" in a culture that thinks of a "bunless burger wrapped in lettuce" or "Atkins diet approved wraps" as desirable food?

I also do not live in the world of my great-grandmothers, who would bake their families' bread with their own hands, and, before cutting a fresh loaf, make the sign of the cross over it. Neither is this my culture of origin, where bread was, indeed, "daily," never mind rich and nourishing. Nowadays, I eat my bread in the land of fast food. Eating in this land is, above all, quick and efficient. It is also highly individualized. Frozen microwaveable TV dinners are real, not a caricature. Food is industrially produced and, as often as not, highly artificial, multiply removed from the "real." Instead of bread, there is the commercially sweetened cereal, or a Danish, or—more upscale—the Raspberry Cream Cheese Croissant, focaccia, and nutrition bars. No wonder that people's relationship to food, in this land of fast food, is highly ambiguous. Children, to begin with, are taught to play with food, gluing beans or rice on cardboard and stringing cereals together as beads. Obesity has become the second leading cause of death in the United States; and it is only one of several forms of eating disorders that plague this land. At the same time, twenty million people here live at or below the poverty level, struggling to find their daily bread, and as often as not ending up with fast food.

How do I ponder the bread of life in this land? What questions emerge from the gospel that will help me sort through my own lived life in this context?

Food That Perishes

If nothing else, the Gospel of John challenges me to a clear distinction between "food that perishes" and the "bread of life." Since the invention of refrigerators, deep freezers, and preservatives, food that perishes clearly is not the daily problem that it was in Jesus' times (indeed, we nowadays pay more for a bread that has "no artificial preservatives, colors, and flavors"). But embedded in the image of food that perishes is a deeper challenge, namely, to distinguish that which truly nurtures life beyond the moment from that which does not last. Maybe for my own context, the equivalent symbol of the "food that perishes" might be the fast lane and the quick fix. Is food that perishes today a life lived hurriedly and on the surface? The bread of life, after all, might simply not be available as fast food and at a drive-through window. Maybe the bread of life can only be eaten slowly.

The questions that emerge for me are these: Do I know how to privilege that which is crucial to life? Do I say no to that which diminishes my life? Do I know how to resist the trivializing of my life and to claim that which is sacred and graced, not only in my own life, but in the world around me? Do I claim and live life as a gift of the living God, as a holy moment, graced in all its limits and brokenness? Jesus encourages me so to distinguish between "food that perishes" and "the bread of life."

Scarcity and Generosity

A second question emerges out of the gospel text. Jesus here embodies the very generosity of God, a God who always seems able to make much out of nothing much. The Gospel of John tells us that not only five thousand were fed, but also twelve baskets of food were left over. I wonder, do I live so generously? Do I live a generous gift of self? In my world, this will mean particular things. The scarcest resource in the land of fast food is no longer food but that which necessitates food being fast, namely, time. Many in this land live extremely busy lives; I happen to know because my life is one of these. Busy-ness, in fact, has become a prime marker of importance. Only the sick, the children, the dying, the unemployed, and the homeless seem to have lots of time.

The questions for me, then, are these: Do I know how to be generous with time and with attention? Do I know how to be present, really present? Can I still listen generously and ponder quietly? Or do I live a life of tight control, both of my own resources, and also of everything around me?

Bread That Satisfies Hunger

A third set of questions emerges from this gospel story. Jesus embodies concern for others: He multiplies food because people are hungry.[1] What an appropriate symbol of God-with-us. God provides food for a world that is so very hungry. My life, too, broken as it may be, is called to embody such giving. What my life offers, however, has to respond to the real needs of real lives. Jesus did not change water into wine when people needed food, nor did he multiply bread when the wine ran out. In a culture such as mine, marked by obesity and eating disorders, Jesus would probably not multiply food. My generosity, in other words, if it is an embodiment of God's own gift, has to respond to what the real needs are. I dare not give my child another toy when his deepest need is for more of my time.

Resisting

Embedded in this Gospel text also is an invitation to faith, but this faith comes with its own challenges. When Jesus says: "*I am the bread of life*," he is also saying that only a God-sustained life can quench all my hunger and all my thirst for life. Is my life open to such a faith? Am I open to the fact that meaning lies not in my own making but in God's? Or do I define my life primarily as my cultural context tells me to, namely, as a consumer, a workaholic, a productive citizen, or a person who has to be in charge? Faith in Jesus has an exclusionary force to it. I have to renounce finding ultimate meaning in anything but God. I am called to resist the temptation to find meaning in things, or "consumer goods," and yes, even in another human being, however deep and passionate my love. I will not pretend that life can be found outside of the life that is God-sustained.

Sorting and Struggling

Finally, in this gospel text, Jesus invites me to a life that carries its own confrontations, struggles, and conflicts—wherever these might be needed for life to flourish. In the Gospel of John, I encounter a Jesus who does not evade conflict, who knows how to challenge and to unmask his hearers' pretenses, who speaks a truth that is hard to hear. Am I willing to live so truth-fully? Am I able to speak truth to power, to confront, unmask, and resist the pretensions and pomposities of my world? Am I ready to challenge abuse wherever it meets me (and everyone is confronted with some versions of this, maybe even in one's own home or in that of a neighboring family)? Am I willing to challenge the abuse of power, or the abuse of the environment, or sexual abuse? Am I willing to create safe spaces for life to flourish, even if that entails struggle and conflict?

As the questions multiply, I realize that the Gospel of John is doing its work. It is helping me to sort through my lived life and to ponder what needs to be left behind for a God-sustained life to flourish. No one ever lives and embodies the Gospel in the way Jesus asked of his followers. But everyone, in confronting their own weaknesses and failings, is invited, with Simon Peter, to find words of life in response to Jesus' challenge. Maybe the words "Your sins are forgiven" are such words of life, too. Christians have the wonderful gift not to fear confronting their own shortcomings, but to sort through them, acknowledge them, and then yet embrace, once again, life itself. The gospel passage I have pondered helps me with such sorting of my lived life, in order that the living of my life can flourish.

Baking Bread in the Land of Fast Food

I suddenly know what to do after the sacrament of reconciliation. I want to take time to make bread with my own hands. I want to see the yeast rising slowly and knead the flour into rich dough. I will bake my bread and let its smell fill the kitchen. And I will make the sign of the cross over the fresh-baked loaf and slowly eat a warm slice. Even in the land of fast food, I will continue to hunger and thirst for the taste of the real bread of life.

The Feast of the Annunciation (March 25)

The Tabernacle of the Womb

T HERE ARE FEW BIBLICAL SCENES that have evoked as much artistic beauty as the moment of the Annunciation, captured in the Gospel of Luke:

> The angel said to her, "Do not be afraid, Mary, for you have found favor with God. And now, you will conceive in your womb and bear a son, and you will name him Jesus." . . . Then Mary said, "Here I am, the servant of the Lord; let it be with me according to your word." (Luke 1:30–31, 38)

Even if many of our contemporaries may know little about the Gospel of Luke, they might be able to conjure up in their minds the Annunciation as depicted by Fra Angelico or Giotto. But Fra Angelico and Giotto are only two in a long tradition of artists, poets, mystics, musicians, preachers, and theologians who have pondered the moment of the Annunciation that Luke describes. And Luke and the artists, mystics, and theologians do not represent a lonely elite when it comes to the Annunciation. Throughout the centuries, people from *all* walks of life have made meaning with this ancient feast (whose origins date back before the Council of Ephesus in 431). Popular religiosity thrived around "Lady Day." Farmers would place an image of the Annunciation in the seed grain to ensure a bountiful harvest, and those predicting the seasons and the weather also found this feast telling ("When Gabriel does the message bring, return the swallows, comes the spring").[1] The traditions around the Feast of the Annunciation are rich indeed.

This richness includes some elements that have largely been forgotten. One such element is the tabernacle Madonnas.[2] These Madonnas, which represent Mary as a eucharistic vessel, not only hold a peculiar beauty of their own but also capture a truth hidden deep within the Feast of the Annunciation. Their truth is this: the first tabernacle, the

The Annunciation [with Mary in priestly vestments!]
Gengenbach Evangeliary (ca. AD 1150)

first vessel to hold the body and blood of Christ, was not a golden receptacle, but a woman's womb.

A Site to Behold

The origins of the tabernacle Madonnas probably lie in the so-called shrine Madonnas, wooden statues of the Madonna that open up, usually on two hinges in front.[3] When opened, such statues of the Madonna transform themselves into altarpieces. Inside these Madonnas can be found either representations of the life of Christ or a representation of the Trinity. Madonnas holding the Trinity within them came to be suppressed by church authorities, who worried about the dogmatic propriety of these representations. Other shrine Madonnas, however, fared better, such as Madonnas that opened in the back to be used as reliquaries, tabernacles, and monstrances. Sometimes a piece of transparent crystal was placed in the Madonna's body to let the faithful see the host inside her womb.

Not surprisingly, shrine Madonnas began to multiply in the thirteenth century, a time that also saw a renewed theological and devotional interest in the Eucharist. Women's religiosity in particular found expression in intense eucharistic devotion.[4] The Feast of Corpus Christi, at whose origins stands the vision of Juliana of Mt. Cornillon, began to be observed in the middle of the thirteenth century. A century later, the observance of Corpus Christi had become obligatory in the Western church. The fourteenth century also saw the proliferation of monstrances, that is, vessels for showing the Blessed Sacrament (from the Latin *monstrare*, to show). Madonna monstrances reached their zenith in the seventeenth century.[5]

Madonnas that double as tabernacles and monstrances may play a minor role in the overall development of both Marian and eucharistic spirituality, but they speak a truth that the tradition has not found easy to capture in words: the body of Christ, which we receive in the Eucharist, first came to be "real presence" in the body of Mary. What the Eucharist "makes," the body and blood of Christ, was first made not by a priest but by the body of a woman—not on an altar, but in a womb. The tabernacle Madonnas give us this site to behold.

"Hosting" the Body of Christ

The realization that there are eucharistic connotations in Mary's "hosting" of the body of Christ emerged much earlier in the Christian tradition than the actual Madonnas that give artistic representation to this insight. The earliest acknowledgment of this insight appears in a text by (Pseudo-)Epiphanius of Salamis. The author has this to say: "'Priest' I call the virgin, and also altar. She has given us, as if she herself were a table, the heavenly bread, Christ, for the forgiveness of our sins."[6] In the following centuries, insistence on Mary's sacerdotal role could be found in the words of theologians as diverse as John Damascene, Bonaventure, Albert the Great, and John Gerson.[7] But there were also other theological voices painstakingly distancing Mary from priestly ministry.[8] Mary's priesthood had to be coded as different from a priesthood reserved exclusively for men. The discourse thus shifts from a narrowly sacerdotal language to a broader eucharistic one. In the thirteenth century, a growing number of spiritual writers spoke of Mary as the actual tabernacle of Christ. The poet Konrad of Würzburg (ca. 1235–87), for example, in one of the most read texts of the Middle Ages, describes Mary as the "host iron of the living bread of heaven" [oblatisen des lebenden himelbrotes] and as "God's tabernacle" [gotes tabernackel].[9]

There were also spiritual writers who continued to rejoice in the parallels between Mary and priestly ministry: Mary offers Jesus at the presentation in the temple, as the priest offers the Mass. Mary makes possible the presence of Christ in her womb with her word, as the priest makes possible the presence of Christ in the Eucharist with the words of institution. The latter theme dominates one of the visions in the Scivias of Hildegard of Bingen (1098–1179). Hildegard ponders the analogies between the mystery of the incarnation and the mystery of the Eucharist:

> for as Divinity displayed its wonders in the womb of the Virgin, it shows its secrets also in this [eucharistic] oblation. How? Because here are manifested the body and blood of the Son of God. . . . For, as the body of my Son came about in the womb of the Virgin, so now the body of My Only-Begotten arises from the sanctification of the altar. . . . As My Son miraculously received humanity in the Virgin, so now this oblation miraculously becomes his body and blood on the altar. . . . As she bore Him in her virginity to be pure and stainless, now the bread that is truly consecrated as His flesh and is pure in its integrity should be received by the faithful in purity of heart.[10]

Is it a coincidence that a woman sees the analogy between the incarnation and the Eucharist with such clarity? Hildegard, of course, not only saw but also heard. And this is what God told her about the analogy she saw: "when the priest does his office as is appointed him, invoking Me in sacred words, I am there in power, just as I was there when My Only-Begotten, without discord or stain, became incarnate."[11]

Mary: Virgin Priest

In the eighteenth and nineteenth centuries, a lively devotion to Mary as "virgin priest" emerged, and in 1907, Pope Pius X himself approved a prayer that explicitly invoked Mary as *Maria Virgo Sacerdos*.[12] The prayer was short-lived. Its papal approval was revoked twenty years later (in all likelihood because questions about the non-ordination of women to priestly ministry had surfaced).

Representations of Mary in priestly vestments also were forbidden at the beginning of the twentieth century, although these representations date back at least to the twelfth century. In the twelfth-century Evangeliary of the Benedictine monastery of Gengenbach, the illumination for the Annunciation shows Mary wearing Eucharistic vestments and a stole, her arms extended in prayer and the Spirit descending on her.[13] Mary, with the angel next to her, is clearly styled analogously to the priest at the moment of consecration. Images of Mary as the one actually giving the Eucharist to the faithful can be found in a number of missals dating back to the fifteenth century. And there are accounts of visions by medieval women, in which they see themselves or Mary (or both) assisting with, and presiding at, the Eucharist. This is the case, for example, in the visions of Elisabeth of Schönau, Juliana of Mt. Cornillon, Mechthild of Magdeburg, and Ida of Leuwen.[14]

In Utero—The "Where" of the Incarnation

It is unfortunate that the fearful distancing of women's bodies from priestly ministry has occluded the deeper truth to which these representations and, particularly, the tabernacle Madonnas point. In a sense, these Madonnas could be taken as a simple commentary on the biblical truth first announced by the angel: "you will conceive *in your womb*" (Luke 1:31). The Latin version of the Scriptures that was the Bible of the Western Church for most of its history—the *Vulgate*—is precise in its translation: "*concipies* in utero" is what the angel announces. But whether in Greek, Latin, or English, the angel's words are confirmed for Mary by Elizabeth, who experiences the truth of the Annunciation in her own womb. Elizabeth's unborn child, John the Baptist, leaps within her, leading her to speak a blessing to Mary: "blessed is the fruit of your womb . . . the child in my womb leaped for joy" (Luke 1:42–44). God's self-disclosure in Mary's womb thus found its first confirmation in the womb of Elizabeth.

It is hard to imagine what else Luke could have done to impress upon us the importance of the maternal body in God's ultimate revelation of God's self. Again, only artistic representation has outdone Luke's narrative powers. There is an early fourteenth-century visitation group from the Dominican convent of Katharinenthal in which both Mary's and Elizabeth's wombs are made of transparent crystals. The wombs of the two mothers are turned toward each other, and the two women's hands touch just below the crystal wombs.[15]

In a sense, these crystal-wombed women continue the affirmation of the Gospel of Luke. Behold (they invite us to believe), the ultimate site of revelation is female bodiliness, a woman's womb.[16] Like the tabernacle Madonnas, they challenge us to take seriously the "where" of the incarnation. What happens when we ponder the where of the incarnation, rather than the "who," or the "how," or the "what," or the "what for"? The answer to the question "where"—namely, a womb—does not seem to have inspired the same intensity of reflection as the answers to any of the other questions. It is hard not to see at work in this inattentiveness what Grace Jantzen has described as the dominant Western imagery focused on renunciation, contemptus mundi, mortality, and overcoming. The incarnation, on the other hand, is part of an imagery of bodiliness and of natality. As Jantzen puts it: "every person who has ever lived has been born, and born of a woman. Natality is a fundamental human condition. It is even more basic to our existence than the fact that we will die, since death presupposes birth."[17] In the incarnation, such natality comes to be a very part of God: "when the fullness of time had come, God sent his son, born of a woman" (Gal. 4:4). But with God assuming natality as God's own, the locus of revelation also shifts and does so in quite profound ways.

The where of God's self-disclosure, after all, does matter in the history of God with the cosmos. The burning bush, a high mountain, the whirlwind—they all speak a truth about the One who chooses to disclose God's self there rather than anywhere else. With the Annunciation, the mode of God's self-disclosure came to be natality, and its site could only be a woman's body, specifically her womb. The maternal body, in the Annunciation, becomes the ultimate site of God's revelation. In light of a Western tradition that dominantly associates woman and her body with weakness, lust, irrationality, and impurity, this is startling indeed.

For those, on the other hand, who come to this startling revelation from the Hebrew Scriptures, this new site of God's self-disclosure would actually not be so startling. In the Hebrew Scriptures and in the language in which they were written, the key word for God's compassionate mercy, *rachamim,* is rooted in the Hebrew word for womb, *rechem.* Phyllis Trible poignantly speaks of a "journey from the wombs of women to the compassion of God" in the Hebrew Scriptures.[18] She notes that this metaphor of a god of the womb "journeys from the concrete to the abstract. 'Womb' is the vehicle; 'compassion,' the tenor. . . . The womb protects and nourishes but does not possess and control. It yields its treasure in order that wholeness and well-being may happen. Truly, it is the way of compassion."[19]

At the moment of the Annunciation, this womb-compassion of God takes flesh. In many ways, the Middle Ages, with their shrine and tabernacle Madonnas, had a much more profound sense of these links between woman, bodiliness, and the body of God than most of us have today.[20]

Mary: Here Is My Body, for You

I dare to go one step further. For the incarnation to have happened, Mary must have given her *fiat.* This is not primarily a mental assent but (contra the dominant theological tradition) an embodied "yes." Mary gives up her own body for Jesus' body to find life. Mary gives up her own blood (quite literally, she gives up the cycle of her own bleeding) for Jesus to live. For medieval minds, the matter was more straightforward still. The unborn was thought to feed on the mother's blood in the womb, and breast milk was thought of as blood "twice cooked."[21] But whether one assumes a medieval or a modern understanding of how women's blood and pregnancy are related is irrelevant; the simple fact remains that both cultures know there to be a connection. Given such a connection, the theological question becomes this: In giving of her own body and blood, did Mary not pattern the deepest mystery of Jesus' life, the life she made possible with her own? Is she not the pattern he would have to follow? As she did in this defining moment of her life, so will he, many years later, in the defining moment of his life, give up his body: "this is my body, . . . for you." Long before these words formed on his lips, they had been embodied in her womb.

Thus the deepest bond between Mary and the Eucharist might not be that this woman was the first to give us the body and blood of Christ—although she certainly was that. She was more. She was the one who gave her own body so that He might live. This is what we celebrate in the Feast of the Annunciation then: the moment in which a woman said to God, "Here is my body, for you."

Holy Week

In the Presence of Women: The Passion of God

Entering Holy Week

ACH YEAR, journeying through Holy Week seems a different task. Not that the liturgies themselves ever change much; the basic elements of this core of the Christian calendar have remained constant over many centuries. What does change from year to year—sometimes dramatically so, sometimes less—is the context of our lives in which Holy Week unfolds. In any given year, what we confront as the "cross of the real" and as crucified lives takes a different form. These changes affect our grasp of the passion. Some years ago, for example, we entered Holy Week amidst disclosures of the sexual abuse of children and youth by priests. By the time Good Friday came, I could not help but envision an abused adolescent body on the cross, fusing with the crucified body of the Redeemer. Sadly, the sexual abuse of children and youth by priests in that troubled year was not the only experience of suffering to intrude into our solemn remembering of the suffering of Jesus. There was, during that Holy Week, also an escalation of violence in the Holy Land, including the news of a suicide bombing by a sixteen-year old Palestinian girl. There was a powerful earthquake in Afghanistan that left at least six hundred people dead and thousands homeless in freezing rain. And those were just three experiences of suffering that made headline news, merely scratching the surface of human pain, which does not stop when Christians enter Holy Week.

Crossing, once again, the threshold into Holy Week, I want to take the cross of the real with me intentionally this year. Remembering the Crucified God will have to fuse with attentiveness to the presence of crucified human beings in this world, whoever they are. In what follows, I will ask particularly about the real presence and the lived lives of women. There is, after all, a peculiar memory about the presence of women at the heart of the gospel. Not only was a woman there at the beginning of it all, consenting to bear a child and to give birth amid pain, blood, and lonesomeness. Women also were the ones present throughout the end, amid all the pain, blood, and lonesomeness. Is it a wonder that women were the ones to witness the dawn of the new beginning?

Palm Sunday: When and How?

In the liturgical calendar, Holy Week begins with Palm Sunday. In 2004, however, Holy Week really began on Ash Wednesday, with the visual onslaught of the film *The Passion of the Christ*. Reflections on the film were legion and predictably divergent, but no one paid much attention to the clear *gendering* of the passion in this film. On the one side, there is male betrayal, power, and cruelty or, on the receiving end, heroic suffering and compelling agony. On the other side, there is female passion, mostly in the form of women's (powerless?) compassion, presence, and tears. (Tellingly, the one site of gender ambiguity in this film is Satan.) Some of the extrabiblical scenes forcefully underline the dominant images of female compassion, be it Veronica's encounter with Jesus, or Pilate's wife giving burial linens to Mary of Nazareth. At best, Mary Magdalene's active compassion in the film means trying to find male help. It is also worth noting that the women around Jesus are conventionally attractive. The film's official Web site says of the "beautiful young" actress portraying Mary Magdalene that "Her slinky black & white TV commercial for Dolce & Gabbana stimulated pulse rates around the world." The actress portraying Pilate's wife won the Miss Teenage Italy pageant in 1987.

Is this what Holy Week teaches us about the passion of God and the presence of women, namely, that it is men who "do," and women who "are," whether beautiful, present, sensitive, tearful, powerless, or a combination of these (with God, of course, being on the male side of things)? Fortunately, the Christian tradition is much richer than such a gendered stereotype of conceiving of the passion of God and the presence of women. In order to see that richness, however, one needs to look broadly and in some unusual places. One of these is the night sky.

Monday of Holy Week: A Paschal Moon

The paschal moon this year rises on the Monday of Holy Week. This moon—proclaiming that Easter is soon to come—is the first full moon after the spring equinox. Its appearance decides the date of Easter every year. Not many Christians know that behind the ever-changing date for Easter stands a lunar calendar: Easter Sunday always is the first Sunday after the first full moon after the spring equinox. A lunar calendar thus determines the core date of the Christian year. The date for Easter, of course, is not the only rhythm determined by the moon. The ocean tides and the cycles of women's bodies, too, follow a lunar rhythm. Again, not many are aware of these connections between the liturgical cycle, the lunar cycle, and the rhythm of women's bodies, but this does not mean that the connections are not real. Neither does it mean that Christians of other times and cultures were not aware of these connections. In the early centuries especially, Christians lived in a context of a vibrant lunar religiosity and mythology. In Hebrew, Greek, and Latin (as in many other languages), the moon is gendered female and considered a symbol of fecundity.[1] Greco-Roman culture knew a number of female lunar-related deities (Selene/Luna, Artemis/Diana). Not surprisingly, several early Christian theologians, among them Origen, Ambrose, and Augustine, wrote eloquently about the deeper meaning of the lunar cycle.[2] Augustine, in fact, had to go to some length to defend Christians from the charge of astrology and magic, since the moon decided the key date in the Christian calendar.[3]

As night falls this Monday evening of Holy Week, I slip out into the clear and cold darkness, leaving behind, for a precious moment, the dishes, the laundry, and the homework. The paschal full moon protrudes out of the night sky, stunningly large. It is like a woman's full belly, ready to birth new life. I ponder the moon's promise of life after all the waning and weakening, only to wonder whether Jesus had the comfort of the full moon on the night he has betrayed. Did he look up into the night sky in his agony in the garden? Did he see the moon's silent promise that vanishing does not always have to be the last word? Did the moon keep awake with him when all others slept?

Tuesday of Holy Week: Passion Devotion (long before the film)

I spend much of the day reading about late-medieval passion devotions. The sheer ubiquity, bloodstained intensity, and devotional multiplicity of these devotions—including calculations of the number of strokes and of the drops of Jesus' blood as well as the length of his side wound—put Mel Gibson's *Passion of the Christ* in historical context. A fifteenth-century Flemish image of the Crucified, for example, has

Jesus' body oozing streams of blood from his head, arms, hands, torso, side, legs, and feet. An indulgence of eighty thousand years was the reward for gazing on this image and praying.[4] There was also, in late medieval England, a fervent devotion to the Three Nails. We have not come far with the contemporary sale of Passion Nail Pendants, Nail Zipper Pulls, and Nail Key Rings. But in the late Middle Ages, there was also a peculiar fascination with the side wound of Christ, and this wound could be seen as feminine.[5] Visually, its pointed oval flesh resembled female genitalia. Moreover, the side wound of Christ did as women do: it bled, birthed new life, offered itself as a breast at which to suckle, and, finally, invited penetration. A crucial image of mystic union, after all, was that of entering Christ's wound. Nothing in our current fascination with the passion of Christ allows for this kind of gender ambiguity or invites the destabilization of binary gender stereotypes in quite the same way. Might this be a loss? Obviously, the medieval responses to the image of the Crucified are foreign to most of us and cannot simply be resurrected. But are our own binary gender stereotypes really constructive for the journey through Holy Week, and beyond?

Wednesday of Holy Week:
Stations of the Cross, in the Real

I attend Stations of the Cross at my son's Catholic school. "And why did he use a kiss. . . . That's not what a kiss is for," the children sing to a haunting melody. Their Jesus is skinny and pale, Veronica chubby and cheerful, and the Virgin Mary clearly embarrassed. I am thankful that I do not have to witness yet another passion where all the women are beautiful and tearful and Jesus has the body of a male model. In the children's Stations of the Cross, some of the soldiers who crucify Jesus are girls, the angel at the tomb wears braces, and this particular Veronica hopefully will never be able to grace a Dolce & Gabanna ad. As I ponder anew the Way of the Cross, I give thanks for the real of our lives, which, precisely in its real-ness, points to the reality of Christ's living and dying as one of us.

Maundy Thursday: Were They There?

Were they there when he broke the bread that night? Were they there, these women who had accompanied him from Galilee to

Jerusalem? Were they there when he made his body become food, like that of a nursing mother? Most paintings of the Last Supper show a Jesus at table with twelve male disciples. But why, for heaven's sake, would the women not be present? They had been with Jesus from the beginning of his ministry (and one of them from the very beginning of his life). Besides, women and men customarily celebrated Passover together in Jesus' time. There is no indication that Jesus told his disciples to divide into two groups, male and female, with the women being left behind as the evening meal approached.

But maybe the question about the bodily presence of women at the Last Supper is based on too narrow a vision anyway. I am struck by some of the medieval texts I have been reading this week, and by their suggestion that Jesus' human body had feminine qualities, at no point more so than during the passion. Jesus' whole body, not only the side wound, did what women's bodies do: it nurtured, bled, and gave new life.[6] Jesus' body had seemed peculiarly feminine to these writers anyway by reason of the incarnation, since Jesus did not have a human father, only a mother. His human body "is from her body," as Bonaventure put it.[7] If one looks at the Last Supper through these lenses, then Jesus' body on Maundy Thursday does indeed become like that of a nursing mother offering her own body as food. "This is my body . . . for you."

There is an image of the Last Supper by Australian painter Margaret Ackland, in which Jesus shares this meal with women, men, and children.[8] Most striking in this image is the woman whom Jesus faces across the table. This woman has a child at her breast whom she nurses. She thus feeds someone with her own body as Jesus speaks of his body becoming food. The scene is even more startling when one knows that in Jesus' time, mother's milk was thought to be the woman's blood, changed by God into milk (transubstantiated, so to speak) during her pregnancy.[9] A mother who nursed therefore was understood to give her child her own blood to drink. "This is my blood . . . shed for you."

Is it surprising that in the Christian tradition, the Eucharist has been imaged as God nursing God's children with life-giving food? Even if texts and rituals using this image were never dominant in the Christian tradition, they are there. In the early centuries, some Christian communities blessed a chalice with milk and honey along with bread and wine for the newly baptized at the Easter Vigil. We have texts of ancient prayers of consecration over this milk-and-honey chalice.[10] A thousand years later, Julian of Norwich wrote of the Eucharist in a similar vein: "The mother can give her child to suck of her milk, but our precious Mother Jesus can feed us with himself, and does, most courteously and most tenderly, with the blessed sacrament, which is the precious food of true life."[11]

Yet another seven hundred years later, here I am, at a solemn Maundy Thursday liturgy. I have taken Margaret Ackland's image of Jesus at table with a nursing mother—both sharing their bodies as food—to church with me. I want to render present the ancient tradition of thinking about the gift of this night with the image of God nursing us. One of my women friends, sitting next to me, misses much of the sermon because she is fascinated with this image I brought to the liturgy.

Good Friday: The Real Presence of Women

If Maundy Thursday is about Jesus' self-giving in ways that might be named feminine, then Good Friday continues the rich interplay between the presence of women and the passion of God. To begin with, there is the biblical memory of women's peculiar presence throughout the passion, crucifixion, and burial of Jesus. The women are there through it all, pure and simple.[12] This real presence of women is not nothing. In at least three ways, this presence bears significance. First, presence is the opposite of absence; the presence of women disciples meant that Jesus did not die deserted. Second, being present to suffering is a form of suffering-with, of comPassion.[13] Such comPassion is hard labor, as anyone who ever had to be with a loved one who suffered will know. Not being able to alleviate suffering, yet remaining present to a beloved is as hard as, if not harder than, suffering oneself. Third, presence means witness; and this witness becomes a crucial part of the telling of the passion story to all future generations. The eyewitnesses are the ones who authenticate, after all. They were there and saw with their own eyes.

Yet again, maybe the real presence of women at the cross is not all there is, important as this real presence surely was. Maybe the women who were there, in the midst of that agony, also rendered present a knowledge born from within their own female bodies. The knowledge is this: that unimaginable pain searing through a body, and water breaking forth, and flesh being torn, and blood flowing profusely are not signs of death alone. They are also the signs of a woman laboring to birth new life. Will any of the women, maybe Mary, his mother, have wondered about the similarity?

The thought of Jesus' death as a form of birthing is not as far-fetched as it might seem at first. This was especially true in Jesus' time when the experiences of childbirth and of dying were clearly linked. Maternal mortality was high. A womb and a tomb were not strangers to each other. Jesus himself evoked the image of a woman in childbirth on the night before he died: "When a woman is in labor, she has pain, because her hour has come. But when her child is born, she no longer remembers the anguish . . ." (John 16:21). Indeed, Jesus' approaching death came to be described with the very same words: "When Jesus knew that his hour had come . . ." (John 13:1). More poignantly, Jesus died with the psalm on his lips that images God as a midwife. Psalm 22, which begins with the haunting "My God, my God, why have you forsaken me?," sharpens the sense of divine betrayal by reminding God of the midwifery God practiced at the psalmist's birth:

> Yet it was you who took me from the womb;
> You kept me safe on my mother's breast.
> On you I was cast from my birth,
> And since my mother bore me you have been my God.

It is precisely this contrast between "you are my God from my mother's womb" (in the translation of the ICEL Psalter) and the sense of now having been forsaken that gives this psalm its bitter depth.

For some medieval writers, it was this imagery of birthing in connection with Jesus' agony on the cross that captured their imagination. Anselm of Canterbury (ca. 1033–1109), for example, meditated: "Truly, Lord, you are a mother; . . . It is by your death that they [your children] have been born."[14] A century after Anselm, the Cistercian monk Aelred of Rievaulx wrote about the crucifix to his confrères that it will "bring before your mind his Passion for you to imitate, his outspread arms will invite you to embrace him, his naked breasts will feed you with the milk of sweetness to console you."[15] And another hundred years later, the Carthusian mystic, Marguerite d'Oingt prayed thus:

> Are you not my mother and more than mother? . . . when the hour of the birth came you were placed on the hard bed of the cross where you could not move or turn around or stretch your limbs as someone who suffers such great pain should be able to do; . . . And surely it was no wonder that your veins were broken when you gave birth to the world all in one day.[16]

Not only medieval mystics cherished the image of Jesus on the cross as maternal labor, however. The sixteenth-century Protestant lay reformer Katharina Schütz Zell put it thus:

> [Christ] gives the analogy of bitter labor and says: "A woman when she bears a child has anguish and sorrow" [John 16:21] and He applies all of this to His suffering, in which He so hard and bitterly bore us, nourished us and made us alive, gave us to drink from His breast and side with water and blood, as a mother nurses her child.[17]

As I go forward on this particular Good Friday, at the solemn Veneration of the Cross, I venerate the body of Christ and all its labored pain. I venerate and adore the body of a God who passionately labors to birth new life, amidst searing pain, breaking water, and much blood.

Only later do I learn that as I venerated the body of Christ Crucified, a woman was found unconscious in a vacant lot not far away. She had been sexually assaulted and savagely beaten. In the hospital, doctors tried for six hours to repair her broken body. *Injuries to her face prevented officers from being able to determine her identity as of Friday evening.* She remains in a coma, the damage to her brain in all likelihood permanent. The woman assaulted on Good Friday is not alone. She is the third within a month. One woman had been beaten to death, another seriously injured. *There are similarities in the cases, police said, without providing specifics.*[18]

Why? Is Jesus' agonized "Why" on the cross large enough to hold all our whys? Why does a woman have to carry this cross of the real, this savage and senseless violence? How many more crucified lives can this earth, can God bear?

Holy Saturday: Jesus' Descent into the Hell of a Woman's Life

As I wake up, the faceless woman in a coma in a hospital room enters my consciousness. Will she ever wake up? If Holy Saturday is about Jesus descending "into hell" (as the Apostles' Creed has it), what redemption is there for the hell this woman was battered into? Did Jesus descend not only into the hell of the past on Holy Saturday, but maybe also somehow, mysteriously, into all hells to come? Can I believe that the hell this woman was beaten into on Good Friday AD

2004 is one Jesus himself entered on Holy Saturday AD 33? Does Jesus know from within the hells of women's lives ever since that Saturday?

Restless, I try to bake a traditional Easter bread, in the shape of a lamb—the kind my mother used to bake every year on Easter Saturday. But the delicate biscuit dough does not cooperate with my wishful struggle for glimpses of wholeness and goodness. On the contrary, my Easter lamb ends up a baking disaster. With it, however, comes the recognition that God always easters in real lived lives,[19] not in some dream or fantasy world, nor in some eternity beyond time.

Easter Sunday and the Cross of the Real

It is an unexpectedly dreary day outside—or is it inside? I struggle with the coerciveness of the Easter liturgy and its relentless Alleluias. Is there room for those who are forced to continue to hang on the cross of the real? The woman assaulted on Good Friday remains in a coma, her body nailed to a hospital bed.

The only thing that captures my imagination during the Easter liturgy is a little azalea plant. In a sea of white, yellow, pink, and purple flowers, this little plant—in the first row, no less—simply droops. I watch the priest take notice of the little azalea (he knows something about plants) and quickly give it some water before Mass. For much of the unfolding Easter liturgy, I contemplate the plant. With a sense of relief, I see that the little azalea simply refuses to cooperate with the theme of resurrection and continues to droop. With its silent sadness, the plant whispers to me that Easter is not a command performance. Neither does it always easter in our lived lives when the liturgical calendar tells us so.

Easter Monday: Women Who Defy
the Finality of Violence

It is evening when, for some reason, I am drawn back to one of the traditional Easter scriptures about women going to the tomb at dawn.[20]

> But at daybreak on the first day of the week they took the spices they had prepared and went to the tomb. They found the stone rolled away from the tomb; but when they entered, they did not find the body of the Lord Jesus. While they were puzzling over this, behold, two men in

dazzling garments appeared to them. They were terrified and bowed their faces to the ground. They said to them, "Why do you seek the living one among the dead? He is not here, but he has been raised. Remember what he said to you while he was still in Galilee, that the Son of Man must be handed over to sinners and be crucified, and rise on the third day." And they remembered his words. Then they returned from the tomb and announced all these things to the eleven and to all the others. The women were Mary Magdalene, Joanna, and Mary the mother of James; the others who accompanied them also told this to the apostles, but their story seemed like nonsense and they did not believe them. (Luke 24:1–11 NAB)

The women came to the tomb that morning to engage in traditional rites of mourning, often a woman-identified task.[21] This task carried with it the stigma of ritual impurity, since it involved contact with a dead body. What these women faced, however, was not only a dead body and its contaminating powers, but the dead body of a loved one who had been savagely abused. And while in life one can still try to soothe and heal wounds, death finalizes the marks of violence on a body. One cannot heal the wounds of someone who has died. The women's comPassion that morning must have been strong. They were willing to confront the finality of violence on a body they loved. In the middle of their willingness, God eastered.

God shattered the finality of violence and death when the women committed themselves to let their presence, their hands, and their spices reach this dead body in a final defiant "no" to the abuse wrought on it. That Easter morning, God and the women con-spired on the body of Jesus of Nazareth. Violence will not be the final word, they say. There are caresses, even beyond death, and gentleness, and spices and perfume. There will be life because there are women's hands that know how to love, and a God who knows how to honor their passionate presence.

As dark settles on this Easter Monday, I finally can affirm again the ancient truth of the first Easter dawn, when women defied the finality of an abused human body, and God graced their defiance with the revelation of ultimate life. May God easter this year in a hospital room where a faceless woman is entombed in a coma brought on by violent abuse. May this tomb also open to becoming a womb, able to birth life where there is nothing but death.[22]

A Day in May, Mary's Month

A Gypsy Mother and the Mother of God

Sal - ve, Re - gi - na, ma - ter mi - se - ri - cor - di - ae;

Hail, holy queen, mother of mercy[1]

It is your month, the month of May, Mary's month. I make my way through Rome's sunlit streets to the ancient Basilica of Santa Maria in Trastevere, the very first church in Rome to be dedicated to you, Mother of God. I know there to be beauty in Santa Maria in Trastevere, the richness of a veneration of you that spans the centuries and the millennia.

vi - ta dul - ce - do et spes no - stra, sal - ve.

our life, our sweetness, and our hope

For seventeen hundred years, in this your church, women's lives and your life have fused. Our lives and your life, our sweetness and our hope. Our lives and all our bitterness, our despair and our experience of the dying of hope.

At the entrance to the ancient church, at the foot of one of its classical arches, cowers a gypsy woman, her body and face almost completely hidden in dark clothes, her head bowed deep. She could not be any more shadowy and anonymous.[2] But in her lap, for all to see, she holds the listless life of a child, a dark-haired little gypsy girl. It is obvious that the child is not simply asleep, but almost unconscious. The girl's exposed face would be called beautiful if it were not so deadly still. The gypsy mother holds out her hand, begging.

From high above her, you look out over the Piazza of Santa Maria in Trastevere: the medieval icon shows you, Mother of God, enthroned, offering your bare breast to your baby's eager mouth and hands.

Ad te cla - ma - mus, ex - su - les fi - li - i E - vae.

To thee do we cry, poor banished children of Eve.

More painful than the sight of the gypsy mother and her little girl at the doors to your church is the knowledge that this woman will have done what many beggars like her do. She will have drugged her child so that the girl's near-comatose body will evoke the predictable response from passers-by: helpless pity, taking the form of money.

The gypsy has chosen her site wisely, mother of mercy. Your church, Santa Maria in Trastevere, has not only become one of the famous tourist sites of Rome; it also is a prominent place of prayer, gathering as many as a thousand people for communal prayer every evening. I wonder whom they see first as they approach the church, you nursing your child high above in the façade, or the gypsy mother cradling her drugged child at the foot of the portico?

Ad te sus - pi - ra - mus, ge - men - tes et flen - tes in hac la - cri - ma - rum val - le.

To thee do we send up our sighs, mourning and weeping in this valley of tears.

How often in its past seventeen hundred years has the beauty of Santa Maria in Trastevere morphed into a valley of tears in the encounter with real women's lives?

I enter the ancient church with nothing but rage, rage at the gypsy mother's blatant abuse of her child.

The coolness and the softness of the chanting inside pledge to take me beyond any valley of tears. But I cannot leave the gypsy mother behind so easily. I know her to cower on the other side of the basilica's doors, in her own valley of tears that no chanting, however soft, will make disappear. I know she will be there when I leave your church. Her image is more powerful than all the precious, centuries-old images of you that grace the inside of Santa Maria in Trastevere. I walk by your famous icon, Lady of Mercy, without even realizing it is there; I am haunted by the woman at the entrance of the church whose life does not seem to know mercy, at least not for her child.

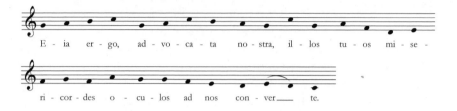

Turn then, most gracious advocate, thine eyes of mercy toward us.

Mary, most gracious advocate, your church has become the site of this gypsy mother and child intertwined in such merciless complicity. Do your eyes of mercy see her, the mother who seems to know no mercy, but whose body nevertheless models itself after yours, holding a lifeless child? A gypsy pietà, with a child's body that has suffering inscribed all over it, but a suffering inflicted by her own mother.

Turn thine eyes of mercy toward us. I only came to Santa Maria in Trastevere to venerate you, not to wrestle with a gypsy mother-with-child who places herself in my path to you.

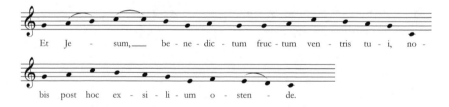

And after this our exile, show unto us the blessed fruit of thy womb, Jesus.

How can the fruit of your womb, Blessed Mother, be redemption for the fruit of the gypsy's womb? I long to see the little girl running around the piazza, skipping across the stones, climbing up the ancient octagonal fountain, enjoying the sunlight on the water that bursts forth into shells of stone.

It is much more likely that the girl will end up, with all the signs of an overdose, in the local children's hospital. I hope to God that she encounters there one of the sisters who have dedicated themselves to working with gypsy women. I vow to leave with them the money I will not put into the gypsy mother's outstretched hands. I cannot but refuse to make myself an accomplice in the drugging of this child by proving it profitable. And yet, I can find nothing redemptive in my resistance.

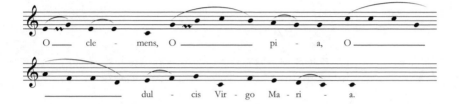

O clement, O loving, O sweet Virgin Mary.

I do know with frightening clarity that the gypsy mother has placed herself and her child in my path for longer than that afternoon at the entrance of Santa Maria in Trastevere. For every time I now pray to you, O sweet Virgin Mary, the bitter vision of the gypsy mother stands between you and me. I can no longer come to you except through and with her. And I find myself pleading with you for the life of this mother and her child, as if their redemption and mine have been forever fused.

A Novena before Pentecost

She Is God Dwelling in Us

A CATHOLIC BISHOP IS REPORTED to claim that inclusive language is "intrinsically incapable of expressing the mysteries of our faith."[1] I wonder.

The traditional novena before Pentecost—the nine consecutive days in which the faithful pray for the coming of the Holy Spirit—seems a good moment for refuting the bishop's claim, not with theological arguments (which would be simple) but with prayer.[2] Praying for the coming of the Holy Spirit has always been a rich moment in women's lives, not least of all because the Spirit is gendered feminine in parts of our tradition, such as the Hebrew Scriptures, and also in early Syriac and Armenian thinking.

I choose as my prayer for the nine days of the novena before Pentecost a text by Karl Rahner (hopefully someone a Catholic bishop will recognize as a theological authority). I change only one element of Rahner's text. Since his mother tongue, German, knows grammatical gender—that is, masculinity is not per se implied by the use of masculine pronouns—I render the grammatically masculine language for God feminine in this English version of Rahner's prayer. Whoever now prays with these words will have to decide for herself whether such feminine language is "intrinsically incapable of expressing the mysteries of our faith"—or whether, on the contrary, it is an authentic way of invoking the ever deeper coming of the Holy Spirit into our lives.

> . . . we have Your Holy Spirit. She is the anointing oil and the eternal seal of our innermost being. She is the fulfillment of all the bottomless depths of our existence. She is the life in us through which we have already overcome death. She is the unbounded happiness, which has dried up the very last streams of our tears, even when their floodwaters had risen over all the lowlands of our experience. She is God dwelling in us, the holiness of our heart, its secret rejoicing, its strength, which is always wonderfully there, even when our own strength fails and we are at our wits' end. She is in us, giving us faith

and inward knowledge, although we are blind fools. For she is all-knowing and she is ours. She is the hope in us, which does not founder in any of the shipwrecks of our own despair. She is the love in us, which loves us and which makes us love, generously, exultantly in spite of our cold, small and narrow hearts. She is eternal youth in us, in the despair-filled senility of our time and of our hearts. She is the laughter which sounds softly behind our tears. She is the confidence which bears us up, the freedom, the winged happiness of our souls. We are greater than we know.[3]

The Feast of Pentecost

Your Daughers Shall Prophesy

IT IS THE DAY OF PENTECOST.
I am standing in a circle of women in the middle of an ancient church. Slowly, the circle of women begins to move. We are dancing, moving gently, harmonizing our steps and our bodies: old and young women; able-bodied and differently-abled; lesbian, bisexual, and straight women; fifty women and no man. In the center of the circle, on the floor, stands a beautiful clear glass bowl full of water, with floating candles and a bright red rose. The Mass of "Wisdom's Power" has begun, a mass of women among women.

It is the day of Pentecost.

I am far from home, and away from my own Catholic Church.

The women who have gathered like this for almost ten years now have invited me to share in their liturgy. We come from different Christian traditions. I do not speak the language in which the liturgy is celebrated. I know none of the songs, and have to learn the dance steps as we move. I trust that I will understand these daughters who prophesy. I trust that the Holy Spirit, Wisdom's Power, will enable me to hear in my own language the words of life which the women share.

It is the day of Pentecost.

The woman priest who presides over the liturgy and also leads the dance is slender and beautiful. Her grey shoulder-length hair surrounds a face that is radiant. Her body moves subtly; she was a dancer before becoming a priest. When she lifts up the loaf of bread and deftly breaks it in two, the sun falling through the stained-glass windows suddenly alights on her. Her red priestly vestments are on fire.

It is the day of Pentecost.

As bread and wine are shared, I realize that there is a figure who has refused to join our circle. A petite woman, in a black cassock, her greying hair in a tight bun, sits in one of the pews toward the back of the church. She observes us closely, her face set in stone. I will learn later that she also is a priest, one of the parish priests in the church that is our gathering space for this Mass of "Wisdom's Power." Although she considers a Mass of women among women wrong, she is present at every one. But she never dances, and she never receives bread and wine.

It is the day of Pentecost.

Your daughters shall prophesy, promises the Spirit.

Your daughters

all of them.

Trinity Sunday

Co-laboring for Life

I WENT TO SEE A MOVIE in the week between Pentecost and Trinity Sunday, a movie that rendered alive the message of both Sundays in unforeseen ways. *Chocolat*—the movie I saw—was a powerful reminder that the Spirit moves where She wills, sometimes in profound challenges to what sees itself as church. But *Chocolat* also made me realize that glimpses of the Trinity come in manifold guises, some of them as ordinary and as startling as three women co-laboring for the sake of life.

I had first heard about this film in a sermon during Lent, of all places.[1] The priest had suggested that *Chocolat*'s central character, a woman, might be a Christ-figure. It does not happen that frequently that I hear women described as icons of Christ in sermons; I welcomed the image. Seeing the film myself between Pentecost and Trinity Sunday, however, my icons differed significantly from what the priest had seen.

If anything, Vianne, the central character of *Chocolat*, is a compelling (even if distinctly transtraditional) symbol of the Holy Spirit. Here is how. Vianne enters the film, and the little French village in which the film is set, in a long red cape which completely envelops her body. She is moved, quite literally, by a strong wind. When this wind blows her into the village, it also blows open the doors of the parish church where Mass is being celebrated that moment. Where Vianne comes from remains unclear for much of the film; whither she goes, until the very end. But her life is one that is vibrant and life-giving for others (her very name bears resonance with words for "life" in Romance languages). Vianne moves among the villagers, breaking open lives in ever-surprising ways, breathing passion into stale relationships, giving new life to a woman abused, healing broken relationships, opening paths to love for people who had grown old without it.

At the end of the film, when Vianne's spirit has blown through much of the little village, it finally reaches even within the church. The young priest finds his own voice to affirm life. It is telling, though, that there remains a fine line between the chocolaterie and the church. Vianne never enters the church, and the priest never tastes the chocolates in the chocolaterie. In the only scene that places him in proximity to both, he remains standing in the door.

Vianne's spirit does not move alone. She has co-laborers. Josephine, the abused woman with the marks of physical violence visible on her body is raised to new life (if there is a Christ-figure in this film, it is surely she). Armande, the feisty old woman, chooses to live life to its fullest, even if it threatens her own. She lives on, in the end, in the Café that Josephine takes over from the abusive husband. There are glimpses of a colorful trinity of women here, co-laboring for the sake of life: the old women whose name evokes "love," the woman with marks of violence on her body who is raised to new life, and the woman whose spirit blows where it wills and breathes new life into dead realities.

Embodied in the film (unbeknown to both producers and actors if one takes the slick Web site of the film as a guide) is a powerful critique of the church, its liturgies and its traditions. *Chocolat* challenges the church as the ultimate or primary locus of life, especially for women. Throughout the film, the vibrant new spirit blowing through the little village in the person of Vianne is fought from within the church—whose doors are reclosed resolutely when Vianne first enters the village accompanied by a strong wind. The pulpit and the confessional are key sites of this struggle. Three men, each with his own forms of distance from women's lives, embody the resistance to Vianne's spirit: the mayor, the young priest, and the abusive husband. The church becomes the dominant site for the articulation of this resistance. The liturgical season of Lent is the negative foil against which Vianne's spirit has to move.

The film's denial of the church as a primary focus of life is performed, however, precisely in appropriating key ecclesial symbols. The chocolaterie, rather than the church, is the key site of conversion to life and of resistance to evil. The chocolaterie is the place where communion becomes possible, and where life is shared in small pieces of food. The contrast between the thin white host which the abusive husband is made to receive in a doomed attempt to change him, and the rich dark chocolate Vianne places in people's hands and mouths is startling. The chocolaterie is a sanctuary, a safe space for women. When evil enters that space by force, two women co-labor to expel the demons of male violence.

Is it a sheer coincidence that in the end these three women (even if one of them only in the memory of the other two and the name of their Café) own key places where the village people gather to eat and drink? Where the Spirit moves and where we co-labor for the sake of life, the power to make communion might just end up in women's hands.

Sunday in Ordinary Time

She Calls Together Her Friends

IT WAS AN ORDINARY MONDAY AFTERNOON—except for the fact that the doctor had just detected a lump in her breast. She will have to go to the nearby hospital for a diagnostic mammogram as soon as possible. The appointment is made for her as she waits. She hears the secretary describing the specifics of what the doctor just found. Walking out of the office dazed, the sunshine seems painfully unreal.

It is not the first time she has been confronted with diagnostic tests that demand further tests. She is no complete stranger to mammograms, ultrasounds, biopsies, and the intense waiting that surrounds all of these. Nor has her circle of women friends remained untouched by cancer. After all, more than two hundred thousand women are diagnosed with breast cancer every year. More than forty thousand women die from breast cancer every year. And unnumbered people are affected by the struggle for early detection and various treatments to fight the disease. Fear wells up inside of her. Her life has just been exposed, yet again, in all its fragility.

Should she say anything to people in her parish? It does not seem that easy to speak to a priest of a lump in her breast, especially not to a priest for whom, supposedly, women's bodies are unknown territory. And she does not want to have to speak in cautious riddles. She needs to tell someone in no uncertain terms that it is that particular part of her body that has become the source of fear. She calls two women friends; they understand immediately. But during the night, she has a strange dream. A priest walks by her as if she were invisible, simply unable to see her pleading gesture. Upon waking, a profound sense of sadness lingers in her memory.

On Friday morning, she arrives at the hospital early, but several other women are already seated in the waiting room. The women are young and old, white, black, and brown, immaculately dressed and in sweats. How many of them would know firsthand that by age fifty, one in fifty-four women will be diagnosed with breast cancer, and by age sixty it will be one in twenty-three? Studying the women waiting with her, she begins to wonder about her parish. There are more than one thousand women in this church. Breast cancer must be a reality among them, but she does not remember it ever surfacing as a concern. She recalls a friend, an ordained Methodist minister, speaking of her own battle against breast cancer and how all of a sudden other women in her congregation began to reveal their battles with the disease. Would it make a difference to have a woman priest, and one who had just had a mastectomy, lift the bread and wine above her head at the celebration of the Eucharist? Her friend had movingly spoken about how the congregation gently recognized their priest's broken body when she elevated the eucharistic elements for the first time after her breast cancer surgery.

Her turn for the mammogram has come, and she simply tries to cooperate with the technician taking the pictures. It is the usual half-painful half-humorous procedure. After the mammogram comes the ultrasound and then the return to the waiting room. Soon she is handed an envelope. The letter tells her that the mammogram and the ultrasound showed no signs of cancer. She is free to go.

As she leaves the hospital, she wonders how many of the women in the waiting room will go home with other results. Throughout the day, her thoughts return to the women gathered in the waiting room that morning. As evening nears, she decides to acknowledge and mark the results of her mammogram in some small way. She calls her friends and invites them for dinner on Sunday night.

Late Sunday afternoon, she begins to prepare the evening meal. She has decided to cook a lavishly spicy dish. As she mixes the spices, combining the cardamom and cloves, the cinnamon, peppercorns, cumin, saffron, cayenne, ginger, and turmeric, she begins to hum; a soft melody accompanies the work of her hands. Finally she realizes the source of the music. It is a tune from this morning's liturgy. She begins to think back to the worship service. There is not much that has stayed with her. Trying to remember the sermon, she simply draws a blank. What has remained are some of the words of the psalm, beautifully sung by a cantor with a rich alto voice. The words now come back, as she simmers her spice mixture, slowly adding all the other ingredients into the large pot:

> You will show me the path to life,
> fullness of joy in your presence,
> the delights at your right hand forever.[1]

More than the words, it was the rich voice of the woman singing that imprinted this song in her memory. As she turns to setting the table and arranging the plates and silverware, glasses and napkins, another biblical text suddenly comes to mind. She is certain that she has not heard the story recently, but it seems perfect for this Sunday. In between stirring the rich mixture in the large pot on the stove and preparing the side dishes, she tries to remember the story more clearly. A woman had ten silver coins. Losing one of them, she searches diligently. Finally, the coin is found. The woman calls together her friends and neighbors, asking them to rejoice with her. For Jesus—who told the story of this woman's loss, search, and joy—the story ends here.

But what about the woman herself? Surely she will have invited her friends to rejoice with her around a lavish meal. What a pity that Jesus told the story so quickly. He surely must have known that the way to mark defining moments in life is with a meal. He did it himself.

When her friends arrive this Sunday evening, one of them brings an armful of fresh flowers from her garden, roses and phlox in all shades between white and purple. The flowers come to be placed in a large vase in the center of the table. As she opens a bottle of champagne, one of the women toasts her, knowingly. In her joy, she suddenly remembers the other gathering of women, in the hospital room on Friday morning. How are these women spending this beautiful Sunday evening? Will they have called together friends? Will they anxiously await the results of a biopsy? Will they face a resurgence of breast cancer? She breathes a silent prayer. For her, this Sunday *is* a moment of rejoicing, an evening to call together friends to share her joy. The feast begins.

A week later, the friend who had toasted her at the feast calls. A mammogram has detected a lump in her breast, and an ultrasound confirmed that it was solid. A needle biopsy is set for the following week.

Baptism

The Waters of Birth and the Waters of Baptism: Embracing the One Gift of Life

THERE IS A STORY in Walter Wangerin's collection *Miz Lil and the Chronicles of Grace* titled "Baby Hannah."[1] The story tells of a baptism in an African American congregation, Grace Lutheran Church. The pastor is a young woman, the child to be baptized her daughter, birthed into the world a short while ago. As the pastor/mother readies to pour the waters of baptism over her child, she finds herself unable to continue the prayer she began. "Hannah, I . . ." is all she can say before tears flood her eyes. Her own birthing of her daughter and God's birthing of this child in baptism flow together, as a powerful sense of the waters of life being one rises within the mother/pastor. In this fusion of birthing and baptism as part of the all-embracing waters of life, God becomes visible as the One who ultimately calls forth all journeys into life. What the pastor/mother experiences is the transparency of her own birthing of a child for God's gift of life in baptism. Both are part of the precious moment of coming to life. Baby Hannah was birthed both in the waters of her mother's womb and of her church's baptismal font just as surely as she is called into life through both by Her God.

What I find remarkable in this short story is the blurring of the boundaries between creaturely birth and ecclesial initiation, between the waters of birth and the waters of baptism. "Baby Hannah" opens a space for us to embrace both our birth and our baptism as part of the one life that is God-sustained. Such a space is not a given in a Christian tradition in which the experiences of women and the meaning of redemption often appear to be in tension.

Women's Lives and the Reality of Redemption: The Tension

In the Christian tradition, a basic tension appears again and again between the lives of women and the reality of redemption. With regard to baptism, the contrast takes this form: It is not the waters of a human mother's womb that birth into authentic life—so the tradition seems to suggest—but rather the baptismal waters of Mother Church. This contrast between the maternal and the ecclesial body and its birthing is not the invention of late or even of post-Constantinian times; it has profoundly biblical roots. In John 3:3–7, Jesus engages the aged Nicodemus in a conversation about birth, insisting that "no one can see the kingdom of God without being born from above." Nicodemus asks, "How can anyone be born after having grown old? Can one enter a second time into the mother's womb and be born?" Jesus answers with this stark contrast:

> Very truly, I tell you, no one can enter the kingdom of God without being born of water and Spirit. What is born of the flesh is flesh, and what is born of the Spirit is spirit. Do not be astonished that I said to you, "You must be born from above."

Suggested here is a contrast or at least a tension between birth waters and baptismal waters, birth and rebirth, creation and redemption. Other biblical texts corroborate this theme (e.g., John 1:12ff.; 1 Pet. 1:23). The underlying disregard of women's bodies and their powers of birthing lives on in the Christian tradition, for example, in rituals surrounding pregnancy and birth that mark a woman as unclean. But the contrast between birth waters and baptismal waters is not the only dissonance between women's lived lives and the experience of redemption inscribed in the Christian tradition. There are at least two other such experiences of dissonance. Both of these, like baptism, are at the center of Christian faith and life. One such dissonant experience between women's lives and the reality of redemption is found in the Eucharist. The eucharistic tradition seems to say to a woman: It is not the nurturing provided by your body and breast-feeding that really nourish life, but rather the Lord's Body and the Lord's Supper. The other dissonant experience for women's lived lives is embedded in the traditional image of the meaning of redemption. Redemption comes through a male body, bleeding for us and for all, that sins may be forgiven. This image might just signal to women: It is not your monthly flow of blood that has anything to do with true life, but rather, the blood of a man, violently shed for us and for all, that brings true life. These dissonances, whether in baptism, Eucharist, or redemption, seem to suggest that the Christian tradition thrives on a negation of a woman's lived life. Not your body, not your water, not your blood

bring true life—the Christian faith seems to say—but rather baptismal
waters and the Body and Blood of Christ.

Pushing beyond the Tension:
Birth Waters and Baptismal Waters as Accomplices

Can we conceive of the Christian tradition in such a way that this
tension at the heart of our faith tradition is lightened? Can we conceive
of a God who does not negate but rather seems to imitate the lives of
women? Instead of dwelling on the contrast between women's lives
and the reality of redemption, is it possible to see God and the lives of
women as accomplices? Can we imagine a God who says: "Just like you
women, so I also . . ."? Just as you women create life in the birth waters
of your bodies, I will give new life in the birth waters of my body, the
church. Just as you women nurture the newly born at your breasts
with your own bodies, just the same I nurture life with my own being.
Just as you women are able to think of blood and new life not in con-
tradiction, but in unison, so also will I bring redemption.

Where do we find traces of this God who is able to call forth amity
between women's lives and God's own redemptive workings? The
sacrament of baptism actually is a good starting point for this search,
since deeply embedded in this sacrament are images of birthing (even
if often by way of a contrast between human and ecclesial birth, as in
John 3). One of the roots of these birthing images in conjunction with
God claiming our lives in redemption is found in the Hebrew Bible.
In Hebrew, the word for God's mercy (*rachamim*) is rooted in the
word for womb (*rechem*).[2] God's redemptive, all-encompassing presence, in other words, is seen to be like a mother's womb, the life-
giving embrace in which she carries her child. Baptism, then, as God's
claiming our life, can be seen as an expression of God's maternal, all-
encompassing compassion.

This knowledge, in fact, has always been a part of our tradition.
Traces of the fusion of maternal images and that which is redemptive
are there in many theological reflections on the sacrament of baptism.
Suffice it to mention but one example, from the Liturgical Movement
in the first half of the twentieth century. The most prolific female
authors of this movement, Sr. Aemiliana Löhr, OSB (1896–1972),
writes eloquently about the waters of baptism being the "womb of the
church, graced and impregnated by the Spirit of the Lord."[3] Löhr's
Benedictine confrère Athanasius Wintersig (1900–1942), monk of
Maria Laach, similarly ponders the baptismal font as "the maternal

womb of the church." He goes on to say that a parish priest baptizes all the parish's children "in this impregnated font." The priest thereby "exercises his status as proxy bridegroom and father in Christ, while the congregation represents the mother in her joy."[4] Clearly these two authors, as many others before them, link baptismal theology and the imagery of birth.

Listening to What the Women Are Saying …

What or who can assist us today, at the beginning of the twenty-first century, in thinking of birth waters and baptismal waters as accomplices? The answer seems so obvious: It is women who experience birth waters and baptismal waters as continuous in their lives and who long to be able to understand both as one all-embracing movement into life. To put this differently: Women's lived lives have to be taken seriously as a locus of theological insight and truth.[5] I learned this most profoundly during my own experience of the pregnancy, birth, and baptism of my son. The months encompassing pregnancy, birth, and baptism were all of a piece for me, although I had been taught to think about them theologically in quite different ways. This dissonance produced my desire to deconstruct the contrast between birth waters and baptismal waters so that birthing my son in the waters of my womb and bringing him to the waters of baptism could be what in fact they were for me: an embrace of God's one gift of life that was and is this child.

But how to think the waters of birth and the waters of baptism together? Simply taking the sacrament of baptism as the starting point and thinking backwards is problematic, since the focus of that sacrament is on the person to be baptized. The mother's body or her presence is not required for baptism (beyond her role as the one who birthed the child). For the sacrament of baptism itself, it is quite irrelevant what the mother thinks and feels, and how she might bridge her own experience of her birth waters and the baptismal waters of Mother Church.

If baptism is not a good starting point, what might be? There are at least two other possibilities to connect birth waters and baptismal waters. The first possibility is provided by the (re)discovery of the importance of natality for all human life (including life in the church, one would want to presume).[6] In emphasizing natality—the simple fact of all of us having been born—as basic to all human life, we might have a starting point for thinking birth waters and baptismal waters together. Both, after all, are birthing events. And without the natality given through the bodies of human mothers, there would simply be no ecclesial natality, no being born into the life of the church. Baptismal birthing cannot exist without the birthing labor of a woman.

There is a second possibility to think theologically of birth waters and baptismal waters together. This possibility is rooted in the notion of the sacramentality of all created reality, therefore also the sacramentality of pregnancy and birth. The sacramental reality of a woman's pregnancy and birthing prepares the way for the sacrament of baptism. Both are a part of the one sacramental mystery that is life in this God-sustained universe. This way of conceiving of birth and baptism, once again, ameliorates the contrast between birth waters and baptismal waters. The two could just be seen as accomplices, after all. In what follows below, I wish to focus on yet another, third possibility, one that emerged for me during my own pregnancy, birthing, and baptism of my child.

Pregnant with a "Little Heathen"?

Shortly before the baptism of my son, one of my friends joked that the child would soon no longer be a "little heathen." It had never occurred to me during my pregnancy that I could carry such a thing as a "little heathen" inside me. Without being aware of it, I had felt that the growing child and I were journeying together on the path of faith. As I reflected theologically on this experience and on my unborn child's journey, I began to imagine my pregnancy as a "catechumenate" in the womb. The term might sound grandiose but is important to claim here. In contemporary Roman Catholicism, much is made of the adult catechumenate, that is, the journey of unbaptized adults to baptism and into full ecclesial communion. I would like to claim this image of a catechumenate for the *prenatal* journey to faith also, that is the gathering into the church of the unborn and newborn even before baptism. How can such a prenatal catechumenate be conceived? I begin, once again, with the experience of my own pregnancy. From early on, I sensed the human being growing inside of me as *with me* on the path of faith. In my day-to-day experience with the child, I prayed with (not just *for* the child), read the Scriptures aloud with him, sang and worshiped as he began to dance in my womb. The child in my body was blessed many times, as I made the sign of the cross on my ever-expanding belly, or touched the place where I knew the little face to be at the moment of the Kiss of Peace during Mass. And I remember vividly how a few days before the birth a pastor and friend of mine laid her hands on my large belly, blessing both the baby and me for what ended up being an exceedingly arduous birth.

Life in the Womb: Biblical Wisdom and Prenatal Research

Both the wisdom of the Scriptures and recent prenatal research seem to confirm my experiences. A simple browsing through any good bookstore shows how much our culture has begun to think of the life world of the unborn as its own little universe (contradicted starkly, of course, by the ease with which this world comes to be ended). Titles conjure up "life before birth," "contact with the soul of your unborn child," or "the secret life of the unborn child." These books speak volumes about the reality and depth of prenatal existence—newly discovered by medical research and by the publishing industry, but, I suspect, known by many mothers all along. Have theological reflection and pastoral practice kept up with the rapid development of knowledge about prenatal life (apart from the painful moral questions around abortion)? What about an unborn's experience of God in the womb? The idea that an unborn child, in terms of the life of faith, is a blank— or even a "little heathen"—is made nonsensical by many of the insights of contemporary prenatal research. This research tells us, for example, that by the fourth month the unborn has a quite well developed sense of taste and touch. Should she not be able to perceive God? The unborn can distinguish the voice of the mother. Should she not be capable of hearing the voice of God? If an unborn child aligns her waking and sleeping with that of the mother, should she not be awake to the presence of God?

Prenatal research is not alone in allowing us to think that experiences of God are possible *in utero*. The liturgical calendar in fact invites us to celebrate a prenatal encounter with God every year on July 2 in the Feast of the Visitation. This feast day commemorates the meeting between two women who are pregnant with God's future, Mary and Elizabeth. In their encounter, the unborn John the Baptist leaps in his mother's womb as he perceives the presence of God in the child Mary carries under her heart (Luke 1:42–44). With his joyful leap, the unborn John confirms the promise an angel had given to his father, Zechariah: This child will be filled with the Holy Spirit already in the womb (Luke 1:15). In the same way, the Apostle Paul knows that he was set apart and called from birth. In his letter to the Galatians, Paul

The Visitation. Attributed to Master Heinrich Constance
(ca. 1310 AD), from the Dominican Nunnery of Katharinental.
The Metropolitan Museum of Art

writes that God "set me apart from birth and called me by his grace" (Gal. 1:15). The Hebrew Bible also witnesses to such prenatal callings. The prophet Jeremiah, for example, was sanctified by God in his mother's womb: "The word of the Lord came to me, saying, 'Before I formed you in the womb I knew you, before you were born I set you apart; I appointed you as a prophet to the nations'" (Jer. 1:4ff.). Isaiah is called similarly: "Before I was born the Lord called me; from my birth he made mention of my name" (Isa. 49:1). The Psalmist acknowledges God as the one who formed us before birth: "For you created my inmost being; you knit me together in my mother's womb" (Ps. 139:13). Jesus died with a psalm on his lips that images God as a midwife, who brings humankind out of the mother's womb at birth: "Yet you brought me out of the womb; you made me trust in you even at my mother's breast. From birth I was cast upon you; from my mother's womb you have been my God" (Ps. 22:10ff.).

Obviously all of these biblical references have a metaphorical quality. "From my mother's womb" or "in my mother's womb" in biblical terms means: from the very beginning, from the first moment on, God knows us. One psalm puts it thus: "From birth I have relied on you; you brought me forth from my mother's womb. I will ever praise you" (Ps. 71:6). In the book of Isaiah, God points to divine care since the moment of conception: "Listen to me, O house of Jacob, . . . you whom I have upheld since you were conceived" (Isa. 46:3; cf. 44:2). The simple fact that these texts have a metaphorical quality does, however, not mean that they cannot also speak in the real. Quite the opposite: Contemporary prenatal research impressively confirms biblical wisdom at this point. There is life, and therefore the possibility of the experience of God, before birth.

Pregnancy as a Sacramental Time

With all that we now know about the life world of the unborn, it is difficult to think of these tiny human beings as spiritually blank pages. Should their manifold capacities for hearing, moving, and reacting exist only in the biological realm? Would God have excluded the unborn from the faith journey into the heart of the divine presence that is our life's destiny? If the answer has to be no (and I am convinced it is) then the unborn is in fact already on a path of faith. But in that case, how do we understand the time of pregnancy and birth, that is, the time before a child is baptized? This time will have to be perceived as already part of the faith journey of these tiny human beings. The image of a catechumenate is helpful here, since it allows one to embrace the journey of faith before and toward baptism. Catechumens, after all, are no longer regarded as "heathens," but rather as already leaning into full communion with the church.

If we take the notion of a catechumenal journey toward baptism and apply it to the life of the unborn in the womb (I am obviously thinking here of the child/ren of parents committed to living their faith), the following becomes clear. The journey of faith begins in the womb. The pregnant woman who prays, sings, and worships does not do these things without her child. Indeed, during the later months of pregnancy the unborn child inevitably takes part in these experiences, since she already recognizes voices, melodies, and times of rest. She partakes of the food her mother eats (presumably even eucharistic food), and reacts with signs of well-being or indisposition to her environment. The unborn child, thus, is already living in and with the church, before she is born and brought to baptism. Her life is ordered toward ecclesial communion. The unborn, in other words, journeys through something like a prenatal catechumenate in the womb.

The Waters of Birth and the Waters of Baptism: Embracing the One Gift of Life

If pregnancy and birthing are understood as a sacramental journey, what does this mean for baptism? Clearly, baptism can no longer be thought of as a child's very first religious "moment." There simply is no little heathen in a womb, at least not for parents who live their faith. Here, then, is the point at which we can claim the flowing together of birth waters and baptismal waters, and embrace the sacramental journey through prenatal, perinatal, newborn, and into baptismal life. What might such a claim mean for the concrete material realities within which we live the faith today? Three possibilities readily come to mind. First is the need to strengthen the spiritual nature of the time of pregnancy and birth, especially for women, and not to leave this time to the medical establishment to define. There are many resources for this, both in the traditional practices of popular religiosity and in the new women-identified rituals and liturgies. Much can be done, especially in the lives of expecting mothers, to strengthen the experience of embracing together the waters of birth and the waters of baptism.

A second possibility has to do with the ecclesial communion itself, that is, the local church, and its relationship to the unborn. What would it take to conceive of inscribing an unborn into a parish's "Book of Life"? In the adult catechumenate, the candidates for baptism are inscribed by name into such a Book of Life during a lenten liturgy—by the bishop, no less. Why not also recognize an unborn child's faith journey toward baptism? With such an act of inscription in the Book of Life, the child finds herself "under way" in and with this particular congregation. (And no, a final decision on the name for the unborn is not necessary for this; my son was simply listed as "baby boy Berger" in the medical charts before he was born).

Being inscribed in a Book of Life could also be important in the heartbreaking case of a miscarriage or stillbirth. In such a case, parents are often left on their own with the loss of a child who was still faceless to the rest of the community. But when an unborn child who was already recorded in a Book of Life dies, it would be possible to hark back to this inscription. The entire ecclesial community, not just the parents, will have to take leave from this unborn, who had begun the journey of faith into full communion within this church. The life and death of this unborn "catechumen" will be experienced quite differently than as the hidden and lonely parting of the woman and her family from an anonymous fetus.

A third point for reconfiguration is the moment of baptism itself, in which the intrinsic connections between the waters of birth and the waters of baptism could be made more explicit than they are now. I am here thinking particularly of the beautiful prayer that precedes the act of baptism itself. This Blessing over Baptismal Waters traditionally has recounted salvation history by focusing on God's gift of the manifold waters of life. Why not strengthen the peculiarly feminine aspects of salvation history, particularly in relation to waters of birthing? This would be one way to signal the connections between the waters of birth, the waters of baptism, and God's ever-present and always manifold gift of life. When the time for my son's baptism came, I wrote such a prayer for the Blessing over the Baptismal Waters:

Breathing (Women's) Life into an Ancient Text: A Blessing over Baptismal Waters

Living God,
we call you mother

because you are the source of all life.
You have showered us with grace
through sacramental signs
which tell of the wonders of your unseen power.
In baptism we embrace your gift of water
which you have made a symbol
of your own overflowing life.

At the very dawn of creation
you birthed the cosmos
and took it in your arms to nurture it.
Ever since then
mothers have known your creative energy
in the breaking of their waters
when giving birth.

Your Spirit breathed gently on the waters of creation
making them wellsprings of life.
You taught the waves
their words of wisdom
and the ocean depths
their silent song of praise.

The torrential waters of the great flood
became a sign of the waters of baptism
as they brought an end to worlds of violence
and a new beginning of life.
In the rainbow
you gave water
the color of hope.

You showed Hagar a well in the desert
to revive her dying child.
You inspired Hebrew midwives
to save the children of Israel
thus preparing a people
to walk through the waters of the Red Sea.
You moved a Levite woman
to hide her son in a basket
and entrust him to a river.
Miriam sang your praises

as you freed her people from slavery
and drowned Pharaoh's chariots
in the waters of the sea.

Like a mother
you carried your people
through the desert,
providing water in the wilderness.

No wonder your prophets spoke of your grace
as morning dew
as overflowing torrent
as mother's milk.

When the time had come,
your Word took human form
in the water of Mary's womb.
Blessed, indeed, the fruit of this womb:
Jesus.
He was baptized in the waters of the Jordan.
At a well, he spoke truth to an outcast woman
and promised her living waters.
He calmed the storms over the Sea of Galilee
and the wind and waves recognized his voice.

Dying on a cross,
water and blood flowed from his side.
In them, you birthed your church.

Living God
you have made water a symbol of your life
ever since the dawn of creation.
Let your Spirit now breathe gently on these waters of baptism
that they may become for us the waters of life,
the color of hope,
the sound of rain in the desert.
May you birth those to be baptized
into the new creation of water and the Spirit
and take them in your arms to nurture them
from now on until the very end of time
when the river of the water of life will be all in all.

I began with a short story and I would like to end with one. This time, it is my own story of birthing a child. As the time came closer when the waters of my womb would break, I packed a flask of holy water into my bag to take to the hospital with me. I did not think much about the symbolism, I simply wanted to greet my child with something beyond pained delight and the white starkness of a bed in a world class hospital. In some ways, I wanted the church—and all it stands for as a witness to divine life and presence—to be there for the birth of this child. When I look back on this spontaneous gesture now, I realize that with it I tried somehow to mingle birth waters and baptismal waters together. I was saying to myself, to my son, and to the church: Let us embrace as one the journey of life through pregnancy, birth, and baptism. Let birth waters and baptismal waters flow together, so that God will be visible as the One who calls us into all life and allows us to embrace ever more deeply the life that is God Herself.

A Lazy Sunday Afternoon
The Making of Love: An ABC

A

Ama et quod vis fac   "Love and do as you desire." A wonderful motto for a lazy Sunday afternoon, especially since it is attributed to Saint Augustine. Much of the Christian tradition, however, has seen fit to think of Sunday and love-making along other lines. Penitentials from the sixth century onward advised couples to practice sexual abstinence on Sundays and feast days, on fast days and the days of patron saints.[1] The liturgical calendar governed the rhythms of sexual desire and restraint quite explicitly—although the simple fact that we know this from penitentials suggests that people did not necessarily live accordingly.

B

Beloved   "I am my beloved's, and his desire is for me. Come, my beloved . . ." (Song of Songs 7:10). Possible biblical authorization for a lazy Sunday afternoon of love-making—if biblical authorization is needed, that is.

Body image   Fundamental to everything we do as women, from encountering ourselves in the mirror first thing in the morning, to our presence at worship, to love-making. The impact of cultural and especially media representations (many of which degrade, stereotype and sexualize women) on our own body image is well documented.[2]

C

Conjugal communion   A beautiful expression used by Pope John Paul II. Vaticanese for *sex*. The pope does conceive of this conjugal

220

communion as the "first communion."[3] Would the second one be eucharistic communion? And how are the two related? One thing seems clear: Communion can be shared and received more than once on a Sunday.

D

Desire   "Desire in the human context that might be recognized as imitating or sharing in God's love will be precisely the desire . . . for the other's good irrespective of the other's capacity to satisfy me, to meet my lack."[4] Profoundly true.

E

Eve   The first woman mentioned in the Bible. Her name means "living," "life-giver," or "the mother of all living" (Gen 3:20).[5] Eve's primary image in the Christian tradition, however, has been that of a seductress. The same still holds true for American popular culture, where "Adam + Eve" is the name of a company that sells sex toys and porn videos. The last word on Eve in the Book of Genesis, however, is not about her as a seductress. After expulsion from the biblical Garden of Eden, Eve is said to have "created a man together with the LORD" (Gen. 4:1–2a). The "highly unusual language" suggests "the awesomeness of female creativity, akin to God's."[6]

Exploitation, of women's bodies   Real and omnipresent, even when we close our bedroom doors. Everything from automobile ads with a half-dressed blonde reclining seductively against the grill of the car to graphic photos of sexual humiliation is carried deep within each of us. We cannot shake this off simply by shedding our clothes.

F

Face to face   A lovely image and reality (cf. 1 Cor. 13:12), but should not be taken to condone only one way of love-making.

Fatigue   Real in women's lives, especially those of mothers. A nap might be more important on a lazy Sunday afternoon than love-making. Both of course assume that the children are taken care of.

Female anatomy   "Women's organs have an intrinsic multiplicity that cannot be easily explained. . . . The hymen and the 'two-lipped vulva,' as noted by Jacques Derrida and Luce Irigaray, suggest fluid, diffuse, multiple, embracing language in place of the linear, unified, and visible language of the phallus."[7]

Flowers   Always beautiful, especially in front of a golden tabernacle, but also next to two human bodies. If no flowers are available, wild summer grass or dried lavender will do. They both carry their own grace and elegance.

Fulfillment   Ever elusive. Built into love-making seems to be the painful realization that there is nothing on this earth that will ever truly still our hunger for life in all its fullness. Daring to make love requires a strong eschatology (i.e., a doctrine of the final destiny of all things).

G

Gift of self   "The total physical self-giving would be a lie if it were not the sign and fruit of a total personal self-giving."[8] Pope John Paul II speaks truth here, although one has to assume he has not lived the reality that he speaks about.

God   "God is Love and in himself he lives a mystery of personal loving communion. . . . Love is therefore the fundamental and innate vocation of every human being."[9] Is there any true love-making without at least the possibility of a glimpse of the divine origin of all love?

Gynergy   Female energy[10] that is both essential for love-making, and a possible result of it. No contraceptive measures should ever be taken.

H

HIV/AIDS   The number of women with HIV/AIDS is increasing steadily worldwide. In 2003, it was at close to twenty million. According to the National Institutes of Health, women are particularly vulnerable to heterosexual transmission of HIV. Four reasons are given: the simple biological fact of women's "substantial mucosal exposure to seminal fluids" during heterosexual intercourse; the frequency of nonconsensual sex forced on women; sex without condom use; and the unknown or high-risk sexual practices of the male partners. Have women not always borne greater risks than men to their own health from sexual encounters (beginning with infections and ending with pregnancies that could be life-threatening)?

I

Internet pornography   With the internet now an integral part of many lives, Internet porn and cybersex are only a click away. The pornography industry boasts an estimated $10 billion of annual sales. There are more than twenty-eight thousand "adult" Web sites.[11] Roughly twelve thousand new hardcore porn videos are released each year.[12] To whom, you ask? To whom not, might be the better question.

Ideals of love, cultural   To be let go as much as possible, for the sake of the real.

J

Jouissance   Maybe best translated into English as "bliss." The notion of *jouissance* is important in postmodern theories of desire and of flourishing, but can also serve as a code for a woman's experience of coming. A good word for subverting the "reductions of the modern cult of orgasm."[13]

K

Know   A verb used in the Hebrew Bible to name sexual union: "Now the man knew his wife Eve, and she conceived . . ." (Gen. 4:1). The Virgin Mary, at the Annunciation, insists, at least in the Greek original, "How can this be . . . I do not know a man?" (Luke 1:34). What knowledges, what ways of knowing are engendered by sexual union, and are these different for men and women?

L

Lips   Invoked at the beginning of the liturgy of the hours: "O Lord, open my lips, and my mouth shall proclaim your praise" (Ps. 51:15). Essential for worship. Note that women are blessed with more than two. Remember: Lips are both sites of praise and of pleasure.

Lover   Essential if one wants to follow St. Augustine's command to love and do as one desires.

M

Messiness   To be welcomed in love-making, as long as the labor of cleanup is shared.

N

Name, of the lover (*see above*)   Given, yes. But also made, in love.

Neruda, Pablo   A poet for a lazy Sunday afternoon. Deserves to be read in his Spanish mother tongue.

No   An essential word in love-making, especially for women when contemplating opening their bodies for another (*also see "yes"*).

O

Orgasm   See *jouissance*

P

Paul, Apostle   Not an easy bedfellow for a lazy Sunday afternoon, but he did write the following: "The husband should give to his wife her conjugal rights . . . the husband does not have authority over his own body, but the wife does" (1 Cor. 7:3ff.).

Penis   Not the center of a woman's universe, even if she regularly receives e-mail messages such as this: "Enlarge your 'tool' naturally: gain up to 3.5+ inches (improved formula); thicken your shaft; gives partner increased pleasure; improves self-esteem & motivation; a longer lasting, healthier erection; all natural, wholesale cost, try it out!" No, thank you.

Pink   Together with red, this seems to be America's favorite color code for love. Can cause nausea if consumed in large quantities, see cards for Valentine's Day. Why not green, or blue, or purple as colors of love? In the liturgy, red mostly denotes suffering and martyrdom, a passion of a different kind.

Pleasure   "Sexuality is a source of joy and pleasure . . . the spouses do nothing evil in seeking this pleasure and enjoyment. They accept what the Creator has intended for them."[14] Amen to that.

Popular culture   Powerfully present in all love-making, no matter how counterculturally we live. Popular culture's fantasies of seduction and of "sexpert" advice provide their own form of commentary on life in contemporary America—for example, "put a donut around your lover's penis and start nibbling." Yeah.

Q

Quality, of erection   Did millions of women all over America roar with laughter when the Levitra ads started, featuring a woman chatting about her lover's EQ (erection quality)? Toward the end of the ad, a warning flashed across the screen: *If you get an erection that lasts more than 4 hours, get medical help right away . . . or lasting damage can happen to your penis.* Most women I know would think that a much shorter erection time span would deserve medical attention, if only for the woman's sake. Who exactly—other than the pharmaceutical industry—benefits from our bodies being forced into sexual hyperactivity? Is there something incongruous about this culture preaching abstinence for teenagers and prizing sexual hyperactivity in everyone else?

R

Real presence   At the heart of the Eucharist, and at the heart of all love-making. To be celebrated and received with utmost devotion. Shoes should be taken off.

Reverence   The loving attentiveness appropriate to all worship of God, as well to our own bodies and the body of a lover.

Rhythm, of women's bodies   To be known, lived with, and enjoyed by both partners wherever possible (PMS, of course, usually simply has to be "lived with").

S

Sacrament   "Sex is a brilliant idea of God's, I think. Almost like a sacrament."[15]

Sexual sins   An ever-present powerful possibility, but these sins might need to be identified more broadly than the dominant Christian tradition has done. Possible examples of such sins include: women undervaluing their own bodies in sexual encounters, selling themselves cheap, faking desire, using sex to get something else, seducing in ways that are disrespectful to the other, or visiting their own (f)rigidities on someone they live with.

Sacred silence   Essential both in liturgy, and in love.

Song of Songs   A biblical book that celebrates the infinite playfulness of two lovers millennia before Dr. Alex Comfort wrote *The Joy of Sex.*

T

Tears, the gift of   To be welcomed. The church used to have a prayer for the gift of tears.

Tongues, the gift of   An important gift both in the sanctuary of the church and in the sanctuary of the bedroom. Not surprisingly, the Apostle Paul mentions the first only—he was writing to a church, after all.

U

Union and procreation   The church teaches "that each and every marriage act must remain open to the transmission of life. This teaching . . . is founded upon the inseparable connection, willed by God and which man [*sic!*] may not break on his own initiative, between the two-fold significance of the conjugal act: the unitive and the procreative significance."[16] As a woman, I find this descrip-

tion of the inseparability of the unitive and the procreative startling. In contradistinction to the male body, my female body can
perform this inseparability only once a month, during the few
hours of ovulation and actual fertility (between menarche and
menopause). For the remainder of the month, each union my body
enacts cannot but be nonprocreative. This simply is the way
women's bodies were created, from the beginning. If theological
and moral reflections began with women's bodies, then the coming
together of the unitive and the procreative would have to be considered the exception, not the rule, I think.

V

Vagina   Despite the success of the *Vagina Monologues*, there are medical professionals who offer to "resculpt" and "rejuvenate" a
woman's vagina with a one-hour laser procedure. Who needs
visions of purgatory in a world that offers that?

Victoria's Secret   Should be renamed Victor's Secret, since it seems to
respond to male fantasies more than to women's bodies and their
comfort. Not essential for love-making anyway.

Violence, sexual   A deadly sin. Seems to have penetrated deeply the
culture we inhabit, which thrives on precisely the combination of
sex and violence.

Virginity   Could be a powerful symbol of female autonomy, but is
now mostly connected with discussions of an intact or broken
hymen. Note: Hymen repair surgery is available nowadays, even if
at considerable cost.

W

Women's bodies   Capable of bearing fruit, as the result of love-
making in all its variety (cf. the Holy Spirit and the womb of the
Virgin).

Worship   1. The proper attitude of human beings toward the divine
presence. 2. Another name for liturgy. 3. What men used to
promise women in the wedding liturgy: "With my body I thee
worship."[17] Nice.

X

X 1. A symbol for Christ. 2. A rating for movies with sexually graphic content. 3. The sex chromosome that determines femaleness when paired with another X.

Note: The lives of women, the living of the gospel, and cultural constructions of femininity are linked, sometimes in quite startling ways (*for details, begin again with "A"*).

Y

Yes An essential word in love-making, especially for women when contemplating opening their bodies for another (*also see "no"*).

Yet . . . An appropriate response to hesitations or negations of love because of the risks involved. Love-making never comes with absolute guarantees, despite exuberant promises, including those of sacramental grace.

Z

Zebidah, Zeresh, Zeruah, Zeruiah, Zibiah, Zillah, Zilpah, Zipporah, Zosara Biblical women whose names begin with Z. Worth reading up on, late on a lazy Sunday afternoon, when all other desires have been fulfilled. Assumes that the children are still taken care of (*also see "fatigue"*).

Notes

Introduction

1. See, for example, the oral history project that seeks to record the faith journeys of Catholic women: Carole Garibaldi Rogers, "Remembering First Communion," *America* 190:16 (May 10, 2004): 18ff.

2. See Teresa Berger, *Women's Ways of Worship: Gender Analysis and Liturgical History* (Collegeville, Minn.: Liturgical Press, 1999), and "Women's Rites: Liturgical History in Fragments," in *The Oxford History of Christian Worship*, ed. Geoffrey Wainwright and Karen Westerfield Tucker (New York: Oxford University Press, forthcoming).

3. For more, see J. Cheryl Exum, *Fragmented Women: Feminist (Sub)versions of Biblical Narratives*, Journal for the Study of the Old Testament Supplement 163 (Sheffield: Sheffield Academic Press, 1993), esp. 12, 176–98.

4. I have learned much from Kathryn Tanner here; see especially her "Theology and Popular Culture," in *Changing Conversations: Religious Reflection & Cultural Analysis*, ed. Dwight N. Hopkins and Sheila Greeve Davaney (New York: Routledge, 1996), 101–20; "Social Theory Concerning the 'New Social Movements' and the Practice of Feminist Theology," in *Horizons in Feminist Theology: Identity, Tradition, and Norms*, ed. Rebecca S. Chopp and Sheila Greeve Davaney (Minneapolis: Fortress, 1997), 179–97; and her book *Theories of Culture: A New Agenda for Theology*, Guides to Theological Inquiry Series (Minneapolis: Fortress, 1997), esp. 128–38.

5. I argue this in more depth in "Prayers and Practices of Women: *Lex Orandi* Reconfigured," *Yearbook of the European Society of Women in Theological Research* 9 (2001): 63–77.

6. The story can be found in Jacques Dalarun, *Robert d'Arbrissel, fondateur de Fontevraud* (Paris: Albin Michel, 1986), 128–29.

7. This is the title of a beautiful song by Bernadette Farrell.

8. Siobhán Garrigan, "Worship in a Violent World: Deconstructing *Ordinary* Liturgies," *Reflections* 91:1 (Winter 2004): 23–31, here 24.

9. The expression is Kathleen Norris's; see her little volume *The Quotidian Mysteries: Laundry, Liturgy, and "Women's Work,"* 1998 Madeleva Lecture in Spirituality (New York: Paulist, 1998).

10. For an insightful map of the current cultural fascination with fragments, see David Tracy, "Fragments: The Spiritual Situation of our Times," in *God, the Gift, and Postmodernism*, ed. John D. Caputo and Michael J. Scanlon,

230 Fragments of Real Presence

Indiana Series in the Philosophy of Religion (Bloomington: Indiana University Press, 1999), 170–84.

11. Matthew is the only gospel writer who mentions this fact; see Matt. 14:20ff. (NRSV): "[T]hey took up what was left over of the broken pieces, twelve baskets full. And those who ate were about five thousand men, besides women and children."

12. It is quite unfortunate that these connections often are lost in translation.

13. For some of the rich exegetical debates around this key chapter in the Gospel of John, see *Critical Readings of John 6*, ed. R. Alan Culpepper, Biblical Interpretation Series 22 (New York: Brill, 1997).

14. Jane S. Webster, *Ingesting Jesus: Eating and Drinking in the Gospel of John*, Academia Biblica 6 (Atlanta: Society of Biblical Literature, 2003), 65.

15. See further Francis J. Moloney, *The Gospel of John*, Sacra Pagina 4 (Collegeville, Minn.: Liturgical Press, 1998), 197–201.

16. David Tracy, "Fragments and Forms: Universality and Particularity Today," in *The Church in Fragments: Towards What Kind of Unity?* ed. Giuseppe Ruggieri and Miklós Tomka, Concilium (Maryknoll, N.Y.: Orbis Books, 1997), 122–29, here 126: "[F]ragments are our best possession."

17. It is worth remembering here, at least in a footnote, Sr. Aemiliana Löhr and her 1934 book *Das Jahr des Herrn*. These meditations on the liturgical year by the most prolific woman author of the Liturgical Movement were translated into several languages (English: *The Year of Our Lord*) and went through repeated editions.

18. Florence S. Berger, *Cooking for Christ: The Liturgical Year in the Kitchen* (Des Moines: National Catholic Rural Life Conference, 1949), preface.

19. Published as "Liturgical Movement and Catholic Women," *Orate Fratres* 8 (1933/34): 564–68.

20. Elizabeth A. Johnson, *Friends of God and Prophets: A Feminist Theological Reading of the Communion of Saints* (New York: Continuum, 1998), 27.

21. As is easy to see, *Fragments of Real Presence* compresses more than simply one liturgical year into its own cycle. Thus, readings from different annual lectionary cycles are included, as well as reflections on events that span more than twelve months.

22. *Fragments of Real Presence* obviously is marked by my own particular subject position. I belong to an ecclesial communion, the Catholic Church, which leaves comparatively little room for women officially to "authorize" liturgy. I am also a scholar of liturgy, committed not only to living but also to interpreting and shaping liturgical tradition. This book has its origins in this rich and conflictual reality. My official liturgical subject-position as a woman in the pew does not divest me of the power to make meaning of liturgy in the crucible of lived life. Moreover, my subject-position is also one of privilege, by virtue of my scholarly work and because of the openness and

richness of my local faith community. As a result of these privileges, I do shape liturgy, sometimes even on the official side.

23. Scholars such as Catherine Bell, Ronald Grimes, Lawrence Hoffman, Graham Hughes, Richard McCarron, Bridget Nichols, and Martin Stringer have stressed this from a number of different angles.

24. Martin Stringer, "Text, Context and Performance: Hermeneutics and the Study of Worship," *Scottish Journal of Theology* 53 (2000): 365–79, here 378.

25. Obviously, I here assign theological meaning to the lived (liturgical) lives of women. Such privileging of the liturgical meaning-making of women is one way of rendering women more central in accounts of "church"—as well as of rendering visible the ever-present power differentials in the life of the church and its liturgy, which continue to mark women's lives so profoundly.

26. Dietrich Bonhoeffer, *Letters and Papers from Prison,* ed. Eberhard Bethge, enlarged ed. (New York: Macmillan, 1972), 215.

27. Ibid., 215. For the German original, see the critical edition *Widerstand und Ergebung: Briefe und Aufzeichnungen aus der Haft,* ed. Christian Gremmels et al., Dietrich Bonhoeffer Werke 8 (Gütersloh: Kaiser/Gütersloher Verlagshaus, 1998), 330ff.

28. Ibid., 219.

29. Caroline Walker Bynum, "In Praise of Fragments: History in the Comic Mode," in *Fragmentation and Redemption: Essays on Gender and the Human Body in Medieval Religion,* 3rd ed. (New York: Zone Books, 1994), 11–26, here 14.

30. I am indebted to Grace M. Jantzen here; see her *Becoming Divine: Towards a Feminist Philosophy of Religion* (Bloomington: Indiana University Press, 1999).

31. See Carol Meyers, "Having Their Space and Eating There Too: Bread Production and Female Power in Ancient Israelite Households," *Nashim: A Journal of Jewish Women's Studies and Gender Issues* 5 (2002): 14–44.

Saint Mary of Magdala (July 22)

1. Luke 8:1–3 (Mary of Magdala is healed by Jesus); Mark 15:40ff./Matt 27:55ff./John 19:25 (Mary of Magdala stands with other women near the cross); Mark 15:47/Matt 27:61 (Mary of Magdala is there at the burial of Jesus); Mark 16:1–8/Matt 28:1–8/Luke 24:1–10/John 20:1f., 11–13 (Mary of Magdala and two other women see the empty tomb on Easter morning); Matt 28:9/John 20:14–18 (the risen Christ charges Mary of Magdala with proclaiming the resurrection); Mark 16:9 (the risen Christ appeared first to Mary of Magdala).

2. For more on the Johannine Mary of Magdala, see Susanne Ruschmann, *Maria von Magdala im Johannesevangelium: Jüngerin—Zeugin—*

Lebensbotin, Neutestamentliche Abhandlungen n.F. 40 (Münster: Aschendorff, 2002).

3. See John Paul II, *Mulieris Dignitatem,* 16, n. 38, for references.

4. See further Karen L. King, *The Gospel of Mary of Magdala: Jesus and the First Woman Apostle* (Santa Rosa, Calif.: Polebridge, 2003).

5. For more on these divergent narratives—and the divergent claims to apostolic authority that undergird them—see Ann Graham Brock, *Mary Magdalene, The First Apostle: The Struggle for Authority,* Harvard Theological Studies 51 (Cambridge, Mass.: Harvard University Press, 2003).

6. The apt expression is Katherine Ludwig Jansen's. See her "Maria Magdalena: *Apostolorum Apostola,*" in *Women Preachers and Prophets through Two Millennia of Christianity,* ed. Beverly Mayne Kienzle and Pamela J. Walker (Berkeley: University of California Press, 1998), 57–96, here 58, 66.

7. Harriet Beecher Stowe, *Woman in Sacred History* (New York: Fords, Howard, and Hulbert, 1873; reprint, New York: Dilithium Press, 1990), 207.

8. See the study of Katherine Ludwig Jansen, *The Making of the Magdalen: Preaching and Popular Devotion in the Later Middle Ages* (Princeton, N.J.: Princeton University Press, 2000).

9. See Jansen, *Making of the Magdalen.*

10. This iconographic theme is rare in Western art until the twelfth century, but does figure in Byzantine cycles of gospel illustration. See *The St. Albans Psalter,* Studies of the Warburg Institute 25 (Leiden: E. J. Brill, 1960), 62. The image can be seen at http://www.abdn.ac.uk/stalbanspsalter/english/commentary/page051.shtml.

11. I do think there is much to learn from *The Da Vinci Code,* but not about Mary Magdalene and early Christian history. The historical "facts" of the novel in any case hardly are the primary reason for seven million people's fascination with the *Code.* A sudden widespread cultural interest in the details of the history of Christian origins would need a miracle larger that Dan Brown can work on his computer. I think the power of Brown's book lies elsewhere. Truly "breaking the Code" will necessitate deciphering the cultural context that has produced it and has welcomed it with such surprising force. In other words, it's about the culture. One trend that is feeding the popularity of the *Code* is a rise of a diffuse spirituality often coded as soft and feminine. Brown's way of reading "divinity" and "femininity" together—by according semidivine status to Mary Magdalene, among other things—feeds into this cultural trend. The other side of Brown's coin, namely, humanizing Jesus of Nazareth, not least of all by forcing him to have sex with Mary Magdalene, is fueling a lot of the evangelical attacks on the book. A Christian response able to go beyond self-defense may want to ask why Christianity has identified divinity and masculinity so closely, especially in the popular imagination and against some of its own best traditions? Second, when questions are raised about the "facts" in the *Code,* the assumption seems to be that the answer will be either true or false. The question itself, however, is misleading.

Brown's novel appeared at a time when there is significant divergence in scholarly reconstructions of Christian origins, particularly the position of women in the early Christian movement. Such divergence is written into the New Testament itself, as becomes evident as soon as one asks who the person was to whom the risen Christ appeared first. While there clearly are areas where Dan Brown is off the chart in his historical reconstruction, there are also some areas where different scholars might give differing readings of the evidence.

12. See http://www.amnestyusa.org/stopviolence/factsheets/sexual violence.html.

13. In the liturgy, Mary Magdalene was the only other woman, besides the Virgin Mary, on whose feast day the creed was recited. See Jansen, "Maria Magdalena," 75.

Sunday in Ordinary Time

1. The text is the appointed reading for the Fourteenth Sunday in Ordinary Time in Cycle C. The text is quoted here from the *Revised New American Bible* used in the *Workbook for Lectors and Gospel Readers* (Chicago: Liturgy Training Publications, 2000), 216.

2. Susan E. Myers, *Workbook for Lectors and Gospel Readers* (Chicago: Liturgy Training Publications, 2000), 216ff.

Sunday in Extra-Ordinary Time

1. Bernadette J. Brooten, "Junia," in *Women in Scripture: A Dictionary of Named and Unnamed Women in the Hebrew Bible, the Apocryphal/Deuterocanonical Books, and the New Testament,* ed. Carol Meyers, Toni Craven, and Ross Shepard Kraemer (Boston: Houghton Mifflin, 2000), 107.

2. I am indebted to my colleague Richard B. Hays for pointing this out to me. See also Robert M. Price, *The Widow Traditions in Luke-Acts: A Feminist-Critical Scrutiny,* SBL Dissertation Series 155 (Atlanta: Scholars Press, 1997), ch. 9: "Justice Blind and Black-Eyed: The Persistent Widow," 191–201.

3. For detailed analyses, see Regina A. Boisclair, "Amnesia in the Catholic Sunday Lectionary: Women—Silenced from the Memories of Salvation History," in *Women and Theology,* ed. Mary Ann Hinsdale and Phyllis H. Kaminski, College Theology Society 40 (Maryknoll, N.Y.: Orbis Books, 1995), 109–35; Marjorie Procter-Smith, "Images of Women in the Lectionary," in *The Power of Naming: A Concilium Reader in Feminist Liberation Theology,* ed. Elisabeth Schüssler Fiorenza (Maryknoll, N.Y.: Orbis Books, 1996), 175–86; Ruth Fox, "Women in the Bible and the Lectionary," in *Remembering the Women: Women's Stories from the Scripture for Sundays and Festivals,* comp. and annot. J. Frank Henderson (Chicago: Liturgy Training Publica-

tions, 1999), 359–67; Elizabeth J. Smith, *Bearing Fruit in Due Season: Feminist Hermeneutics and the Bible in Worship* (Collegeville, Minn.: Liturgical Press, 1999), 75–99.

4. I am using the table of readings from *Sundays, Solemnities, Feasts of the Lord and the Saints*, vol. 1 of *Lectionary for Mass for Use in the Dioceses of the United States of America, Second Typical Edition* (Collegeville, Minn.: Liturgical Press, 1998).

5. Biblical quotations in this text are from the NRSV, unless indicated otherwise.

6. Claudia V. Camp, "Hulda," in *Women in Scripture*, ed. Meyers et al., 96.

7. See Toni Craven, "Judith," in *Women in Scripture*, ed. Meyers et al., 105.

8. For a more detailed account of this, see Gale A. Yee, *Poor Banished Children of Eve: Woman as Evil in the Hebrew Bible* (Minneapolis: Fortress Press, 2003), 111–34.

9. For what follows I am indebted to Patrick D. Miller, "Things Too Wonderful: Prayers of Women in the Old Testament," in *Biblische Theologie und gesellschaftlicher Wandel: Für Norbert Lohfink SJ*, ed. Georg Braulik et al. (Freiburg: Herder, 1993), 237–51.

10. Toni Craven, "'From Where Will My Help Come?' Women and Prayer in the Apocryphal/Deuterocanonical Books," in *Worship and the Hebrew Bible: Essays in Honour of John T. Willis*, ed. M. Patrick Graham, Rick R. Marrs, and Steven L. McKenzie, Journal for the Study of the Old Testament Supplement 284 (Sheffield: Sheffield Academic Press, 1999), 95–109, here 99.

11. Ibid., 98.

12. Quoted in Janet R. Walton, *Feminist Liturgy: A Matter of Justice*, American Essays in Liturgy (Collegeville, Minn.: Liturgical Press, 2000), 50–51.

13. Miriam Therese Winter, "Anna's Psalm," in *WomanWord: A Feminist Lectionary and Psalter, Women of the New Testament* (New York: Crossroad, 1991), 43. Copyright © 1990. Used with permission of the Medical Mission Sisters.

Summer Days

1. The words are an adaptation of the famous claim attributed to Chief Seattle: Every part of the earth is sacred to my God. Feminist theologians such as Rosemary Radford Ruether, Sallie McFague, and Ivone Gebara not only have shown the links between the denigration of nature and the denigration of women but also have developed ecofeminist challenges to these links.

2. "Amnesty International launches global campaign to stop violence

against women," March 5, 2004, at http://news.amnesty.org/Index/ENGACT770212004.

3. Amnesty International's Web site has a "facts and figures" section: http://web.amnesty.org/library/Index/ENGACT770342004?open&of=ENG-373. One general source of information on women's lives is worth mentioning here: *The State of Women in the World Atlas*, ed. Joni Seager, Penguin Reference, new rev. 2nd ed. (New York: Penguin Books, 1997).

4. See Douglas A. Hicks, "Gender, Discrimination, and Capability: Insights from Amartya Sen," *Journal of Religious Ethics* 30 (2002): 137–54.

5. Elisabeth Schüssler Fiorenza, "Introduction," in *Violence Against Women*, ed. Elisabeth Schüssler Fiorenza and M. Shawn Copeland, Concilium (Maryknoll, N.Y.: Orbis Books, 1994) vii–xxiv, here x.

6. As reported in *The Economist*, May 24, 2003.

7. Matthew 15:21–28 is the appointed Gospel for the Twentieth Sunday in Ordinary Time in Cycle A. The text is quoted here from the *Revised New American Bible* used in the *Workbook for Lectors and Gospel Readers* (Chicago: Liturgy Training Publications, 2001), 224. I follow the Revised NAB text here, except for the fact that I have chosen to render the Greek term *theleis*, usually translated in this pericope with "as you wish" with the stronger "as you desire." The range of meanings associated with the Greek word clearly supports this translation. In fact, "as you desire" seems to me more faithful to the meaning of *theleis* in Matthew 15:21–28 than "wish." Cf. *A Greek-English Lexicon of the New Testament and Other Early Christian Literature*, rev. and ed. Frederick William Danker, based on Walter Bauer (3rd ed.; Chicago: University of Chicago Press, 2000), 447ff.

8. The Gospel of Mark identifies the woman as a Syrophoenician.

9. For more on the cultural meaning of demon possession and how this plays out in the case of this girl, see Elaine M. Wainwright, "Not Without My Daughter: Gender and Demon Possession in Matthew 15:21–28," in *A Feminist Companion to Matthew*, ed. Amy-Jill Levine with Marianne Blickenstaff, Feminist Companion to the New Testament and Early Christian Writings 1 (Sheffield: Sheffield Academic Press, 2001), 126–37.

10. Contrary to the story as told in Mark, there is no clear indication in Matt that the girl was absent.

11. I learned much about this pericope from Elaine M. Wainwright, *Shall We Look for Another? A Feminist Reading of the Matthean Jesus*, Bible & Liberation Series (Maryknoll, N.Y.: Orbis Books, 1998), esp. 86–92.

12. Elisabeth Schüssler Fiorenza, *But She Said: Feminist Practices of Biblical Interpretation* (Boston: Beacon Press, 1992), 103.

13. So the Jewish-Christian *Pseudo-Clementine Homilies*, thought to have been composed in the third and fourth centuries; see Schüssler Fiorenza, *But She Said*, 100.

14. The Matthean story differs from the story as told by Mark 7:24–30.

Saint Clare of Assisi (August 11)

An earlier version of this essay appeared in the *Journal of Feminist Studies in Religion* 18 (2002): 53–69. Copyright © The Journal of Feminist Studies in Religion, 2002. Used with permission.

1. The works of Franciscan scholars Margaret Carney, Chiara Augusta Lainati, Ingrid Peterson, and Anton Rotzetter are of special importance here.

2. See Catherine M. Mooney, "*Imitatio Christi* or *Imitatio Mariae*? Clare of Assisi and Her Interpreters," in *Gendered Voices: Medieval Saints and Their Interpreters*, ed. Catherine M. Mooney, Middle Ages Series (Philadelphia: University of Pennsylvania Press, 1999), 52–77, here 53.

3. See the 1972 film *Brother Sun, Sister Moon*, co-scripted by Lina Wertmüller and Franco Zeffirelli.

4. This is what Clare's mother, Ortulana, heard as she prayed during her pregnancy, fearful of the dangers of childbirth. Clare's name reflects this divine promise of radiance for the child. See the *Acts of the Process of Canonization*, Third Witness, 28. All references to writings of Clare or early writings about Clare are taken from *Clare of Assisi: Early Documents*, ed. and trans. Regis J. Armstrong (Mahwah, N.J.: Paulist Press, 1988), here 144.

5. I am grateful to Paula Robinson at the library of Duke's Fuqua School of Business for helping me enter the business side of the world of Clairol.

6. Thus the comments on the back cover of Gerard Thomas Straub's *The Sun & Moon over Assisi: A Personal Encounter with Francis & Clare* (Cincinnati, Oh.: St. Anthony Messenger Press, 2000).

7. Mooney, "*Imitatio Christi*," 52.

8. See Marco Bartoli, *Clare of Assisi*, trans. Frances Teresa (Quincy, Ill.: Franciscan Press, 1993), 132, 226.

9. The wonderful study by Martina Kreidler-Kos, *Klara von Assisi: Schattenfrau und Lichtgestalt*, Tübinger Studien zur Theologie und Philosophie 17 (Tübingen: A. Francke Verlag, 2000), has profoundly shaped my own rethinking of Clare.

10. *Bull of Canonization*, 4, in *Clare of Assisi: Early Documents*, 178 (my italics).

11. *Acts of the Process of Canonization*, First Witness, 8, in *Clare of Assisi: Early Documents*, 131.

12. This is how Caroline Walker Bynum reads these practices in her magisterial study *Holy Feast and Holy Fast: The Religious Significance of Food for Medieval Women* (Berkeley: University of California Press, 1986).

13. For more on this subject, see Caroline Walker Bynum, "Women Mystics and Eucharistic Devotion in the Thirteenth Century," in *Fragmentation and Redemption: Essays on Gender and the Human Body in Medieval Religion*, 3rd ed. (New York: Zone Books, 1994), 119–50.

14. *Fitness* 8 (January 1999).

15. This is well illustrated in Colleen McDannell, *Material Christianity:*

Religion and Popular Culture in America (New Haven: Yale University Press, 1995).

16. Regarding this section heading, recall the famous Clairol advertising campaign from the 1950s, with the slogan "Does she . . . or doesn't she?" *Life* magazine initially considered the slogan so suggestive that it refused to run the ad. In the end, however, the ads ran for eighteen years, in which sales of Clairol more than quadrupled. See Angela Woodward, "Clairol," in *Encyclopedia of Consumer Brands*, vol. 2, *Personal Products*, ed. Janice Jorgensen (Detroit: St. James Press, 1994), 127–29, here 128.

17. *Bull of Canonization*, 13, in *Clare of Assisi: Early Documents*, 181.

18. Clare of Assisi, "Fourth Letter to Blessed Agnes of Prague," 9, in *Clare of Assisi: Early Documents*, 48.

19. "Blessing," 14, in *Clare of Assisi: Early Documents*, 79.

20. Clare of Assisi, "Fourth Letter to Blessed Agnes of Prague," 1, in *Clare of Assisi: Early Documents*, 47. A scholarly edition of Clare's letters to Agnes is now available: Joan Mueller, *Clare's Letters to Agnes: Texts and Sources* (St. Bonaventure, N.Y.: Franciscan Institute, 2001).

21. Clare of Assisi, "Fourth Letter to Blessed Agnes of Prague," 35, in *Clare of Assisi: Early Documents*, 50.

22. Clare of Assisi, "Fourth Letter to Blessed Agnes of Prague," 27–32, in *Clare of Assisi: Early Documents*, 49ff.

23. Clare of Assisi, "First Letter to Blessed Agnes of Prague," 10, in *Clare of Assisi: Early Documents*, 35.

24. Clare of Assisi, "Rule," 24, in *Clare of Assisi: Early Documents*, 64.

25. Similar issues are raised by Wendy M. Wright, "Reading Clare of Assisi in a Dodge Mini Van at the Curbside on a Grade School Soccer Carpool Route," in *Clare of Assisi: A Medieval and Modern Woman*, ed. Ingrid Peterson, Clare Centenary Series 7 (St. Bonaventure, N.Y.: Franciscan Institute, 1996), 219–38.

26. See the wonderful title of Kathleen Norris's book: *Quotidian Mysteries: Laundry, Liturgy, and "Women's Work"* (New York: Paulist Press, 1998).

27. Margaret Carney, *The First Franciscan Woman: Clare of Assisi & Her Form of Life* (Quincy, Ill.: Franciscan Press, 1993), 18. For more on a feminist reading of the communion of saints, see Elizabeth A. Johnson, *Friends of God and Prophets: A Feminist Theological Reading of the Communion of Saints* (New York: Continuum, 1998).

28. *Legend of Saint Clare*, 14, in *Clare of Assisi: Early Documents*, 203.

29. *Legend of Saint Clare*, 38, in *Clare of Assisi: Early Documents*, 224.

30. Caroline Walker Bynum, "In Praise of Fragments: History in the Comic Mode," in *Fragmentation and Redemption: Essays on Gender and the Human Body in Medieval Religion*, 3rd ed. (New York: Zone Books, 1994), 11–26, here 18–19.

31. Quoted in *Working Mother* 24:7 (July/August 2001): 42.

The Nativity of Mary (September 8)

1. Carolingian liturgists assigned this gospel text for the feast in the eighth and early ninth centuries, thus transforming the meaning of the feast as they had received it from Rome. See Margot Fassler, "Mary's Nativity, Fulbert of Chartres, and the *Stirps Jesse:* Liturgical Innovation circa 1000 and Its Afterlife," *Speculum* 75 (2000): 389–434.

2. The biblical translation used throughout is the NRSV.

3. *The Infancy Gospels of James and Thomas*, ed. Ronald F. Hook, Scholars Bible 2 (Santa Rosa, Calif.: Polebridge Press, 1995), 43.

4. Ibid., 27.

5. Ikos on September 8, Anthologion I, 626. Quoted in "Anna," *Marienlexikon* I, ed. Remigius Bäumer and Leo Scheffcyzk (St. Ottilien: EOS Verlag, 1988), 156.

A Day in Extra-Ordinary Time

1. This is part of a reflection entitled "Rich Woman, Poor Woman" written by a working-class Chilean woman in 1973 shortly after Chile's elected socialist president Salvador Allende was overthrown in a bloody military coup. A U.S. missionary translated the work and brought it with her when she was forced to leave Chile. Source: Coordinating Center for Women, New York, N.Y.

2. "Beth's Psalm," in *Facing the Abusing God: A Theology of Protest*, ed. David R. Blumenthal (Louisville, Ky.: Westminster John Knox Press, 1993), 227–32, here 230.

3. E-mail message to the author from the International Center of Bethlehem, October 2001.

4. David Tracy, "Saving from Evil: Salvation and Evil Today," in *The Fascination of Evil*, ed. Hermann Häring and David Tracy, Concilium (Maryknoll, N.Y.: Orbis Books, 1998), 107–16, here 114.

5. Choan-Seng Song, *Third-Eye Theology: Theology in Formation in Asian Settings*, rev. ed. (Maryknoll, N.Y.: Orbis Books, 1991), 119.

6. Karl Rahner (*Encounters with Silence*, 5th ed. [Westminster, Md.: Newman Press, 1965], 23) meditates on the "eloquent sounds" of God's silence. See also Barbara Brown Taylor, *When God Is Silent* (Cambridge, Mass.: Cowley Publications, 1998), 43–82.

7. Dietrich Bonhoeffer, *Letters and Papers from Prison*, ed. Eberhard Bethge, enlarged ed. (New York: Macmillan, 1972), 219.

8. Quoted in *Holy Name Province: 100th Anniversary* (Paterson, N.J.: St. Anthony's Guild, 2001) n.p.

9. I learned about the custom of Lithuanian women to sew a birth-shirt, and about Jewish women's ritual practices of guarding the birthing mother against the "child eater" from *Women, Ritual and Liturgy*, ed. Susan K. Roll et al., *Yearbook of the European Society of Women in Theological Research* 9 (Leuven: Peeters, 2001).

10. See Kathleen D. Billman's use of this story from Exodus as an image of pastoral ministry, in "Pastoral Care as an Art of Community," in *The Arts of Ministry: Feminist-Womanist Approaches*, ed. Christie Cozad Neuger (Louisville, Ky.: Westminster John Knox Press, 1996), 10–38, esp. 21–25.

11. See Denise Ackermann, "Engaging Freedom: A Contextual Feminist Theology of Praxis," *Journal of Theology for Southern Africa* 94 (1996): 33–49, esp. 46–47.

Hildegard of Bingen (September 17)

1. Superlatives about Hildegard abound; the one quoted here is from Peter Dronke, "Hildegard's Inventions: Aspects of her Language and Imagery," in *Hildegard von Bingen in ihrem historischen Umfeld*, ed. Alfred Haverkamp (Mainz: Verlag Philipp von Zabern, 2000), 299–320, here 299.

2. Barbara Newman, "'Sybil of the Rhine': Hildegard's Life and Times," in *Voice of the Living Light: Hildegard of Bingen and Her World*, ed. Barbara Newman (Berkeley: University of California Press, 1998), 1–29, here 1. © 1998 The Regents of the University of California. Used with permission.

3. The centrality of the term *viriditas* for Hildegard has been duly noted in scholarship; see, e.g., Gabriele Lautenschläger, "*Viriditas:* Ein Begriff und seine Bedeutung," in *Hildegard von Bingen: Prophetin durch die Zeiten*, ed. Edeltraud Forster et al. (Freiburg i.B.: Herder, 1997), 224–37.

4. Hildegard of Bingen, *Scivias*, trans. Mother Columba Hart and Jane Bishop, Classics of Western Spirituality (New York: Paulist Press, 1990), 59ff. Copyright © 1990 by Abbey of Regina Laudis, Bethlehem, Connecticut. Used with permission.

5. See *The Life of Hildegard*, book II, ch. 2, in *Jutta and Hildegard: The Biographical Sources*, ed. Anna Silvas, Brepols Medieval Women Series (University Park: Pennsylvania State University Press, 1999), 158.

6. I owe a profound depth of gratitude to Lorna Collingridge for nurturing my scholarly interest in Hildegard and in her liturgical compositions.

Lorna's dissertation "Music as Evocative Power: The Intersection of Music with Images of the Divine in the Songs of Hildegard of Bingen" (Ph.D. thesis, Griffith University, 2004) is accessible on the Australian Digital Theses Program Web site: http://www4.gu.edu.au:8080/adt-root/public/adt-QGU2004 0624.110229/index.html.

7. For more, see Barbara Newman, "Three-Part Invention: The *Vita S. Hildegardis* and Mystical Hagiography," in *Hildegard of Bingen: The Context of Her Thought and Art,* ed. Charles Burnett and Peter Dronke, Warburg Institute Colloquia 4 (London: Warburg Institute, 1989), 189–210; and "Seherin—Prophetin—Mystikerin: Hildegard von Bingen in der hagiographischen Tradition," in *Hildegard von Bingen: Prophetin durch die Zeiten,* 126–52. English translation: "Hildegard and her Female Hagiographers: The Remaking of Female Sainthood," in *Gendered Voices: Medieval Saints and Their Interpreters,* ed. Catherine M. Mooney, Middle Ages Series (Philadelphia: University of Pennsylvania Press, 1999), 16–34.

8. For the English text, see "Eight Readings To Be Read on the Feast of St. Hildegard," in *Jutta and Hildegard: The Biographical Sources,* 211–19.

9. For a detailed account of this unsuccessful process of canonization, see Georg May, "Der Kanonisationsprozeß Hildegards im 13. Jahrhundert, " in *900 Jahre Hildegard von Bingen: Neuere Untersuchungen und literarische Nachweise,* ed. Wolfgang Podehl, Verzeichnisse und Schriften der Hessischen Landesbibliothek Wiesbaden 12 (Wiesbaden: Hessische Landesbibliothek, 1998), 27–43.

10. For what follows, I am indebted to German scholars who have treated the subject of the veneration of Hildegard, especially Helmut Hinkel, "St. Hildegards Verehrung im Bistum Mainz," in *Hildegard von Bingen 1179-1979,* ed. Anton Ph. Brück, Quellen und Abhandlungen zur mittelrheinischen Kirchengeschichte 33 (Mainz: Selbstverlag der Gesellschaft für Mittelrheinische Kirchengeschichte, 1979), 385–411; idem, "Hildegard von Bingen: Nachleben," in *Hildegard von Bingen 1098-1179,* ed. Hans-Jürgen Kotzur (Mainz: Verlag Philipp von Zabern, 1998), 148ff.; Josef Krasenbrink, "Die 'inoffizielle Heilige': Zur Verehrung Hildegards diesseits und jenseits des Rheins," in *Hildegard von Bingen: Prophetin durch die Zeiten,* 496–510.

11. See Hinkel, "Hildegard von Bingen," 149. For a history of the relics of Hildegard, see Adelheid Simon, "Die Reliquien der Heiligen Hildegard und ihre Geschichte," in *Hildegard von Bingen 1179-1979,* 371–83; Werner Lauter, "Hildegard von Bingen—Reliquien und Reliquiare: Versuch eines Überblicks," in *Im Angesicht Gottes suche der Mensch sich selbst,* ed. Rainer Berndt, Erudiri Sapientia: Studien zum Mittelalter und seiner Rezeptionsgeschichte 2 (Berlin: Akademie Verlag, 2001), 503–43.

12. For this and what follows, see the fascinating essay by Hans-Joachim Schmidt, "Geschichte und Prophetie: Rezeption der Texte Hildegards von Bingen im 13. Jahrhundert," in *Hildegard von Bingen in ihrem historischen Umfeld,* 489–517.

13. See Schmidt, "Geschichte und Prophetie," 495ff.

14. For the reception of Hildegard in late medieval England, see Kathryn Kerby-Fulton, "Hildegard and the Male Reader: A Study in Insular Reception," in *Prophets Abroad: The Reception of Continental Holy Women in Late-Medieval England,* ed. Rosalynn Voaden (Cambridge: D. S. Brewer, 1996), 1–18.

15. Information on the Web site of the Abbey of Saint Hildegard: http://www.abtei-st-hildegard.de/english/hildegard/momentum.htm.

16. These are available, for example, in Adelgundis Führkötter's edition of the Latin text of *Hildegardis Scivias* in the series Corpus Christianorum: Continuatio Mediaevalis 43–43A (Turnholt: Brepols, 1978).

17. Available from BridgeBuilding Images at www.BridgeBuilding .com.

18. This song first appeared in an earlier form on the CD *Walking in the Wilderness* by Seeds of Wild Honey (privately published by Lorna Collingridge and Adele Neal, Australia, 1995). The text has been changed, although the melody remains the same. Used with permission. For more information and full settings of all music by Lorna Collingridge, see her Web site at www.lornacollingridge.net.

19. Hildegard of Bingen, Letter to the Monk Guibert [no. 103r], in *The Letters of Hildegard of Bingen,* vol. 2, ed. and trans. Joseph L. Baird and Radd K. Ehrman (New York: Oxford University Press, 1998), 23. Copyright © 1998 by Oxford University Press, Inc. Used with permission.

20. The antiphon is sung, and the verses are said while the accompanist improvises. The psalm is Psalm 18:2–7, 47–51, in the ICEL translation: *The Psalter: A faithful and inclusive rendering from the Hebrew into contemporary English poetry, intended primarily for communal song and recitation* (Chicago: Liturgy Training Publications, 1995).

21. See Hildegard, Letter to Abbot Bernard of Clairvaux [no. 1], in *The Letters of Hildegard of Bingen,* vol. 1, trans. Joseph L. Baird and Radd K. Ehrman (New York: Oxford University Press, 1994), 28.

22. Hildegard of Bingen, *The Book of the Rewards of Life,* trans. Bruce W. Hozeski, Garland Library of Medieval Literature 89 Series B (New York: Garland, 1994), 136. Copyright © 1994 by Bruce W. Hozeski. Used with permission.

23. Hildegard of Bingen, *Scivias,* trans. Mother Columba Hart and Jane Bishop, Classics of Western Spirituality (New York: Paulist Press, 1990), 336. Copyright © 1990 by Abbey of Regina Laudis, Bethlehem, Connecticut. Used with permission. [I have chosen to render Hildegard's Latin *homo* as "human beings."]

24. The Latin text for "*Caritas Habundat*" is taken from *Symphonia: A Critical Edition of the Symphonia Armonie Celestium Revelationum of Hildegard of Bingen,* ed. Barbara Newman, 2nd ed. (Ithaca: Cornell University Press, 1998), 140, except that Newman's spelling "karitas" is amended to the more familiar "caritas." The English translation is by Lorna Collingridge,

with assistance from Dr. Drina Oldroyd. The music of *"Caritas Habundat"* was transcribed by Catherine Jeffreys from the Dendermonde, St.-Pieters & Paulusabdij Codex 9, fol. 157r, and is used with permission. Jeffreys's version includes three additional notes at the end of the chant, which she adapted from the later *"Riesenkodex."* Lorna Collingridge has omitted these last three notes here, suggesting that the unfinished ending might, in fact, have been intended by Hildegard. The contemporary "Divine Love" was written by Lorna Collingridge, using both the visionary words and some melodic ideas from Hildegard's chant.

25. *The Life of the Holy Hildegard by the Monks Gottfried and Theoderic,* book III, ch. 27, trans. Adelgundis Führkötter, and James McGrath (Collegeville, Minn.: Liturgical Press, 1995), 99ff. Copyright © 1995 by The Order of St. Benedict, Inc. Used with permission of The Liturgical Press, Collegeville, Minn.

26. Hildegard, Letter to the Prioress [no. 140r], in *The Letters of Hildegard of Bingen,* vol. 2, 80.

Saint Teresa of Ávila (October 15)

1. How some women of Teresa's time used patronage to influence religious life can be seen in Jodi Bilinkoff, *The Ávila of Saint Teresa: Religious Reform in a Sixteenth-Century City* (Ithaca, N.Y.: Cornell University Press, 1989), 35–52.

2. See Ronald E. Surtz, *Writing Women in Late Medieval and Early Modern Spain: The Mothers of Saint Teresa of Ávila,* Middle Ages Series (Philadelphia: University of Pennsylvania Press, 1995).

3. See further Gillian T. W. Ahlgren, *Teresa of Ávila and the Politics of Sanctity* (Ithaca, N.Y.: Cornell University Press, 1996).

4. All quotations are from *The Collected Works of St. Teresa of Ávila,* trans. Kieran Kavanaugh and Otilio Rodriguez, 3 vols. (Washington, D.C.: Institute of Carmelite Studies, 1976–85).

5. For more on Teresa's rhetorical strategies, see Alison Weber, *Teresa of Ávila and the Rhetoric of Femininity* (Princeton, N.J.: Princeton University Press, 1990).

Blessed Mother Teresa (October 19)

1. Virginia Burrus is right to insist that the lives of the saints can (and should) be read as sites of an "exuberant eroticism"; see *The Sex Lives of the Saints: An Erotics of Ancient Hagiography* (Philadelphia: University of Pennsylvania Press, 2004), 1.

2. Cf. Michael D. Whalen, "In the Company of Women? The Politics of Memory in the Liturgical Commemoration of Saints—Male and Female," *Worship* 73 (1999): 482–504.

3. This holds true even if one acknowledges that virginity, like all other gendered identities, is constructed and therefore ever changing. "[T]he concept of virginity encompassed a range of meanings well beyond the simple inviolate female body, the sealed vessel" (Samantha J. E. Riches, "St. George as a Male Virgin Martyr," in *Gender and Holiness: Men, Women, and Saints in Late Medieval Europe*, ed. Samantha J. E. Riches and Sarah Salih, Routledge Studies in Medieval Religion and Culture 1 [New York: Routledge, 2002], 65–85, here 68).

4. Address of John Paul II to the pilgrims who had come to Rome for the Beatification of Mother Teresa, http://www.vatican.va/holy_father/john_paul_ii/speeches/2003/october/documents/hf_jp-ii_spe_20031020_pilgrims-mother-teresa_en.html.

5. Homily of John Paul II, for the Beatification of Mother Teresa, http://www.vatican.va/holy_father/john_paul_ii/homilies/2003/documents/hf_jp-ii_hom_20031019_mother-theresa_en.html.

6. Address of John Paul II to the pilgrims who had come to Rome for the Beatification of Mother Teresa, http://www.vatican.va/holy_father/john_paul_ii/speeches/2003/october/documents/hf_jp-ii_spe_20031020_pilgrims-mother-teresa_en.html [emphasis mine].

7. See Eileen J. Stenzel, "Maria Goretti: Rape and the Politics of Sainthood," in *The Power of Naming: A Concilium Reader in Feminist Liberation Theology*, ed. Elisabeth Schüssler Fiorenza (Maryknoll, N.Y.: Orbis Books, 1996), 224–31.

8. See Beverly Mayne Kienzle and Nancy Nienhuis, "Battered Women and the Construction of Sanctity," *Journal of Feminist Studies in Religion* 17 (2001): 33–61.

9. See Catherine M. Mooney, "Voice, Gender, and the Portrayal of Sanctity," in *Gendered Voices: Medieval Saints and Their Interpreters*, ed. Catherine M. Mooney, Middle Ages Series (Philadelphia: University of Pennsylvania Press, 1999), 1–15, here 7.

10. See Robert A. Orsi, *Thank You, St. Jude: Women's Devotion to the Patron Saint of Hopeless Causes* (New Haven: Yale University Press, 1996).

11. Donald Weinstein and Rudolph M. Bell, *Saints and Society: The Two Worlds of Western Christendom, 1000–1700* (Chicago: University of Chicago Press, 1982), 220 [emphasis mine].

12. Elizabeth Stuart, *Spitting at Dragons: Towards a Feminist Theology of Sainthood* (New York: Mowbray, 1996); Elizabeth A. Johnson, *Friends of God and Prophets: A Feminist Theological Reading of the Communion of Saints* (New York: Continuum, 1998).

13. Caroline Walker Bynum, *Holy Feast and Holy Fast: The Religious Sig-*

nificance of Food to Medieval Women (Berkeley: University of California Press, 1987), 193.

14. See further Caroline Walker Bynum, "Women Mystics and Eucharistic Devotion in the Thirteenth Century," in *Fragmentation and Redemption: Essays on Gender and the Human Body in Medieval Religion*, 3rd ed. (New York: Zone Books, 1994), 119–50.

15. See further Susan Ashbrook Harvey, "Women in Early Byzantine Hagiography: Reversing the Story," in *That Gentle Strength: Historical Perspectives on Women in Christianity*, ed. Lynda L. Coon, Katherine J. Haldane, and Elisabeth W. Sommer (Charlottesville: University Press of Virginia, 1990), 36–59, esp. 46ff.; Lynda L. Coon, *Sacred Fictions: Holy Women and Hagiography in Late Antiquity*, Middle Ages Series (Philadelphia: University of Pennsylvania Press, 1997), 71–94.

16. See Elizabeth Robertson, "The Corporeality of Female Sanctity in the Life of Saint Margaret," in *Images of Sainthood in Medieval Europe*, ed. Renate Blumenfeld-Kosinski and Timea Szell (Ithaca, N.Y.: Cornell University Press, 1991), 268–87, here 269ff.

17. See Mooney, "Voice, Gender, and the Portrayal of Sanctity," 12–13; and Robertson, "The Corporeality of Female Sanctity in the Life of Saint Margaret," 268–87.

18. See, e.g., Carolyn Muessig, "Paradigms of Sanctity for Thirteenth-Century Women," in *Models of Holiness in Medieval Sermons: Proceedings of the International Symposium* (Kalamazoo, 4–7 May 1995), ed. Beverly Mayne Kienzle et al., Textes et études du Moyen Age 5 (Louvain-la-Neuve: Fédération internationale des instituts d'études médiévales, 1996), 85–102.

19. Thus at least Mooney, "Voice, Gender, and the Portrayal of Sanctity," 10–12.

20. Homily of John Paul II, for the Beatification of Mother Teresa, http://www.vatican.va/holy_father/john_paul_ii/homilies/2003/documents/hf_jp-ii_hom_20031019_mother-theresa_en.html.

21. Samantha J. E. Riches and Sarah Salih, introduction to *Gender and Holiness*, 5. The cover of the book puts it thus: "the pursuit of holiness can destabilize a binary conception of gender. Though saints may be classified as masculine or feminine, holiness may also cut across gender divisions and demand a break from normally gendered behavior."

22. Quoted by Cardinal José Saraiva Martins in his homily at the Thanksgiving Mass for the Beatification of Mother Teresa, October 20, 2003, http://www.vatican.va/roman_curia/congregations/csaints/documents/rc_con_csaints_doc_20031020_beat-mother-teresa_en.html.

23. Thomas Merton, *The Seven Storey Mountain* (New York: Harcourt, Brace and Co., 1948), 353.

24. Ibid.

25. Ibid.

26. Ibid., 355.

Our Lady of Guadalupe (December 12)

1. The term *Abya Yala* has emerged as a way of naming this hemisphere without the conceptualization of coloniality presupposed by such terms as "pre-Columbian cultures" or "the Americas." *Abya Yala* means "continent of life" and was apparently used by the Kuna peoples of Panama and Colombia to name this hemisphere.

2. For more on this encounter as perpetrating the greatest genocide in human history, see, e.g., Tzvetan Todorov, *The Conquest of America: The Question of the Other* (New York: Harper & Row, 1984), esp. 132–45.

3. See, e.g., the essays in *Goddess of the Americas: Writings on the Virgin of Guadalupe*, ed. Ana Castillo (New York: Riverhead Books, 1996).

4. I am indebted for the following to Richard Nebel, *Santa María Tonantzin, Virgen de Guadalupe: Religiöse Kontinuität und Transformation in Mexiko*, Neue Zeitschrift für Missionswissenschaft, Supplementa 40 (Immensee: Neue Zeitschrift für Missionswissenschaft, 1992).

5. Edwin E. Sylvest, Jr., *Nuestra Señora de Guadalupe: Mother of God, Mother of the Americas*, Bridwell Library Publications, New Series (Dallas, Tex.: Bridwell Library of Southern Methodist University, 1992), 9.

6. I am choosing to avoid the protracted question of historicity here; there are more important questions when it comes to devotion to *La Guadalupana* and the lives of women.

7. The italicized quotations, from the earliest written account of the appearance of the Virgin of Guadalupe, are taken from Virgil Elizondo's translation in *Guadalupe, Mother of the New Creation*, 5th ed. (Maryknoll, N.Y.: Orbis Books, 2001), 5–22, here 7. Copyright © 1997 by Virgil Elizondo. Used with permission.

December 17 to December 23

1. For background on the O-Antiphons, especially their many biblical allusions, see J. D. Crichton's little study *Preparing for Christmas* (Blackrock, Ireland: Columba Press, 1998).

2. I use the Latin text as it appears in the Divine Office, including the punctuation marks; see *Liturgia Horarum: Iuxta Ritum Romanum*, vol. 1 (Rome: Typis Polyglottis Vaticanis, 1977). I do not, however, give the marks added for emphasis in reading.

3. Leigh Eric Schmidt, *Consumer Rites: The Buying & Selling of American Holidays* (Princeton, N.J.: Princeton University Press, 1995), 6.

4. Ibid., 5.

5. The expression is Elizabeth H. Pleck's, *Celebrating the Family: Ethnicity, Consumer Culture, and Family Rituals* (Cambridge, Mass.: Harvard University Press, 2000), 44. Pleck identifies two discordant systems of meaning,

the sentimental and the postsentimental approaches to Christmas. I would argue that there are more than these two.

6. Schmidt, *Consumer Rites,* 191.

7. The information in this paragraph comes from Robert Verdisco, "Gender-specific Shopping," *Chain Store Age* 75:2 (1999): 26. My thanks to Paula Robinson from the Library of the Fuqua School of Business at Duke University for her generous help and advice.

8. "Corporate profile" from the company's Web site.

9. This is Gail Ramshaw's question; for her beautiful answer, see *A Metaphorical God: An Abecedary of Images for God* (Chicago: Liturgy Training Publications, 1995), 83–86.

10. Eve Kosofsky Sedgwick, *Tendencies,* Series Q (Durham, N.C.: Duke University Press, 1993), 8. Sedgwick describes the term "queer" in this way. One could argue that God becoming human is decidely queer and "identity-fracturing," even if along different lines from the ones theorized so ably by Kosofsky Sedgwick.

11. The expression is Dietrich Bonhoeffer's; see *Letters and Papers from Prison,* ed. Eberhard Bethge, enlarged ed. (New York: Macmillan, 1972), 282.

Fourth Sunday of Advent

1. Luke 1:39–45 is the appointed reading for the Fourth Sunday of Advent in Year C.

Christmas

1. See Christine E. Gudorf, "The Erosion of Sexual Dimorphism: Challenges to Religion and Religious Ethics," *Journal of the American Academy of Religion* 69 (2001): 863–91, here 874ff.

2. Thomas Aquinas speaks of a "natural resemblance" between sacramental signs and that which they signify. In its 1976 Declaration *Inter Insigniores,* the Congregation for the Doctrine of the Faith used Thomas's affirmation of a "natural resemblance" in order to substantiate its own claim that the priest has to be male, since otherwise "it would be difficult to see in the minister the image of Christ" (*Inter Insigniores,* in *The Order of Priesthood: Nine Commentaries on the Vatican Decree "Inter Insigniores"* [Huntington, Ind.: Our Sunday Visitor, 1978], 1–20, here 12).

3. Karl Rahner, *Schriften zur Theologie* 16 (Zurich: Benziger, 1984), 330–31 (translation mine).

4. See further Elizabeth A. Johnson, "Wisdom Was Made Flesh and Pitched Her Tent Among Us," in *Reconstructing the Christ Symbol: Essays in Feminist Christology,* ed. Maryanne Stevens (New York: Paulist Press, 1993), 95–117; Elisabeth Schüssler Fiorenza, *Jesus: Miriam's Child, Sophia's Prophet: Critical Issues in Feminist Christology* (New York: Continuum, 1994).

5. Eusebius, *The History of the Church from Christ to Constantine* (London: Penguin Books, 1989), 145.

6. Johannes Betz, "Die Eucharistie als Gottes Milch in frühchristlicher Sicht," *Zeitschrift für Katholische Theologie* 106 (1984): 1–26, 167–85, here 184 (translation mine).

7. Julian of Norwich, *Showings,* trans. Edmund Colledge and James Walsh (New York: Paulist Press, 1978), 298.

8. Anselm of Canterbury, "Prayer to St Paul," in *The Prayers and Meditations of St Anselm with the Proslogion,* trans. Sister Benedicta Ward, Penguin Classics (Harmondsworth: Penguin, 1973), 153ff. Copyright © Benedicta Ward, 1973. Reproduced by permission of Penguin Books Ltd., London.

9. See also Caroline Walker Bynum, "'. . . And Woman his Humanity': Female Imagery in the Religious Writing of the Later Middle Ages," in *Fragmentation and Redemption: Essays on Gender and the Human Body in Medieval Religion* (New York: Zone Books, 1992), 151–79, here 158.

10. *The Writings of Margaret of Oingt, Medieval Prioress and Mystic,* trans. with an introduction, essay, and notes by Renate Blumenfeld-Kosinski, Focus Library of Medieval Women (Newburyport, Mass.: Focus Information Group, 1990), 31. For the original Latin text, see *Les Oeuvres de Marguerite d'Oingt,* ed. and trans. Antonin Duraffour et al., Publications de l'Institut de Linguistique Romane de Lyon (Paris: Belles Lettres, 1965), 77–79.

11. Anselm of Canterbury, "Prayer to St Paul," 155.

12. Julian of Norwich, *Showings,* 295.

13. Quoted in Elsie Anne McKee, "Katharina Schütz Zell and the 'Our Father,'" in *Oratio: Das Gebet in patristischer und reformatorischer Sicht,* ed. Emidio Campi et al., Forschungen zur Kirchen- und Dogmengeschichte 76 (Göttingen: Vandenhoeck & Ruprecht, 1999), 239–47, here 242f.

14. Teresa of Ávila, "Meditations on the Song of Songs" 4:4, in *The Collected Works of St. Teresa of Ávila,* vol. 2, trans. Kieran Kavanaugh and Otilio Rodriguez (Washington, D.C.: Institute of Carmelite Studies, 1980), 244ff.

15. See further Caroline Walker Bynum, "The Female Body and Religious Practice in the Later Middle Ages," in *Fragmentation and Redemption,* 181–238, here 181.

16. See Peter Dinzelbacher, "Rollenverweigerung, religiöser Aufbruch und mystisches Erleben mittelalterlicher Frauen," in *Religiöse Frauenbewegung und mystische Frömmigkeit im Mittelalter,* ed. Peter Dinzelbacher and D. R. Bauer (Cologne: Bohlau, 1988), 1–58, here 43–44.

Christmastime

1. Maureen Dowd, "Father Knows Worst," *The New York Times* (March 20, 2002).

2. Kenneth L. Woodward, "Bing Crosby had it right," *Newsweek* (March 4, 2002).

3. Bob O'Gorman and Mary Faulkner, *The Complete Idiot's Guide to Understanding Catholicism* (New York: Alpha Books 2000), 36.

4. See Mary Gordon, "Father Chuck: A Reading of *Going My Way* and *The Bells of St. Mary's,* or Why Priests Made Us Crazy," in *Catholic Lives, Contemporary America,* ed. Thomas J. Ferraro (Durham, N.C.: Duke University Press, 1997), 65–75.

5. See Hans Küng, *My Struggle for Freedom: Memoirs* (Grand Rapids: William B. Eerdmans, 2003), 106, 431.

A Day of Prayer for Peace in the World

1. This is the case not least of all because for many Christians the question of praying together with people of other faiths will be answered in the negative. For an interesting theological reflection on this question, see Gavin D'Costa, *The Meeting of Religions and the Trinity,* Faith Meets Faith Series (Maryknoll, N.Y.: Orbis Books, 2000), 143–71.

2. We used a modified version of a text by Hildegard of Bingen (1098–1179), in a rendition of Betty Wendelborn. The song can be found in Wendelborn's collection, *Sing Green: Songs of the Mystics,* 2nd ed. (Auckland, N.Z.: Pyramid Press, 1999), 1. For more information, see Betty Wendelborn's Web site: www.muzique.infi.net.nz.

3. My paraphrase, from the Hebrew.

4. Sara Ruddick, *Maternal Thinking: Toward a Politics of Peace,* 2nd ed., with a new preface (Boston: Beacon Press, 1995).

5. J. Michael Joncas, "God ever-faithful." Copyright © (1994) by GIA Publications, Inc. All Rights Reserved. Printed in U.S.A. 7404 S. Mason Ave., Chicago, IL 60638. www.giamusic.com. 800.442.1358. Used with permission.

Ash Wednesday

1. Literally: "Remember, man, you are dust, and to dust you will return." The words are based on God's words to Adam after the eating of the forbidden fruit (Gen. 3:19). In the current Sacramentary, this sentence is but one possibility for the imposition of ashes. In many Ash Wednesday liturgies, another possibility is chosen: "Turn away from sin and be faithful to the gospel."

2. As trends do, the cultural avoidance of death has produced its own alarmed running commentary on this phenomenon as well as a number of countertrends. Among these countertrends are expanding forms of care at the end of life, an interest in rituals of dying, and a growing scholarly interest in death studies across a variety of disciplines.

3. I owe this "expert" description to Marshall Kapp, who is quoted in the moving article by Mary Lee Freeman, "Caring for the Dying: My Patients,

My Work, My Faith," *Commonweal* (Jan. 30, 2004): 11–15, here 14. I am grateful to my colleague Stanley Hauerwas for pointing me to this essay.

4. See Philipp Harnoncourt, "Die Vorbereitung auf das eigene Sterben: Eine verlorene Dimension spiritueller Bildung," in *Im Angesicht des Todes: Ein interdisziplinäres Kompendium*, vol. 2, ed. Hansjakob Becker et al., Pietas Liturgica 4 (St. Ottilien: EOS Verlag, 1987), 1371–89.

5. Angela Berlis, Psalm 71. English translation by Teresa Berger. Copyright © 2004. Used by permission of Angela Berlis and Teresa Berger. The (slightly longer) German original can be found in *Psalmen leben: Frauen aus allen Kontinenten lesen biblische Psalmen neu*, ed. Bärbel Fünfsinn and Carola Kienel, Christlicher Glaube in der einen Welt 6 (Hamburg: EB-Verlag, 2002), 155–57.

6. See, e.g., *Now and at the Hour of Our Death: Important Information Concerning My Medical Treatment, Finances, Death and Funeral*, rev. ed. (Chicago: Liturgy Training Publications, 1999).

7. I would add to these a signed Organ Donation Card and a Declaration of Life, which affirms that if I should die as a result of violent crime, I would not wish the person found guilty to be subjected to the death penalty under any circumstances.

8. See Bernhard Einig, "'*Somnus est imago mortis*': Die Komplet als allabendliches '*memento mori*'," in *Im Angesicht des Todes*, 1299–1320.

9. Night Prayer as it appears in *Worship: A Hymnal and Service Book for Roman Catholics*, 3rd ed. (Chicago: GIA, 1986), nos. 19–23.

10. Ibid., no. 20.

11. Ibid., no. 1183.

12. The contemplative practice of Music-Thanatology currently attempts to render present the power of music to the process of dying.

13. The full hymn text is available in the Cyber Hymnal at http://www.cyberhymnal.org.

14. Francis of Assisi, "The Canticle of Brother Sun," in *Francis and Clare: The Complete Works*, trans. Regis J. Armstrong et al., Classics of Western Spirituality (New York: Paulist, 1982), 39. It is unfortunate that the English translation uses the ambiguous term "man" when Francis's sentence clearly speaks about each and every "human being."

15. At least according to the Gospel of Luke (23:46).

Lent

1. The title is that of a book by Elizabeth Jordan, *Reconciling Women: A Feminist Perspective on the Confession of Sin in Roman Catholic Tradition* (Strathfield: St Pauls Publications, 2000).

2. Found in *Healing Priesthood: Women's Voices Worldwide*, ed. Angela Perkins and Verena Wright (London: Darton, Longman & Todd, 2003), 121–23, here 122.

An Examination of Conscience

1. Gail R. O'Day rightly points out that the text itself does not actually mention the crowd's hunger as a motivation for Jesus' gift of food; see her "John 6:1–15," *Interpretation* 57 (2001): 196–98.

The Feast of the Annunciation (March 25)

1. Francis X. Weiser, SJ, has documented some of these traditions in his *Handbook of Christian Feasts and Customs: The Year of the Lord in Liturgy and Folklore* (New York: Harcourt, Brace and Company, 1952), 302.

2. There is no accepted English translation, other than the literal "shrine Madonna," for the German *Schreinmadonna* (French: *vièrge ouvrante*) or the more particular type of the *Platyteramonstranz* (French: *vièrge-tabernacle*).

3. The definitive study of the shrine Madonnas is still that by Christoph Baumer, "Die Schreinmadonna," *Marian Library Studies* 9 (1977): 239–72.

4. See Caroline Walker Bynum, "Women Mystics and Eucharistic Devotion," in *Fragmentation and Redemption: Essays on Gender and the Human Body in Medieval Religion* (New York: Zone Books, 1992), 119–50.

5. See Gregor Martin Lechner, *Maria Gravida: Zum Schwangerschaftsmotiv in der bildenden Kunst,* Münchner kunsthistorische Abhandlungen (Munich: Verlag Schnell & Steiner, 1981), 149–55; and Lechner, "Platyteramonstranzen," in *Marienlexikon,* vol. 5, ed. Remigius Bäumer and Leo Scheffcyzk (St. Ottilien: EOS Verlag, 1993), 253.

6. [Ps-]Epiphanius, "Homilia V," in "Laudes Sanctae Mariae Deiparae," in *Patrologia Graeca* 43, 497–98. Cf. *Clavis Patrum Graecorum* II, 335.

7. See Paul Y. Cardile, "Mary As Priest: Mary's Sacerdotal Position in the Visual Arts," *Arte Cristiana* 72 (1984): 199–208. Curiously, the author does not seem to know the twelfth-century depiction of Mary in priestly vestments in the Evangeliary of Gengenbach.

8. For these other theological voices, see Gregor Martin Lechner, "Priestertum," in *Marienlexikon,* vol. 5, ed. Remigius Bäumer and Leo Scheffcyzk (St. Ottilien: EOS Verlag, 1993), 314–18.

9. Konrad von Würzburg, *Die Goldene Schmiede,* ed. Edward Schröder (Göttingen: Vandenhoeck & Ruprecht, 1926), lines 495 and 1274.

10. Hildegard of Bingen, *Scivias,* trans. Mother Columba Hart and Jane Bishop, Classics of Western Spirituality (New York: Paulist Press, 1990), 244, 246, and 254. Copyright © 1990 Abbey of Regina Laudis, Bethlehem, Connecticut. Used with permission.

11. Ibid., 259.

12. See Lechner, "Priestertum," 315ff.

13. Württembergische Landesbibliothek Stuttgart, Cod. Bibl. fol. 28. See illustration 3.

14. See Peter Dinzelbacher, "Rollenverweigerung, religiöser Aufbruch und mystisches Erleben mittelalterlicher Frauen," in *Religiöse Frauenbewegung*

und mystische Frömmigkeit im Mittelalter, ed. Peter Dinzelbacher and D. R. Bauer (Cologne: Böhlau, 1988), 43–44; and Anne L. Clark, "The Priesthood of the Virgin Mary: Gender Trouble in the Twelfth Century," in *Journal of Feminist Studies in Religion* 18 (2002): 5–24.

15. See illustration 4. The statue itself is now housed in the Metropolitan Museum of Art, New York.

16. More than three hundred years later, an Asian theologian will put it thus: "God has chosen the human womb to manifest God's presence in the world and God's salvation for humankind." Choan-Seng Song develops his "theology of the womb," in *Third-Eye Theology: Theology in Formation in Asian Settings*, rev. ed. (Maryknoll, N.Y.: Orbis Books, 1991), 150ff.

17. Grace M. Jantzen, *Becoming Divine: Towards a Feminist Philosophy of Religion* (Bloomington: Indiana University Press, 1999), 144. Interestingly, Pope John Paul II emphasizes such a symbolism of natality in his meditation on "motherhood in relation to the covenant," in *Mulieris Dignitatem* 19: "The history of every human being passes through the threshold of a woman's motherhood; crossing it conditions 'the revelation of the children of God'" (*"Mulieris Dignitatem*: On the Dignity and Vocation of Women," *Origins* 18:17 [1988]: 275).

18. Phyllis Trible, *God and the Rhetoric of Sexuality*, Overtures to Biblical Theology (Philadelphia: Fortress Press, 1978), 34.

19. Ibid., 33.

20. See Caroline Walker Bynum, "The Body of Christ in the Later Middle Ages," in *Fragmentation and Redemption*, 101.

21. See Caroline Walker Bynum, "The Female Body and Religious Practice," in *Fragmentation and Redemption*, 214.

Holy Week

1. See Othmar Keel, *Goddesses and Trees, New Moon and Yahweh: Ancient Near Eastern Art and the Hebrew Bible*, Journal for the Study of the Old Testament, Supplement 261 (Sheffield: Sheffield Academic Press, 1998), esp. 102–9, on the importance of the moon-related calendar in Israel. Note that Isa 3:18 chastises Israelite women for wearing crescent pendants.

2. See further Hugo Rahner, "Mysterium Lunae," in *Symbole der Kirche: Die Ekklesiologie der Väter* (Salzburg: Otto Müller, 1964), 91–139.

3. See Augustine, especially Letter 55 to Januarius.

4. See R. N. Swanson, "Passion and Practice: The Social and Ecclesiastical Implications of Passion Devotion in the Late Middle Ages," in *The Broken Body: Passion Devotion in Late-Medieval Culture*, ed. A. A. MacDonald et al., Medievalia Groningana 21 (Groningen: Egbert Forsten, 1998), 1–30, here 2ff.

5. See further Flora Lewis, "The Wound in Christ's side and the Instruments of the Passion: Gendered Experience and Response," in *Women and the Book: Assessing the Visual Evidence*, ed. Lesley Smith and Jane H. M. Taylor,

British Library Studies in Medieval Culture (London: British Library, 1997), 204–29.

6. See Caroline Walker Bynum, "The Female Body and Religious Practice in the Later Middle Ages," in *Fragmentation and Redemption: Essays on Gender and the Human Body in Medieval Religion,* 3rd ed. (New York: Zone Books, 1994), 181–238.

7. Quoted in Bynum, "Female Body," 212.

8. *A Place at the Table: Women at the Last Supper,* ed. Judi Fisher and Janet Wood (Melbourne: Joint Board of Christian Education, 1993), 51.

9. See Tal Ilan, *Jewish Women in Greco-Roman Palestine: An Inquiry into Image and Status,* Texte und Studien zum Antiken Judentum 44 (Tübingen: J. C. B. Mohr, 1995), 119–21.

10. See Johannes Betz, "Die Eucharistie als Gottes Milch in frühchristlicher Sicht," *Zeitschrift für Katholische Theologie* 106 (1984): 1–26, 167–85.

11. Julian of Norwich, *Showings,* trans. Edmund Colledge and James Walsh (New York: Paulist Press, 1978), 298.

12. The historical and textual questions surrounding the presence of women in the passion narratives are, of course, complex. Raymond E. Brown provides a map for navigating these complexities (*The Death of the Messiah: From Gethsemane to the Grave,* vol. 2, Anchor Bible Reference Library [New York: Doubleday, 1994], 1013–26, 1275–77).

13. The term is Swanson's; see "Passion and Practice," 14.

14. Anselm of Canterbury, "Prayer to St Paul," in *The Prayers and Meditations of St Anselm with the Proslogion,* trans. Sister Benedicta Ward, Penguin Classics (Harmondsworth: Penguin, 1973), 153ff.

15. Quoted in Caroline Walker Bynum, ". . . And Women His Humanity': Female Imagery in the Religious Writing of the Later Middle Ages," in *Fragmentation and Redemption,* 151–79, here 158ff.

16. *The Writings of Margaret of Oingt, Medieval Prioress and Mystic,* trans. with an introduction, essay, and notes by Renate Blumenfeld-Kosinski, Focus Library of Medieval Women (Newburyport, Mass.: Focus Information Group, 1990), 31.

17. Quoted in Elsie Anne McKee, "Katharina Schütz Zell and the 'Our Father,'" in *Oratio: Das Gebet in patristischer und reformatorischer Sicht,* ed. Emidio Campi et al., Forschungen zur Kirchen- und Dogmengeschichte 76 (Göttingen: Vandenhoeck & Ruprecht, 1999), 239–47, here 242f.

18. The quotations in italics are from *The Associated Press* and *The Charlotte Observer* news reports on this crime. All three victims had been sexually assaulted and their faces smashed beyond human recognition.

19. For "Easter" as a verb, see the poem by Gerard Manley Hopkins, "The Wreck of the Deutschland."

20. For a fascinating reading of the biblical stories of the women at the tomb, see Carolyn Osiek, "The Women at the Tomb: What Are They Doing There?" in *A Feminist Companion to Matthew,* ed. Amy-Jill Levine with Mari-

anne Blickenstaff, Feminist Companion to the New Testament and Early Christian Writings 1 (Sheffield: Sheffield Academic Press, 2001), 205–20.

21. For more details on burial customs in Jesus' time, see Byron R. McCane, *Roll Back the Stone: Death and Burial in the World of Jesus* (New York: Trinity Press International, 2003), esp. 98–106.

22. The woman whose life was shattered on Good Friday died on August 1, 2004, without ever awakening from her coma. I write in memory of her, and in honor of the ministry of her pastor, the Rev. Alice Johnson-Curl.

A Day in May, Mary's Month

1. The "*Salve Regina*" is one of the oldest Marian antiphons, dating back to the turn of the eleventh to the twelfth century. The melody used here was transcribed by Lorna Collingridge from the old prayer-book with which I first learned to sing this ancient Marian hymn.

2. A note about Europe's gypsies is in order to guard against popular misconceptions: The "gypsies," or better, Romani, are an ethnic minority of about six to eight million people, found across Europe. They came (from northern India?) in medieval times, and for centuries have kept some of their own cultural particularities, such as a distinct linguistic tradition, that is, Romani dialects, and distinct patterns of migration. Where gypsies embraced Christianity, their faith practices were often shaped by forms of popular religiosity, particularly in the devotion to Mary. European society mostly ostracized the gypsies. Half a million gypsies died in concentration camps. A recent United Nations report noted growing poverty among European gypsies, finding that many often go hungry and that one in six is "constantly starving" (*New York Times*, January 17, 2003). The popular romantic image of the gypsy was that of a carefree wanderer; gypsy women (cf. Esmeralda in Disney's *The Hunchback of Notre Dame*) were sexualized and darkly exoticized, but also imaged as beggars, fortune-tellers, palm-readers, and petty thieves. Elements of the imaginary and the real do, on occasion, meet, as they did for me in Rome that day in May. See also the poem by Patricia Flower Vermillion, "Dancing with Gypsies in Piazza Santa Maria Novella," *Theology Today* 55 (1998): 242–43.

A Novena before Pentecost

1. Quoted in *National Catholic Reporter* 37:36 (August 10, 2001): 6.

2. See also Joan Chittister, *Life Ablaze: A Woman's Novena* (Franklin, Wis.: Sheed & Ward, 2000).

3. Karl Rahner, *Prayers for a Lifetime*, ed. Albert Raffelt (New York: Crossroad, 1984), 96. English Translation of Karl Rahner, *Gebete des Lebens*, ed. Albert Raffelt (Freiburg: Herder, 1984), 16ff. Copyright © 1984. All rights reserved. Used with permission of The Crossroad Publishing Company, New York.

The Feast of Pentecost

I dedicate this meditation, in gratitude and joy, to the women of *Kvinnor i Svenska kyrkan,* with whom I celebrated the Feast of Pentecost in Stockholm, Sweden, in the year 2001.

Trinity Sunday

1. The 2001 film *Chocolat* is based on the novel by Joanne Harris, *Chocolat: A Novel* (New York: Penguin Books, 1999). When I turned to the novel after having seen the film, I was astounded by how much starker and more pronounced the struggle between "church" and "chocolaterie" is in the book. To begin with, there is a clear focus in the novel on two protagonists only, Vianne and the parish priest, a focus that is underlined by the story switching between these two as narrators. There is no manipulative mayor behind the priest—the figure of the mayor is an invention of the film. There are only two other priests, each with his own evil history. Together, these three priests are embodiments of the "Black man" who haunts the narrative of Vianne. At the end of the story, the "Black man" disappears, together with the parish priest, and the chocolate festival takes place *instead of* the Easter Mass!

The novel also does without the romantic couples who emerge in the film: the older couple who find passion again with the chocolates Vianne has chosen for them, Guillaume and the woman he has loved from afar for decades, the mayor and his secretary, and finally Vianne and Roux as a couple that will last. These are all (later) inventions of the film. In the book, there are no simplistic romantic relationships at all.

The starkest contrast between the novel and the film, however, lies in the depth of evil associated with ecclesial life. In the novel, there is the parish priest who at age twelve already was an eager arsonist (and murderer). There is the older priest who condoned and absolved—and also, as slowly becomes clear, had a sexual relationship with the young priest's mother. There is the priest to whom Vianne's mother attempted to confess and who with his stark response sent her fleeing. But besides the particulars of this unholy male clerical trinity, the book's whole language about the church is painfully negative: "aggressively whitewashed," "rigid," "the barbed and poisonous weapon of the righteous," "unforgiving, hard, and strangely envious," "the unanswerable voice of authority, a specious logic that keeps you frozen, obedient, fearful." In short, there is no redemption for the church in this book. The struggle between "church" and "chocolaterie" is envisioned as one of life and death, of either-or. In the novel, the church loses, and life wins. It is telling that the film could not bear the starkness of this opposition, and instead ends with a clear message of both-and: There is an Easter Mass in the film, and there is a chocolate festival too.

The book with its stark contrast between "church" and "chocolaterie" clearly is part of a broader cultural trend that labels the church as authoritarian, rigid, and death-dealing. I remain dissatisfied with the superficiality of the book's counterclaim that all that matters in life is "happiness." I want to know much more precisely what constitutes and comes to be counted as happiness. And I blur the starkness of *Chocolat*'s contrast in my own life, since I claim the knowledge of the church as life-giving as well as of ordinary sites as graced. In that sense, the film with its own blurring of the novel's irredeemable contrast speaks a message close to where I find myself. The starkness of the novel, however, holds a truth of its own, painful as this is to acknowledge. There are reasons why a woman writes a novel at whose heart stands a powerful conflict between the "church" and a "chocolaterie." I am afraid that all too often, the church and those of us who inhabit it have fallen short of rendering visible the church's life-giving potential, especially for women. The novel *Chocolat*, with its stark indictment of the church, invites us to write stories with our own lives in which women find life not only in a chocolaterie located "immediately opposite" from the church, but also in the church itself. Or, to re-imagine both the end of the novel and the end of the film: What would it look like, and what would it take for Vianne to end up sharing chocolate *and* communion with the villagers?

Sunday in Ordinary Time

1. From Psalm 16, appointed for the 13th Sunday in Ordinary Time, Cycle C.

Baptism

I am profoundly grateful to my colleague, Dr. Mary Deasey Collins, for her translation of my original German text into English.

1. Walter Wangerin, Jr., *Miz Lil and the Chronicles of Grace* (New York: HarperCollins, 1988), 185–96.

2. See further Phyllis Trible, *God and the Rhetoric of Sexuality*, Overtures to Biblical Theology (Philadelphia: Fortress Press, 1978), 34–59.

3. Aemiliana Löhr, "Das Priestertum der Frau im Lichte der kath. Liturgie," *Die Seelsorge* 8 (1930/31): 346–54, here 349 (translation mine).

4. Athanasius Wintersig, "Pfarrei und Mysterium," *Jahrbuch für Liturgiewissenschaft* 5 (1925): 136–43, here 138ff. (translation mine).

5. See further Susan A. Ross, *Extravagant Affections: A Feminist Sacramental Theology* (New York: Continuum, 1998); Verena Wodtke-Werner, "Geh hin, frag die Schwangere: Schwangerschaft, Geburt und Stillen im religiösen Brauchtum und in der Theologie," in *Kraftfelder: Sakramente in der Lebenswirklichkeit von Frauen*, ed. Regina Ammicht-Quinn and Stefanie Spendel (Regensburg: Friedrich Pustet, 1998), 161–83; Thelma Aldcroft, "Childbirth, Liturgy, and Ritual—A Neglected Dimension of Pastoral Theol-

ogy," in *Life Cycles: Women and Pastoral Care,* ed. Elaine Graham and Margaret Halsey (London: SPCK, 1993), 180–91.

6. The philosophical interest in natality, quite pronounced in recent feminist philosophical work, emerges with the work of Hannah Arendt. See Grace M. Jantzen, *Becoming Divine: Towards a Feminist Philosophy of Religion* (Bloomington: Indiana University Press, 1999).

A Lazy Sunday Afternoon

1. See further Hubertus Lutterbach, *Sexualität im Mittelalter: Eine Kulturstudie anhand von Bußbüchern des 6. bis 12. Jahrhunderts,* Beihefte zum Archiv für Kulturgeschichte 43 (Cologne: Böhlau, 1999), 76–80.

2. See, e.g., the series of documentaries *Killing Us Softly,* Cambridge Documentary Films, Cambridge, Massachusetts.

3. John Paul II, Apostolic Exhortation *Familiaris Consortio* §19.

4. Rowan Williams, "The Deflections of Desire: Negative Theology in Trinitarian Disclosure," in *Silence and the Word: Negative Theology and Incarnation,* ed. Oliver Davies and Denys Turner (New York: Cambridge University Press, 2002), 115–35, here 132.

5. See Carol Meyers, "Eve," in *Women in Scripture: A Dictionary of Named and Unnamed Women in the Hebrew Bible, the Apocryphal/Deuterocanonical Books, and the New Testament,* ed. Carol Meyers, Toni Craven, and Ross Shepard Kraemer (Boston: Houghton Mifflin, 2000), 79–82.

6. Ibid., 82. The translation of Gen. 4:1–2a here quoted is Meyers's.

7. Bonnie J. Miller-McLemore, "Epistemology or Bust: A Maternal Feminist Knowledge of Knowing," *Journal of Religion* 72 (1992): 229–47, here 242.

8. John Paul II, Apostolic Exhortation *Familiaris Consortio* §11.

9. Ibid.

10. See Mary Daly, with Jane Caputi, *Websters' First New Intergalactic Wickedary of the English Language* (Boston: Beacon Press, 1987), 77.

11. See Frederick S. Lane, *Obscene Profits: The Entrepreneurs of Pornography in the Cyber Age* (New York: Routledge, 2000), 129.

12. The figures are reported by Robert Jensen, "A Cruel Edge—Pornography," in *Ms.* 13:4 (Spring 2004): 54–58, here 56.

13. Virginia Burrus, *The Sex Lives of the Saints: An Erotics of Ancient Hagiography* (Philadelphia: University of Pennsylvania Press, 2004), 2.

14. *Catechism of the Catholic Church,* 2nd ed. (Vatican City: Libreria Editrice Vaticana, 2000), no. 2362.

15. Father Joseph Warrilow, OSB, as quoted by Tony Hendra, in *Father Joe: The Man Who Saved My Soul* (New York: Random House, 2004), 126.

16. Pope Paul VI, *Humanae Vitae* §11ff.

17. *Book of Common Prayer:* "With this ring I thee wed, with my body I thee worship, and with all my worldly goods I thee endow . . . ."

Index

Abelard: on Mary of Magdala, 18
Ackland, Margaret, 188
Advent: and consumerism, 115
Aelred of Rievaulx: on Jesus as mother, 190
agency: gender asymmetry and, 98–99
Agnes (sister of Clare of Assisi), 44–45
Agnes of Prague
    letter of Clare of Assisi to, 50–52
    Rule of, 55
All Souls' Day, 12
Ambrose: and lunar cycle, 186
Amnesty International
    on sexual exploitation of women, 22
    on violence against women, 37
Anna (mother of Mary)
    barren one giving birth, 62-63
    reconstruction of prayer of, 35–36
Anne Trinitaire, 63
Annunciation
    depictions of, in art, 176–77
    Feast of, 176–83
Anselm of Canterbury: on Jesus as mother, 131, 132, 190
Aquinas. *See* Thomas Aquinas
Arbrissel, Robert d', 5–6
Assisi World Day of Prayer for Peace (2002), 142
Augustine
    on love, 220
    and lunar cycle, 186

baptism, 207–19
Barbara, Saint, 162
Barefield, Laura,
Bathsheba: in genealogy of Jesus, 61, 64
beatification
    of Luigi and Maria Beltrame Quat-trochi, 96
    of Mother Teresa, 93

beauty business, 38, 46–57
Benevenuta, Blessed, 133
Berger, Florence S., 9–10
Bernard of Clairvaux: on Mary of Mag-dala, 18
Betz, Johannes, 130
Bible
    androcentric bias of, 26–27, 33–34
    politics of translation of, 26–27
    readings that render women voiceless, 27–29
    readings that resonate with women's lives, 24–25, 26
    story of secondary wife of Levite (Judg. 19–20), 4
    women at prayer in, 31–33
Birgitta of Sweden, Saint, 162
Bonaventure: on Jesus' body, 188
Bonhoeffer, Dietrich
    execution of, 68
    on fragmentation of life, 14–15, 69
bread
    making of, 16
    significance of: in feeding story, 8–9
breast cancer, 204–6
Brown, Dan, *Da Vinci Code* by, 17, 21, 232n. 11
Burton, Katherine, 10
Bynum, Caroline Walker
    on fragments, 15
    on gender and sanctity, 98
    on heritage of female communities and visions, 56

calendars, 12
    civil, 12
    liturgical, 11-12, 77, 87; and gender asymmetry in ranks in, 95–97
    lunar: and date of Easter, 12, 185–86
    See also cycles

257

About the Author

Teresa Maria Berger was baptized into the Roman Catholic Church on April 30, 1956, at the ripe age of ten days old. She grew up in post-War (West) Germany and studied theology at St. John's College, Nottingham, and the Universities of Mainz, Heidelberg, Münster, and Geneva. She holds doctorates in dogmatic theology and liturgical studies. Since 1984, Teresa Berger has lived in the United States, teaching theology on the faculty of The Divinity School of Duke University in Durham, NC. Teresa Berger has written extensively on liturgy and women's lives. Her recent publications include *Women's Ways of Worship: Gender Analysis and Liturgical History* (1999) and *Dissident Daughters: Feminist Liturgies in Global Context* (2001). Together with her nine-year-old son Peter, she is a part of Immaculate Conception Catholic Church in Durham, NC. In 2003, Teresa Berger received the distinguished *Herbert Haag Prize for Freedom in the Church*.